Patent Litigation in China

**MEDTRONIC COPORATE
PATENT DEPARTMENT**

PATENT LITIGATION IN CHINA

Douglas Clark

OXFORD
UNIVERSITY PRESS

UNIVERSITY PRESS

Oxford University Press, Inc., publishes works that further Oxford University's objective of excellence in research, scholarship, and education.

Oxford New York
Auckland Cape Town Dar es Salaam Hong Kong Karachi Kuala Lumpur Madrid Melbourne
Mexico City Nairobi New Delhi Shanghai Taipei Toronto

With offices in
Argentina Austria Brazil Chile Czech Republic France Greece Guatemala Hungary Italy
Japan Poland Portugal Singapore South Korea Switzerland Thailand Turkey Ukraine
Vietnam

Copyright © 2011 by Oxford University Press, Inc.

Published by Oxford University Press, Inc.
198 Madison Avenue, New York, New York 10016

Oxford is a registered trademark of Oxford University Press
Oxford University Press is a registered trademark of Oxford University Press, Inc.

All rights reserved. No part of this publication may be reproduced, stored in a retrieval system, or transmitted, in any form or by any means, electronic, mechanical, photocopying, recording, or otherwise, without the prior permission of Oxford University Press, Inc.

_____
Library of Congress Cataloging-in-Publication Data

Clark, Douglas.
  Patent litigation in China / Douglas Clark.
     p. cm.
  Includes bibliographical references and index.
  ISBN 978-0-19-973025-4 ((pbk.): alk. paper)
 1. Patent suits—China. 2. Patent laws and legislation—China.
 I. Title.

KNQ1215.C53 2011
346.5104'86—dc22   2011006686
_____

1 2 3 4 5 6 7 8 9
Printed in the United States of America on acid-free paper

Note to Readers
This publication is designed to provide accurate and authoritative information in regard to the subject matter covered. It is based upon sources believed to be accurate and reliable and is intended to be current as of the time it was written. It is sold with the understanding that the publisher is not engaged in rendering legal, accounting, or other professional services. If legal advice or other expert assistance is required, the services of a competent professional person should be sought. Also, to confirm that the information has not been affected or changed by recent developments, traditional legal research techniques should be used, including checking primary sources where appropriate.

(*Based on the Declaration of Principles jointly adopted by a Committee of the
American Bar Association and a Committee of Publishers and Associations.*)

You may order this or any other Oxford University Press publication by
visiting the Oxford University Press website at www.oup.com

To Mum and Dad

CONTENTS

Acknowledgments xiii
A Note on Translations xvii

1. Introduction   1
   1.1 Intellectual Property Rights in China   1
   1.2 Scope of This Book   2
   1.3 History of Patent Law in China   2
   1.4 Modern Patent Law   3
   1.5 Patents in China   3
   1.6 Weaknesses in the Chinese Patent System   4
2. Sources of Patent Law   7
   2.1 Principal Legal Provisions Covering Patent Law   7
   2.2 Other Relevant Legislation   8
   2.3 Amendments to the Patent Law   9
   2.4 Renumbering of Articles After Amendment   9
   2.5 Transitional Provisions Applying to the Most Recent Amendments   9
   2.6 Case Law   10
   2.7 Supreme Court Judicial Interpretations and Opinions   11
   2.8 Interpretations and Opinions of the Lower Courts   12
3. Introduction to China's Administrative and Judicial Patent Systems   13
   3.1 Introduction   13
   3.2 Administrative System   13
   3.3 Judicial System   13
   3.4 State Intellectual Property Office   14
   3.5 Patent Review and Adjudication Board   15
   3.6 Structure of the Chinese Judicial System   16
   3.7 Intellectual Property Chambers   17
   3.8 Courts That Handle Patent Cases   17
   3.9 Appeals   18

3.10 The Judiciary   18
3.11 Adjudication Committees   19
4. Administrative Enforcement   21
    4.1 Administrative Enforcement   21
    4.2 The Procedure for SIPO Administrative Actions   22
    4.3 Mediation by the SIPO   25
    4.4 General Administration for Customs   27
5. Patents   31
    5.1 Introduction   31
    5.2 Types of Patents   31
    5.3 Filing Requirements   32
    5.4 Term of Protection   33
    5.5 Grace Periods   34
    5.6 Patent Examination Guidelines   34
    5.7 Preliminary Examination   35
    5.8 Substantive Examination   36
    5.9 Rejection   37
    5.10 Re-Examination   38
    5.11 Appeal of the Re-Examination Decisions to the Court   39
6. Grounds for Invalidating a Patent   41
    6.1 Introduction   41
    6.2 Statutory Grounds   41
    6.3 Definitions of Invention and Utility Model   42
    6.4 Confidentiality Examination   43
    6.5 Novelty   44
    6.6 Inventiveness   48
    6.7 Practical Applicability   51
    6.8 Sufficiency of Disclosure   52
    6.9 Claims Must Be Supported by the Description   54
    6.10 Amendments   56
    6.11 Claims Must Contain the Essential Technical Features   58
    6.12 Divisional Applications Must Not Go Beyond Scope of Original Application   59
    6.13 Law, Morality, or Public Interest   59
    6.14 Breach of Law or Regulations Relating to Genetic Resources   61
    6.15 Prohibited Inventions   61
    6.16 Earlier Application   62
7. Patent Revocation Proceedings   63
    7.1 Introduction   63
    7.2 Application for Revocation   63
    7.3 Invalidation Procedures   64

  7.4 Grounds for Invalidation 68
  7.5 Evidence 69
  7.6 Oral Hearing 74
  7.7 Appeal of PRAB's Invalidation Decision 75
  7.8 Effect of a Final Invalidation Decision 77
8. Civil Litigation in China 79
  8.1 Introduction 79
  8.2 Summary of Civil Proceedings 79
  8.3 Judging Panel 79
  8.4 Filing Fees 79
  8.5 The Complaint 80
  8.6 Acceptance of the Complaint 81
  8.7 Service of the Complaint 81
  8.8 Defense 82
  8.9 Proceedings in the Absence of a Party 82
  8.10 Mediation 82
  8.11 Evidence Collection and Admissibility 83
  8.12 Evidence Exchange 83
  8.13 Trial 84
  8.14 Judgment 85
  8.15 Appeals 85
  8.16 Effect of an Appeal 87
  8.17 New Evidence on Appeal 87
  8.18 Review of the Decision by the Supreme Court or Procuratorate 87
9. Preliminary and Interlocutory Issues 89
  9.1 Introduction 89
  9.2 Powers of Attorney 89
  9.3 Limitation Periods 91
  9.4 Jurisdiction 93
  9.5 Search Reports for Utility Model and Design Cases 96
  9.6 Pretrial or Interim Injunctions 97
  9.7 Asset-Freezing Orders 100
  9.8 Declaration of Non-Infringement 100
  9.9 Stay of Infringement Proceedings 101
10. Evidence 105
  10.1 The Importance of Evidence 105
  10.2 Permitted Evidence 106
  10.3 Best Evidence Rule 107
  10.4 Notarized Evidence 107
  10.5 Foreign Evidence: Notarization and Legalization 108

10.6 Foreign Language Evidence   108
10.7 Expert Evidence   108
10.8 Evidence Preservation Orders   109
10.9 Evidence Collection by the Court   111
10.10 The Burden of Proof Does Not Shift If the Other Party Does Not Comply with an Evidence Request   111
10.11 Penalties for Destroying Evidence   111
10.12 Investigations by the Parties   112
10.13 Inadmissibility of Illegally Obtained Evidence   113
10.14 Admissibility of Pretext or Trap Purchases   114

11. Patent Infringement Litigation—Invention Patents and Utility Models   117
    11.1 Introduction   117
    11.2 The Rights of Patentees and Related Injured Parties to Bring Action   118
    11.3 Acts of Infringement   119
    11.4 Indirect Infringement   120
    11.5 Joint Infringement   121
    11.6 Reverse Burden of Proof If the Patent Relates to a Method of Making a *New Product*   122
    11.7 Claim Interpretation   122
    11.8 Doctrine of Equivalents   125
    11.9 File Wrapper Estoppel   128
    11.10 Interpretation of Claims to Rectify Mistakes   129
    11.11 Proving Infringement   129

12. Defenses   131
    12.1 Types of Defense   131
    12.2 Invalidity   132
    12.3 Non-Infringement   132
    12.4 Prior Art Defense   133
    12.5 Exhaustion of Rights   134
    12.6 Prior Use Defense   134
    12.7 Temporary Entry into China   136
    12.8 Research and Development   136
    12.9 Clinical Trials   136
    12.10 Innocence   137
    12.11 Limitation Defense   138
    12.12 Breach of Anti-Monopoly Law   138
    12.13 Patent Incorporated into Standard   139

13. Design Patents   141
    13.1 Introduction   141
    13.2 Stay of Infringement Proceedings   141
    13.3 Grounds for Invalidating Design Patent   141
    13.4 Definition of Design   142
    13.5 Design Rights Shall Not Belong to an Existing Design   143
    13.6 Identical or Not Substantially Different Designs   143
    13.7 Conflict with Prior Legal Rights   145
    13.8 Two-Dimensional Designs that Mainly Serve as Indicators   145
    13.9 The Design Drawing Should Clearly Identify the Design   146
    13.10 Amendments Beyond the Scope of the Initial Application   146
    13.11 Contrary to Law or Social Morality, or Detrimental to the Public Interest   146
    13.12 Identical Invention-Creation   147
    13.13 Infringement of Design Patents   147
    13.14 Designs Incorporated into Other Products   149
    13.15 Defenses   149
    13.16 Prior Art Defense   150
    13.17 Damages   150
14. Remedies   151
    14.1 Remedies Available in China   151
    14.2 Injunctions   152
    14.3 Circumstances in Which an Injunction Will Not Be Granted   152
    14.4 Reasonable Fee for Pre-Grant Use   154
    14.5 Damages for Post-Grant Infringement   154
    14.6 Eliminating Ill Effects   159
    14.7 Apology   159
    14.8 The Enforcement of Damages Awards   159
    14.9 The Enforcement of Injunctions   159
Concluding Remarks   161
Tables   163
    Patent Applications   163
    Patent Infringement Litigation   164
    Patent Prelitigation, Litigation Official Court, and Enforcement Cost Projections   165
Appendices
    1. Patent Law of the People's Republic of China   169
    2. Implementing Regulations of the Patent Law of the People's Republic of China   191

3. Interpretation by the Supreme People's Court on Several Issues Regarding Legal Application in the Adjudication of Patent Infringement Cases   245
4. Several Provisions of the Supreme People's Court on Issues Relating to Application of Law to Adjudication of Cases of Patent Disputes   251
5. Several Provisions of the Supreme People's Court for the Application of Law to Pre-trial Cessation of Infringement of Patent Right   259
6. Supreme People's Court Opinion on Certain Issues with Respect to Intellectual Property Judicial Adjudication Under the Current Economic Situation   265
7. List of Courts with Jurisdiction to Handle Patent Cases   281

Table of Cases   283
Table of Legislation   285
Index   287

ACKNOWLEDGMENTS

I have had the opportunity over the past more than twenty years to have worked with and been taught by exceptional lawyers whose contribution to my knowledge of intellectual property law, Chinese law, and Chinese intellectual property law has been immense. Of these, there are four people, in particular, I would like to thank. Taking their contributions in chronological order, I would first like to thank my principal teacher and mentor at Fudan University, Zhang Guangjie, for his great patience and effort during my studies, in teaching me and helping me gain an understanding of the Chinese legal and political system. Second, I would like to thank Stephen Hayward and Henry Wheare, partners at Lovell White Durrant (as it then was) who first supervised me as a junior intellectual property (IP) lawyer. Stephen first took me on as a paralegal and supervised me on my first two patent cases. Henry took over this supervision when Stephen moved to Vietnam. Both Stephen and Henry strongly supported my desire to build an IP practice in China and helped to arrange a secondment for me to Shanghai in 2000. Henry continued to support the development of the firm's China IP practice after Stephen left, and I was proud to become a partner in the firm in 2001. Last, but not least, I must thank Lu Fang Ming, with whom I worked on literally hundreds of IP cases all over China between 1994 and 2004, when he retired. Mr. Lu generously taught me a huge amount about intellectual property law in China. Without his guidance and teaching, I would not have been able to write this book.

I have had the honor of working with many excellent IP practitioners in China in my time at Hogan Lovells. Each one of them has contributed to this book, in ways ranging from the work on cases to discussions over a few drinks late at night. These include, in addition to Steve and Henry, Gabriela Kennedy, Gabrielle Ma, Kim McLeod, Andrew Cobden, Horace Lam, Margaret Yang, Peter Shen, Monique Woo, Sandra Gibbons, Alan Adcock, Deanna Wong, Sebastian Hughes, Judy Chan, Jessica Chan, Katherine Wong, Joanne Harland, Adam Salter, Vivian Chung, Vivian Lui, Lewis Ho, Christine Yiu, Sarah Doyle, Amy Zhang, Michelle Yee, and Brenda Lui, who

I worked with in Hong Kong. I also thank Zhen (Katie) Feng, William "Skip" Fisher, Geoffrey Lin, Rieko Michishita, Georgia Chiu, Eugene Chen, Alex Xia, Julia Peng, Yu-an Chang, and Michael Ni, who I worked with in Shanghai; and Stacy Yuan, Enoch Liang, Rae Yan, Helen Xia, Albert Tsui, Betty Li, David Chen, and Cliff Borg-Mark, who were based in Beijing.

Many people in the Hogan Lovells Shanghai, Hong Kong, and Beijing offices assisted greatly in the preparation of this book or the preparation of research notes or advice that found their way into this book. In particular, thanks must go to Duncan Thomson, who spent a huge amount of time researching the law and preparing a first draft of the book. Special thanks to Geoffrey Lin, Georgia Chiu, and Michael Ni. Chapters on invalidity draw strongly on the work that they have prepared. Alex Xia took on the mammoth job of proofreading the entire book and cross checking citations (any errors that remain are mine) and also contributed greatly in the analysis of the 2010 judicial interpretation. Andrew Cobden also provided useful comments on a draft of the book. A number of summer interns also assisted in proofreading and adding comments to the book. Particular thanks to Daniel Jones, Yi Chen, and Bisola Daramola.

Thank you to Andreas von Falck and Crispin Rapinet for allowing me to work on this book and for their support over the years. I would also like to give special thanks to the IP group of Hogan Lovells, and many others I have worked with over the years at Lovells and Hogan Lovells. Their names are too numerous to mention, but thanks to all.

Outside Hogan Lovells, I have appreciated the many discussions regarding IPRI have had with my fellow members of the European Chamber of Commerce IPR Working Group, in particular, Thomas Pattloch, Paul Ranjard, Joe Rogers, Chris Bailey, and Lewis Ho. Thank you also to Ioana Kraft for her hard work in organizing the Working Group.

A number of my competitors have also been very generous over the years in serving as sounding boards for ideas or pointing me in the right direction to find relevant laws, regulations, or rules. In particular, I would like to thank Luke Minford of Rouse and Co., and Joe Simone, Robert Arnold, and Cliff Borg-Marks, all of whom while at Baker & McKenzie generously provided ideas on the handling of cases, many of which have found their way into this book. (Cliff was also a colleague at Hogan Lovells.) John Slater, now at Simmons and Simmons; Yvonne Chua, Anne Choi, and Andrea Fong at Wilkinson & Grist; Kenny Wong and Rosita Li at Mayer Brown JSM; Matthew Laight and Alison Wong of Bird & Bird also have provided interesting insights into Chinese law.

Frank Holliday at Marks & Clerk was also of superb assistance on many of my early patent cases.

A number of local counsel I have worked with in China have also provided very useful guidance and understanding of the Chinese legal system. In particular, I would like to acknowledge Andy An and his team at An Tian Zhang, Dixon Zhang and his team at Fangda, Ai Hong and his team at ZY Partners, Chen Jianming of Tsinghua University, and Xu Weiqi who has his own firm. A special thanks also to Ding Zhongying who worked with Lu Fangming and me for many years.

Special thanks also to Stephen Weiss and Gregory Fleesler of Mosers and Singer in New York for instructing me as an expert witness on Chinese patent law. The report that I (with much help from Skip Fisher) prepared provided a strong foundation for this book.

Many Chinese judges, officials, and academics have also been very generous with their time and very patient to answer my questions over the years regarding how the system works in practice. To all of you, I give my thanks.

At the end of the day, I have only been able to write this book due to the direct support of many clients who have instructed my firm over many years and shown great patience as we have navigated the treacherous shoals of litigating IP in China. If I were to name one, I would need to name many (and then need to navigate the treacherous shoals of client confidentiality), so I will leave this as a general thank you.

I greatly appreciate the enthusiasm and patience of Matt Gallaway, my editor at Oxford University Press, for commissioning me to write this book and for tolerating with good grace my constantly slipping deadlines.

My family has been supportive and encouraging. I have dedicated this book to my parents and also thank them for their encouragement and support for me to study at high school in Japan and university in China thus starting my Asian odyssey. Thank you also to my siblings, Tanya, Russell (and his wife Michelle), and Nicola for their support and "constructive criticism" that only siblings can give over the years. And, finally my great appreciation and thanks to my wife Tomoko and children Leila, Kai, Ray, and India for your support always.

A NOTE ON TRANSLATIONS

It is difficult to achieve legal translations from Chinese to English that are consistent and 100 percent accurate. Chinese does not have tenses, definite or indefinite articles, or plural forms for nouns. Nor, because Chinese is written using characters, are defined terms indicated by capital letters. As a result, a provision of Chinese law can be accurately translated into English in a number of ways, none of which can be deemed to be inaccurate.

The author has attempted to ensure consistency of translation throughout the book, but certain translations will appear to be inconsistent either with other passages in the book or other translations to which a reader may refer. Ultimately, if the meaning of a word or phrase is important, it is necessary to consult the original Chinese. For this reason, the translations of patent law and other documents in the appendices are provided for reference only.

Other than for quotations from the *Examination Guidelines*, the translations used in the book have been done or checked by the author. For quotations from the *Examination Guidelines*, the author has relied upon the official translation issued by the Patent Office, save the correction of obvious grammatical or spelling mistakes in the official translation.

CHAPTER 1
Introduction

1.1 INTELLECTUAL PROPERTY RIGHTS IN CHINA

1.1.1 The author first studied intellectual property law at Fudan University in Shanghai, the People's Republic of China (PRC or China), in 1989. At that time, there were no courses on intellectual property (IP); only a short section of the course on civil law was devoted to intellectual property. At the time, studying the enforcement of intellectual property rights in China was more theoretical than practical.

1.1.2 In 1993, I started working as an intellectual property paralegal based in Hong Kong. At that time, I handled the filing of some patents in China but no patent litigation. During the 1990s, most of the work of intellectual property practitioners in China revolved around anti-counterfeiting with some general advice on patent law.

1.1.3 As China's economy grew, more and more foreign companies invested in higher technology production in China, and the filing of patents increased substantially. After China joined the World Trade Organization (WTO) in 2001, there was a further marked increase in filings. From about 2003, we also started to see foreign and domestic companies become more and more involved in patent litigation. In the past five years, the majority of my practice has been devoted to handling patent litigation matters in China, including a number of cases involving cross-border patent disputes.

1.1.4 In 2008, China became the world's second largest economy, behind the United States (U.S.), and surpassed Germany to become the second largest exporter in the world.[1] Many foreign companies have no choice but

---

1. World Economic Outlook Database, International Monetary Fund, 2009.

to invest in and transfer technology to China. Increasingly, they have to rely on the Chinese legal system to protect their rights.

1.1.5 A number of problems remain in the Chinese legal system, including that law is not above politics; the state owns many large enterprises, and, local protectionism can be strong. Each of these problems is discussed briefly at the end of this chapter.

1.1.6 Nevertheless, the Chinese legal system has over the last eighteen years improved with the growth of the economy. The official policy of the Chinese government is to protect intellectual property rights so as to encourage domestic innovation and move the economy away from the current "world's factory" model whereby foreign products are made in China to be exported elsewhere. Although there will be ups and downs, I expect to see the legal system governing patents to continue to improve.

1.2 SCOPE OF THIS BOOK

1.2.1 This book is intended to provide non-Chinese patent practitioners and others interested in the Chinese patent system an overview of the patent enforcement system so as to allow them to understand the steps that need to be taken to protect or defend their rights.

1.2.2 This book is not a substitute for obtaining legal advice. Although this caveat is always included in texts on legal subjects, it is particularly important that legal advice be obtained in relation to patent matters in China. Laws and regulations can change very quickly, and local rules and practices can make a big difference to whether a case can be brought or defended successfully.

1.3 HISTORY OF PATENT LAW IN CHINA

1.3.1 The concept of intellectual property rights, particularly patent rights, is relatively new in China. Traditionally, no domestic intellectual property laws existed. It was not until the late nineteenth century, when Chinese scholars began to travel and study abroad, and bring ideas back from the West, that palpable notions of intellectual property rights began to be formulated in China. This intellectual development culminated in 1898 when several ordinances relating to intellectual property, including the *Awarding Procedures for Manufacturing Craftsmanship*, were issued by the government of the Qing Dynasty.

1.3.2 This legislation became the first in Chinese history that recognized the rights of inventors; the protection it afforded lasted for a period of between 10 and 50 years. However, after a brief period, the protection of this legislation and all other patent protection vanished, as China fractured and came under the control of warlords in the post-Qing dynasty period. No patent laws were enacted throughout the period of national turbulence that lasted from World War I through the civil war between the Communist and Nationalist forces, and the initial stages of socialism in China that led to the Cultural Revolution. During the Cultural Revolution almost all economic laws were repealed and there was limited protection of economic rights, let alone patent rights.

1.4 MODERN PATENT LAW

1.4.1 After the Cultural Revolution, China entered a period of "reform and opening," which included the development of a market economy as part of the socialist economy. It was recognized that a market economy necessitates a legal system that can protect economic rights, and so steps were taken to create such a system. A new court system was established, and numerous laws, including the General Principles of Civil Law, a mini civil code, and a Civil Procedure Law were enacted.

1.4.2 It was also recognized that to create a market economy, it is necessary to be able to register and protect intellectual property. The first Patent Law was passed in 1984 by the National People's Congress and came into force in 1985. The Patent Law was subsequently amended in 1992, 2000, and 2008, with the third set of amendments coming into force in October 2009.

1.4.3 Trademark, copyright, and unfair competition laws were also enacted.

1.5 PATENTS IN CHINA

1.5.1 According to the official State Intellectual Property Office (SIPO) of the People's Republic of China (Chinese Patent Office) 2010 Statistics, a total of 1,222,286 patent applications were filed in China during 2010. A breakdown of this total figure shows that there were 391,177 invention patent applications, 409,836 utility model applications, and 421,273 external design patent applications. Foreigners submitted 112,858 of the applications, while domestic applications accounted for 1,109,428 of the total of 1,222,286 patent applications.[2]

---

2. See http://www.sipo.gov.cn/sipo_English/statistics/ for detailed statistics.

1.5.2 In 2010, China ranked fourth in the world for the number of patent applications made through the Patent Cooperation Treaty according to the World Intellectual Property Organization (WIPO).[3]

1.5.3 In June 2008, the Chinese government issued the 2008 National Intellectual Property Rights Strategy (National IPR Strategy), which outlines the plan for the development of China's intellectual property rights law in China up to 2020. In the National IPR Strategy, the Chinese State Council noted that China is among the countries that grant the most invention patents, and foreign applications for Chinese domestic patents have substantially increased.[4] The document made clear that the Chinese government understands that the race for patent technology is a priority for governments worldwide, and that patents relating to sectors such as advanced energy, modern agriculture, space flight, and environmental resources will support the development of China's high-technology industry.[5] Furthermore, it is understood that China has to accept international standards regarding patents and must actively participate in their formulation.[6] Moreover, the document states that China's official policy includes encouraging employees to make inventions,[7] and managing the relationship between patent protection and public interest.[8]

1.6 WEAKNESSES IN THE CHINESE PATENT SYSTEM

1.6.1 The Chinese legal system is still in a developmental stage and deficiencies remain in both the legal system itself and the enforcement of IP rights. Problems likely to be encountered include local protectionism, poorly trained and inexperienced judges, and, in some cases, corruption.

Political Aspects of Bringing a Case

1.6.2 China is a one-party state, and the government and the party retain an ability to influence the legal system.[9] There have been strong efforts to

---

3. "China's international patent filings on 56.2-pct jump last year: WIPO," China Daily, 10 February 2011.
4. 2008 National Intellectual Property Rights Strategy, Article 7.
5. 2008 National Intellectual Property Rights Strategy, Article 16.
6. 2008 National Intellectual Property Rights Strategy, Article 17.
7. 2008 National Intellectual Property Rights Strategy, Article 18.
8. 2008 National Intellectual Property Rights Strategy, Article 20.
9. See the discussion on the judiciary in Chapter 3, "Introduction to China's Administrative and Judicial Patent Systems."

develop a neutral legal system, whereby cases are decided solely on merit as determined by the law. I purposefully use the word *neutral* and not *independent* because, despite Article 126 of the Chinese Constitution, which provides that courts should exercise judicial power independently, there has never been a genuine policy in China to develop a truly independent judiciary. Although this question goes beyond the scope of this book, a truly independent judiciary would conflict with the "leadership of the communist party" enshrined in the four cardinal principles set out in the Preamble of the Constitution, and the socialist state prescribed in Article 2 of the Constitution.

1.6.3 Nevertheless, the legal system has improved substantially, particularly in larger cities in recent years. For example, in Shanghai and Beijing, judges of the IP chambers are well educated and professional; there is little corruption, and political influence is only apparent in the most important of cases.

Government Ownership

1.6.4 Lawsuits brought against infringers where the alleged infringer is a state-owned enterprise can be especially problematic. State-owned enterprises usually have close relationships with local governments at the place where the enterprises are located. If the IP owner has operations at the same location, filing a suit against the infringer may seriously undermine the IP owner's relationship with the local government. Therefore, the IP owner should diligently consider all the potential risks before filing a suit against an infringer that is owned by the government.

Local Protectionism

1.6.5 A patentee also needs to consider the economic consequences of filing a lawsuit. An infringer may, for example, launch a media campaign against the IP owner, inciting nationalistic sentiments (should the plaintiff be a foreign organization). In large cities, this is usually not a serious concern. In smaller cities, however, the local government will have strong incentives to protect any opposing party that is a large employer of workers, and/or a large source of tax revenue. Courts, law enforcement agencies, and administrative bodies in the area where the state-owned enterprise is located may refuse to cooperate fully with the court particularly where the plaintiff is seeking to use legal or administrative processes to gather evidence or enforce a judgment. This makes it more difficult for the IP owner to not only win the case, but also enforce any judgments handed down by the courts.

CHAPTER 2
Sources of Patent Law

2.1 PRINCIPAL LEGAL PROVISIONS COVERING PATENT LAW

2.1.1 The main legislation or judicial and administrative provisions governing patent law in the People's Republic of China (PRC or China) are the following:

(a) The Patent Law, which was enacted in 1984 and amended in 1992 and 2000 and 2008 promulgated by the National People's Congress, the highest legislative body in China. The third amendment of the Patent Law came into force on October 1, 2009.

(b) The Implementing Regulations of the Patent Law (Patent Law Implementing Regulations), promulgated by the State Council on January 21, 2010, which provide detailed regulations for implementing the Patent Law, and came into force on February 1, 2010.

(c) The Supreme Court Interpretation on Several Issues Regarding Legal Application in the Adjudication of Patent Infringement Cases (2010 Judicial Interpretation), which was issued on December 28, 2009, and came into force on January 1, 2010. This Interpretation provides that, in case of inconsistency with any other interpretations, the 2010 Judicial Interpretation will prevail.[1]

(d) The Guidelines on the Application of the Law Regarding Trials of Patent Infringement Cases (2001 Patent Trial Guidelines), which were issued by the Supreme People's Court of China (Supreme Court or Supreme People's Court) on June 19, 2001, and govern court proceedings at all levels involving patent infringement. The 2001 Patent Trial Guidelines came into force on July 1, 2001.

(e) Several Provisions of the Supreme People's Court for the Application of Law to Pre-trial Cessation of Infringement of Patent Right Adopted at

---

1. 2010 Judicial Interpretation, Article 20.

the 179th Meeting of the Adjudication Committee of the Supreme People's Court on June 5, 2001 (2001 Patent Interim Measures Rules), which became effective from July 1, 2001.

(f) The Supreme Court Opinion on Handling of Certain Issues in Intellectual Property Cases During the Current Economic Situation, which was issued on April 21, 2009 (2009 Economic Situation Opinion).[2]

(g) The Guidelines for Patent Examination (Examination Guidelines), issued by the State Intellectual Property Office (SIPO) on January 21, 2010, detail the requirements for patentability and are used by patent examiners to examine applications and by the Patent Re-examination and Adjudication Board when making decisions on the validity of patents. The Examination Guidelines came into force on February 1, 2010.

(h) Measures for Administrative Enforcement of Patents (2001 Administrative Patent Measures), which were issued by SIPO on December 29, 2010, and came into force on February 1, 2010.

The first six of these provisions are included in this book as appendices in a bilingual format.

2.2 OTHER RELEVANT LEGISLATION

2.2.1 Other laws or judicial provisions, though directly not related to patents, which govern certain aspects of patent enforcement are the following:

(a) The General Principles of Civil Law, adopted at the Fourth Session of the Sixth National People's Congress on April 12, 1986, which became effective on January 1, 1987.

(b) The Civil Procedure Law, which was promulgated by the Fourth Session of the Seventh National People's Congress on April 9, 1991, and amended in 2007 with the amendments taking effect from April 1, 2008.

(c) The Administrative Litigation Law (also translated as the Administrative Procedure Law), which was adopted at the Second Session of the Seventh National People's Congress on April 4, 1989, and became effective as of October 1, 1990.

(d) Provisions of the Supreme People's Court on Certain Issues Concerning the Application of the Statute of Limitations to Civil Case Trials (2008 Limitation Provisions), which became effective on September 1, 2008.

---

2. The 2009 Economic Situation Opinion is a hybrid document that is part policy and part legal provisions. It is nevertheless an important document as it provides certain regulations to assist the handling of patent cases.

(e) Regulations for IP Customs Protection (IP Customs Regulations), which became effective on April 1, 2010, and replaced regulations issued in 2003, which in turn replaced regulations issued in 1995.

(f) The Several Provisions of the Supreme People's Court on Evidence in Civil Proceedings (Supreme Court Evidence Rules) were adopted at the 1201st meeting of the Judicial Committee of the Supreme People's Court on December 6, 2001, and came into effect on April 1, 2002.

2.2.2 There are other laws and regulations that have an impact on intellectual property cases cited in this book. The above are the main laws and regulations.

2.3 AMENDMENTS TO THE PATENT LAW

2.3.1 The Patent Law was first enacted in 1984 and came into effect in 1986. It has been amended three times since it was first enacted in 1992, 2000, and 2009. Each amendment has made changes to the substantive law and, in general, has improved the law.

2.4 RENUMBERING OF ARTICLES AFTER AMENDMENT

2.4.1 Readers should note that if a law or other legal provision is amended in China and articles of the law are deleted or added, the law is renumbered in its entirety. There is, therefore, no consistency between the numbering of laws pre- and post-amendment. Unless otherwise noted, in this book, references to all statutes and other legal provisions are to their current versions.

2.5 TRANSITIONAL PROVISIONS APPLYING TO THE MOST RECENT AMENDMENTS

2.5.1 As part of the enactment of the 2008 amendments, a number of transitional provisions have been introduced. These included:

(a) For acts of infringement committed before the new law took effect on October 1, 2009, the previous law will be applied by both courts and administrative agencies.[3]

---

3. 2010 Judicial Interpretation, Article 19 and State Intellectual Property Office's Transitional Rules regarding the Application of the Amended Patent Law, Article 4.

(b) In determining the validity of patents, for patents applied before the new law came into effect, the previous law will apply. The new law will apply to patents applied for on or after October 1, 2009.[4]

2.5.2 The impact of these transitional provisions on infringement litigation is limited. The main changes in terms of acts of infringement introduced in the law are that the offer to sell a product protected by a design patent is now an act of infringement, and the maximum possible statutory damages have been increased from one-half to one million renminbi. (*Statutory damages* are damages the court may award when it is difficult to calculate damages under other heads of damage.)

2.5.3 For the validity of patents, the main change in the law is to introduce absolute novelty. That is, prior use (and not just prior publication) outside of China prior to the priority date of the patent can also be used to challenge the validity of the patent.

2.5.4 This book will therefore focus on the current patent law and subsidiary legislation and judicial opinions while noting any major differences with the previous version of the law. Readers should be alert to consider whether the acts of infringement predate October 1, 2009, or the date of patent grant is prior to October 1, 2009, in considering whether the new or old law will apply. This will be of limited concern after October 1, 2001, for infringement cases because the limitation period for bringing action is, generally, two years. In considering the validity of a patent, this will need to be borne in mind for the life of the patent, which could be up to twenty years after 2009.

2.6 CASE LAW

2.6.1 China is a civil law jurisdiction. As such, the Chinese legal system does not have a rule of binding precedent. Chinese courts do not have to follow the earlier decisions of other courts, even higher courts. However, the decisions and opinions of some courts, such as the Supreme People's Court and Beijing and Shanghai Higher People's Court, are sometimes cited.

2.6.2 This book makes limited reference to case law. The reason for this is twofold, as follows:

(a) The courts and lawyers in China do not often make reference to case law when arguing or deciding cases. Rather they rely on the provisions of the

---

4. State Intellectual Property Office's Transitional Rules regarding the Application of the Amended Patent Law, Article 2.

law and any judicial interpretations or opinions that are relevant to the case. If reference is made to case law, it is to cases from the Supreme People's Court as the final decider of the law. In a local region, there may be references to the decisions of the Higher People's Courts of that region.

(b) For various reasons, such as political influence, the decisions of the Chinese courts are not consistent even within the same chambers. The Supreme People's Court addressed this issue in the 2009 Current Economic Situation Opinion in that it encouraged the courts to make consistent decisions in the same type or similar types of cases[5] as well as to avoid local protectionism and treat domestic and foreign parties equally.[6]

2.6.3 If cases are referred to, and if possible, reference is made to decisions of the Supreme People's Court of the People's Republic of China (Supreme People's Court or Supreme Court). In the case of appeals from invalidation decisions, reference is made to certain decisions of the Beijing First Intermediate Court and Beijing Higher People's Courts; there is some consistency in their decision making because they are the only courts in the country to hear such appeals. Certain other cases are referred to illustrate how courts can apply certain provisions of the law.

2.7 SUPREME COURT JUDICIAL INTERPRETATIONS AND OPINIONS

2.7.1 The judicial interpretations of the Supreme People's Court play a significant role in the legal system in China. Despite there being no doctrine of precedent, the Supreme People's Court and other higher level courts in China are authorized to and do issue interpretations and opinions of the law.

2.7.2 The National People's Congress has authorized the national supreme judicial authorities (i.e., the Supreme Court or the Supreme People's Prosecutor's Office) to issue judicial interpretations on questions relating to specific application of laws in their judicial practices. The basic effect of judicial interpretations is to provide guidance to judicial authorities when they handle cases. This is especially needed in relation to business law, as the Chinese economy has been developing rapidly and legislation is failing to keep up with the pace of change.

2.7.3 On June 10, 1981, the Standing Committee of the National People's Congress adopted the Resolution on Strengthening the Work of Law Interpretation (the Resolution). Article 2 of the Resolution prescribes that

---

5. 2009 Current Economic Situation Opinion, paragraph 19.
6. 2009 Current Economic Situation Opinion, paragraph 19.

all questions arising from court trials concerning the specific application of laws and regulations shall be interpreted by the Supreme People's Court. Based on the Resolution, the Supreme Court has the authority to formulate judicial interpretations. Since 1995, the Supreme People's Court has formulated many judicial interpretations in relation to numerous laws, and such interpretations have helped to interpret the law in numerous fields, such as banking, arbitration, and intellectual property.

2.7.4 These interpretations go well beyond just interpretation of provisions of a law and are often very long and include detailed provisions, such as in patent law, for claim interpretation. The interpretations are to this extent more akin to legislation and are generally interpreted by the courts as such.

2.7.5 The Supreme People's Court may issue four types of judicial explanations: interpretations, provisions, replies, and decisions.[7] For patent cases, the most important of these has been mentioned above. Certain other provisions, replies, and decisions are referred to in this book.

2.8 INTERPRETATIONS AND OPINIONS OF THE LOWER COURTS

2.8.1 Lower courts can issue interpretations on the laws which cover their jurisdiction. In patent law, the Beijing Higher People's Court in 2001 issued an Opinion on Issues Regarding the Establishment of Patent Infringement (Beijing Patent Opinion). This was not binding on other courts in China but did have persuasive authority. Given the amendments to the Patent Law and new judicial interpretations that have been issued, the Beijing Patent Opinion has lost much of its persuasive authority. Reference is made to it in this book, if there are no other opinions of other courts covering the issue under discussion.

---

7. Regulations of the Supreme People's Court Concerning Judicial Explanation Work, Article 6.

CHAPTER 3

Introduction to China's Administrative and Judicial Patent Systems

3.1 INTRODUCTION

3.1.1 The People's Republic of China (PRC or China) has a dual administrative and judicial system for enforcing patents. Patent enforcement actions may be brought to administrative bodies or to the courts.

3.1.2 The chapter provides an introduction to the:

(a) State Intellectual Property Office (SIPO) and the Patent Review and Adjudication Board (PRAB, also called the Patent Re-examination Board) as the key administrative body handling patent related matters and
(b) Chinese judicial system.

3.2 ADMINISTRATIVE SYSTEM

3.2.1 Patent validity is determined by an administrative body, the Patent Review, and Adjudication Board.

3.2.2 Administrative patent enforcement administrative actions are brought to the local branches of the SIPO where the infringement is occurring.

3.2.3 The General Administration of Customs (GAC) also can take action to seize imports or exports of products that infringe a patent.

3.3 JUDICIAL SYSTEM

3.3.1 The courts may handle all infringement cases directly, but have no power to handle validity cases other than on appeal.

3.3.2 Appeals from decisions of the PRAB on validity cases may be made to Beijing First Intermediate Court with a subsequent appeal available to the Beijing Higher People's Court. In all other cases of administrative enforcement, appeals lie to the courts where the administrative body is located.

3.4 STATE INTELLECTUAL PROPERTY OFFICE

3.4.1 The SIPO is the government department responsible for patents. It is designated by the State Council to be responsible for accepting patent applications, examining patent applications, and granting patent rights.[1] It is a directly subordinate organization of the State Council, according to the *Notice of the State Council Concerning the Establishment of Organizations*.[2] The SIPO only has eighty-five staff members, among which there is one commissioner, four assistant commissioners, and nineteen deputy commissioners.[3] There are a total of seven internal departments in SIPO and twelve subordinate organizations that report directly to SIPO. The seven internal departments of the SIPO are the General Office Department, the Treaty and Law Department, the Protection Coordination Department, the International Cooperation Department (incorporating the Hong Kong, Macau, and Taiwan Offices), the Patent Management Department, and the Personnel Department. The General Office Department is responsible for work including communications, daily organizational work, policy research, and the financial and administrative affairs of the SIPO.[4] Foreign-related patent issues, including the amendment of international intellectual property (IP) treaties, foreign negotiations relating to intellectual property, and the preparation of intellectual property laws relating to patents is undertaken by the Treaty and Law Department.[5] Coordination of intellectual property enforcement activities and related work is the responsibility of the Protection Coordination Department.[6] Any patent affairs that are international in nature, which also covers any patent affairs regarding Hong Kong,

---

1. Patent Law, Article 3.
2. State Council Notice, No. 11, 2008.
3. Notice of the General Office of the State Council Concerning Regulation of the Main Duties, Internal Structures, and Staff of the State Intellectual Property Office, Article 3.
4. Notice of the General Office of the State Council Concerning Regulation of the Main Duties, Internal Structures, and Staff of the State Intellectual Property Office, Article 2(1).
5. Notice of the General Office of the State Council Concerning Regulation of the Main Duties, Internal Structures, and Staff of the State Intellectual Property Office, Article 2(2).
6. Notice of the General Office of the State Council Concerning Regulation of the Main Duties, Internal Structures, and Staff of the State Intellectual Property Office, Article 2(3).

Macau, and Taiwan, including international communication and cooperation, is managed by the International Cooperation Department.[7]

3.4.2 Patent infringement mediation disputes, the investigating of patent counterfeiting, and policies for standardizing patent technology transfers are handled by the Patent Management Department.[8]

3.4.3 The Development Plan Department guides and supervises the management of the subordinate organizations in the SIPO.[9] Personnel management is managed by the Personnel Department, which is made up of cadres and the Party Committee.[10] The twelve subordinate organizations of the SIPO are the Patent Review and Adjudication Board, the Intellectual Property Rights Publishing House, the China Patent Information Centre, the China Intellectual Property Rights Newspaper, the China Patent Technology Development Company, the China Intellectual Property Rights Training Center, the China Intellectual Rights Research Committee, the Patent Search Advisory Center, the Patent Examination Coordination Center, the China Patent Protection Association, the National Patent Attorney Association, and the China Invention Association.

Local Intellectual Property Offices

3.4.4 The SIPO central office is located in Beijing. Nevertheless, local intellectual property departments are located throughout China in the provinces, autonomous regions, or directly controlled municipalities.

3.5 PATENT REVIEW AND ADJUDICATION BOARD

3.5.1 The Patent Review and Adjudication Board is responsible for reviewing patent applications rejected by SIPO and handling patent invalidation actions.[11] The procedures for the re-examination and invalidation of patent will be discussed below.

---

7. Notice of the General Office of the State Council Concerning Regulation of the Main Duties, Internal Structures, and Staff of the State Intellectual Property Office, Article 2(4).
8. Notice of the General Office of the State Council Concerning Regulation of the Main Duties, Internal Structures, and Staff of the State Intellectual Property Office, Article 2(5).
9. Notice of the General Office of the State Council Concerning Regulation of the Main Duties, Internal Structures, and Staff of the State Intellectual Property Office, Article 2(6).
10. Notice of the General Office of the State Council Concerning Regulation of the Main Duties, Internal Structures, and Staff of the State Intellectual Property Office, Article 2(7).
11. Patent Law Implementing Regulations, Chapter IV, Articles 59–72.

3.5.2 The PRAB is established under the SIPO.[12] The technical and legal panelists of the PRAB are selected by the SIPO. The chairman of the PRAB is required to be a member of the SIPO.[13] The purpose of the PRAB is to ensure the impartiality of administrative decisions related to the application and invalidation process. Any member of the PRAB who has previously conducted an examination of the patent or has a vested interest in the outcome of any re-examinations required should not take part in the ensuing procedures.[14]

3.6 STRUCTURE OF THE CHINESE JUDICIAL SYSTEM

3.6.1 The Chinese judicial system follows the structure of the Chinese political system. The Supreme People's Court of China (Supreme Court or Supreme People's Court) is located in Beijing. Under this court, in each province, autonomous region, or directly controlled city is a Higher People's Court, which is the highest court for that region. Under the Higher People's Courts are Intermediate People's Courts in major cities, and Primary People's Courts in smaller areas and suburbs of cities. The main trial courts are the Primary People's Courts and Intermediate People's Courts, although the Higher People's Courts and Supreme Court do have first instance jurisdiction in certain cases. There is one level of appeal to the next highest court.[15] There is also a system of military courts that is not discussed in this book.

3.6.2 A flow chart of the system is set out below:

The Supreme People's Court	The Supreme People's Court is the highest court. It tries the following: (1) cases of first instance over which it has jurisdiction according to law; (2) cases of first instance it deems that it should try; (3) cases of first instance submitted for trial by people's courts at lower level in accordance with law; (4) cases of appeal and review against the judgments and orders of Higher People's Courts and special people's courts; and (5) cases of reviews filed by the Supreme People's Procuratorate in accordance with the procedures of trial supervision.
The Higher People's Court	The Higher People's Court operates at the level of province, autonomous region, and municipality with provincial status. Higher People's Courts try the following: (1) cases of first instance over which it has jurisdiction; (2) cases of first instance submitted for trial by people's courts at lower level according to law; (3) cases of first instance transferred from the Supreme People's Court according to law; (4) cases of appeal and review against judgments and orders of people's courts at lower level; and (5) cases of review filed by people's procuratorate in accordance with the procedures of trial supervision.

12. Patent Law, Article 41.
13. Patent Law Implementing Regulations, Article 59.
14. Patent Law Implementing Regulations, Article 37.
15. The specific structures and powers of courts are set out in the People's Courts Organization Law.

The Intermediate People's Courts	The Intermediate People's Courts operate at the level of prefectures in Chinese provinces; autonomous regions; districts in municipalities with provincial status; cities and autonomous prefectures of provinces and autonomous regions. An Intermediate People's Court hears the following: (1) cases of first instance over which it has jurisdiction; (2) cases of first instance it is empowered by the Supreme People's Court to try; (3) cases of first instance submitted for trial by Primary People's Courts; (4) cases of first instance transferred from courts at higher level according to law; and (5) cases of appeal and review against judgments and orders made by the Primary People's Courts, and cases of review filed by the people's procuratorate according to the procedures of trial supervision.
The Primary People's Court	The Primary People's Courts operate in counties, cities at county level, autonomous counties, banners, and city districts. A Primary People's Court hears criminal, civil, economic, and administrative cases of first instance, except for those cases otherwise stipulated by law. The Primary People's Courts can also guide people through mediation in minor cases that do not require a trial.

3.7 INTELLECTUAL PROPERTY CHAMBERS

3.7.1 The Supreme Court has established an intellectual property chamber that hears intellectual property appeals and is responsible for the drafting of judicial interpretations relating to intellectual property matters.

3.7.2 Higher People's Courts, most Intermediate People's Courts, and certain Primary People's Courts have also established intellectual property chambers that are made up of specialist judges who have been trained in IP law. Some judges of the IP Civil Division have science or engineering background and they all have experience in dealing with IP cases.

3.8 COURTS THAT HANDLE PATENT CASES

3.8.1 All patent infringement cases or appeals from administrative decisions of SIPO or patent cases from the Administration of Customs must be filed to Intermediate People's Courts that have been designated to handle patent cases by the Supreme People's Court or, for infringement cases, if the claimed damages are large, to Higher People's Courts.[16] At the time of writing, seventy-six Intermediate Courts had been designated to handle patent cases.[17] For patent cases, certain Intermediate Courts are granted a wider geographical jurisdiction than normal and may hear patent cases relating to alleged

---

16. 2001 Patent Trial Guidelines, Article 2.
17. A list of Intermediate Courts authorized by the Supreme People's Court to handle patent cases is attached as an appendix. This has been sourced from various material as one consolidated document listing the courts has not been published by the Supreme People's Court.

infringements occurring in cities designated to be in their jurisdiction for patent cases. One Primary People's Court in Yiwu, Zhejiang has been authorised to try utility model and design patent cases on a trial basis.

3.8.2 The number of courts with jurisdiction to try patent cases is limited because of the complex nature of the patent cases. However, despite this, over the years, the number of courts with jurisdiction to try cases has been increased. The reason for this is that many cities wish to have their courts to be designated as patent courts so as to show the technical advancement of the city.

3.9 APPEALS

3.9.1 For infringement cases, an appeal can be made to the next highest court in the hierarchy. As, with one exception, patent cases can only be filed to Intermediate Courts or Higher People's Courts, the next level of appeal is the Higher People's Court of the relevant province or autonomous region or the Supreme People's Court.

3.9.2 Appeals from decisions of the PRAB are heard by the Beijing First Intermediate People's Court with a subsequent appeal available to the Beijing Higher People's Court.

3.9.3 A judgment made by the appellate court is a final decision unless a party successfully petitions the Supreme People's Court to review the case. The Supreme Court has complete discretion whether to review a case and may decide whether to conduct a review on paper or after an oral hearing.

3.10 THE JUDICIARY

3.10.1 Judges are regulated by general laws controlling public servants, as well as specialized laws controlling their profession.

3.10.2 Article 26 of the Chinese Constitution provides:[18]

> The people's courts exercise judicial power independently, in accordance with the provisions of the law, and are not subject to interference by any administrative organ, public organization or individual.

---

18. This is repeated in Article 4 of the People's Court Organization Law.

3.10.3 This concept of judicial independence is further codified in the *Basic Standards of Judges Professional Ethics*, which provides that judges must conduct independent hearings, and not be interfered by any administrative organs, social organizations, or individuals.[19] The *Basic Standards of Judges Professional Ethics* also specifically prohibits money, relationships, or other factors from interfering with judges maintaining their correct legal opinions during hearings and not privately see only one party during the court hearing.[20] Judges are required to maintain their neutrality and equality when protecting the legal rights and interest of all parties, and not be biased towards one particular party.[21]

3.10.4 These rules are not always followed as has been frankly admitted by the Supreme People's Court on numerous occasions. For example, in his work report delivered to the National People's Congress in March 2010, Wang Shengjun, President of the Supreme People's Court, stated that ensuring "clean government" in the courts was a major task and reported that 795 employees of courts had been punished for corruption in 2009, and 137 had been transferred to the prosecutors for prosecution. President Wang also said that improving the quality of judges was a major task.[22]

3.11 ADJUDICATION COMMITTEES

3.11.1 One further restriction on judicial independence in China is the establishment of adjudication committees in all courts. Article 11 of the People's Court Organization Law provides

> All levels of People Courts establish adjudication committees to implement the democratic centralism system. The duties of adjudication committees are to bring together adjudication experience, discuss serious or difficult cases as well as other problems that arise in adjudication work.

3.11.2 An adjudication committee oversees the decisions made by judges and has the power to overrule decisions made by judges either before a decision is made or, if a decision has become effective, after a reference by the chief judge of the court.[23] The adjudication committee is made up of senior

---

19. Basic Standards of Judges Professional Ethics, Article 8.
20. Basic Standards of Judges Professional Ethics, Articles 13 and 15.
21. Basic Standards of Judges Professional Ethics, Article 8.
22. Work Report of the President of the Supreme People's Court to the 3rd Session of the 11th National People's Congress, March 11, 2010, Section 7.
23. *See* Civil Procedure Law, Article 177 for the power of the Chief Judge to refer a matter.

judges who are generally, if not invariably, communist party members. The committees can serve a useful oversight role and ensure that decisions are being made correctly by the panel of judges on a court. The other role is to provide political oversight to cases and ensure that decisions are made are in line with party policy or objectives. The reference to "implementing the democratic centralism system" refers to ultimately maintaining the leading role of the Communist Party.[24]

3.11.3 It is not the purpose of this book to discuss the political structure of the Chinese courts. The role of both adjudication committees and the problems cited by President Wang of the Supreme People's Court should always be considered when handling patent cases in China.

---

24. Democratic Centralism is a Leninist formulation created to justify a one-party state in a "democratic" country. For definitions of Democratic Centralism, as applied in China, see Article 3 of the Chinese Constitution and the Preamble to the Constitution of the Chinese Communist Party.

CHAPTER 4

Administrative Enforcement

4.1 ADMINISTRATIVE ENFORCEMENT

4.1.1 In the People's Republic of China (PRC or China), patentees can initiate administrative actions against an infringer through the State Intellectual Property Office (SIPO) or the General Administration of Customs (GAC).

4.1.2 The advantages of administrative actions are the following:

(a) Administrative actions are much quicker and generally cost less.

(b) An administrative agency may act on less evidence than a court would and sometimes accepts evidence that would be inadmissible in court.

(c) In collecting evidence against the opposing party, the administrative bodies have the power to collect evidence that a patentee may not be able to collect themselves. The evidence can be used either to support the administrative action or in court actions. This approach can be very effective if the intellectual property (IP) owner has a good working relationship with the administrative agency.

4.1.3 The disadvantages of administrative actions are the following:

(a) Monetary damages cannot be ordered.

(b) The relevant administrative agencies have discretion over whether to take on a case, and in general, they are unwilling to do so if the case requires anything other than a straightforward interpretation of the law.

(c) If the opposing party is dissatisfied with the result of an administrative action, it can appeal the administrative agency's decision to a People's Court, so the case often ends up in court in any event.

4.2 THE PROCEDURE FOR SIPO ADMINISTRATIVE ACTIONS

4.2.1 This section describes the procedures for bringing administrative actions through SIPO. It focuses on the procedural aspects of such actions. The substantive law to be applied by SIPO is the same as that discussed in relation to patent infringement litigation.

4.2.2 Article 60 of the Patent Law provides, if a patent dispute arises, a party may bring either a civil case or an administrative case. If the case is brought to SIPO, and it is determined that there is infringement, SIPO "may order the infringer to stop the infringing act immediately." The infringer may appeal a decision within fifteen days. If an appeal is not brought and the order is not complied with, SIPO may approach the People's Court for compulsory execution.

4.2.3 With regard to compensation, under Article 60, SIPO "may, upon the request of the parties, mediate in the amount of compensation for the infringement of the patent right." If the mediation fails, the parties may institute legal proceedings in the people's court for damages.

4.2.4 The specific rules governing administrative action for patent infringement are the contained in the Measures for Administrative Enforcement of Patents (2011 Administrative Patent Measures), issued by SIPO and which took effect from February 1, 2011.

4.2.5 Administrative proceedings generally involve the following steps:

    (a) Submission of a complaint by the patentee, including the submission of evidence;
    (b) Acceptance or rejection of the matter by the SIPO;
    (c) If accepted, inspection of the defendant's premises and records by the SIPO to gather evidence and serve the complaint;
    (d) Submission of a written defense and evidence by the defendant;
    (e) Oral hearing at the discretion of the SIPO; and
    (f) Decision on infringement by the SIPO.

4.2.6 The procedure for commencing the administrative process is to approach the local SIPO and file a formal complaint concerning the act of patent infringement. In serious cases or if infringement is occurring in more than two localities, the local SIPO may refer the matter to a higher level.[1]

---

1. 2011 Administrative Patent Measures Rules, Article 5.

4.2.7 Article 8 of the 2011 Patent Administrative Measures provides that if a party requests SIPO to handle a patent infringement dispute, it should fulfill the following conditions:

1. The applicant is the patent holder or related injured party.
2. There is a clear respondent.
3. There is a clear claim and reasons and evidence to support that claim.
4. It falls within the jurisdiction of that administrative authority for patent affairs.
5. The applicant has not brought proceedings to a people's court with regard to the same dispute.

4.2.8 With regard to who is a related injured party, Article 8(2) of the 2011 Patent Administrative Measures provides that an exclusive licensee or, where the patentee has given up its rights to take action, a sole licensee may submit a request for the handling of a patent infringement dispute as a related injured party under Article 60 Patent Law.

4.2.9 The type of evidence that will need to be submitted is:

(a) Evidence of the right-holder's intellectual property rights or related injured parties' standing;[2]
(b) Evidence obtained concerning the alleged infringement;
(c) Documentary evidence of the alleged infringement;
(d) A sample of the genuine item to enable comparison with the alleged infringing item.

4.2.10 All the necessary documents must be signed and sealed before being filed with the SIPO, and, according to the number of respondents, the applicant must provide enough copies of the request and photocopies of the patent certificate.[3]

4.2.11 SIPOs will, generally, not accept evidence that is not notarized and legalized.

Jurisdiction

4.2.12 Generally, the SIPO closest to the infringer's premises has jurisidction. Due to the risk of local protectionism, the SIPO's links with the infringers should be considered. If there is a risk of local protectionism, the complaint

---

2. 2011 Administrative Patent Measures Rules, Article 5.
3. 2011 Administrative Patent Measures Rules, Article 9.

should be filed with a SIPO at a higher level, which is usually at the provincial level.

Interested Parties

Handling of the Case

4.2.13 If the request conforms to the requirements in the 2011 Patent Administrative Measures, then the SIPO will, within five days of receipt of the request, notify the applicant of the acceptance and appoint three or more personnel to handle the patent infringement case.[4]

4.2.14 For patent infringement disputes involving utility models or design patents, SIPO may request the applicant to submit a search report within fifteen days of receiving the request.[5]

4.2.15 The SIPO, when handling a case, will usually conduct an on-site investigation of the alleged infringer's premises to collect evidence such as samples and documentation relating to the alleged infringement.

4.2.16 If the request does not conform to the requirements in the 2011 Patent Administrative Measures, then SIPO should notify the applicant within seven days of receipt of the request.[6]

4.2.17 SIPO should serve the complaint on the respondent within five days of acceptance and give the respondent fifteen days to file a defense (if any). If a defense is received, it should be sent to the complainant within five days.[7]

4.2.18 If the respondent files an application to invalidate the patent, the SIPO has a discretion whether to stay the action or not.[8] If the action is stayed, it should notify both parties. If a decision is made upholding the patent, the case should resume immediately. If the patent is invalidated, the case should be withdrawn or SIPO will dismiss it.

4.2.19 According to the circumstances of the patent infringement case, the SIPO may decide to conduct an oral hearing with the parties, and will inform the parties of the date and time at least three days prior to the

---

4. 2011 Administrative Patent Measures Rules, Article 11.
5. 2011 Administrative Patent Measures Rules, Article 9.
6. 2011 Administrative Patent Measures Rules, Article 11.
7. 2011 Administrative Patent Measures Rules, Article 12.
8. Patent Law Implementing Regulations, Article 82.

oral hearing.⁹ A written record of the parties attending and the main points of the hearing are kept by SIPO.¹⁰

The Decision

4.2.20 The SIPO may, after investigation, order a party to cease infringing the patent rights.¹¹ However, the SIPO does not have the power to order damages. If the claimant wishes to claim damages, they are required to bring a case to the People's Court. If the respondent does not challenge the decision of SIPO as to infringement, the court's sole role in hearing a claim for damages will be to assess the damages.

The Appeal to Court

4.2.21 Should a party not accept a decision from the SIPO, it may file an administrative lawsuit with the People's Court within fifteen days of notice of the SIPO notification in accordance with the Administrative Litigation Law.¹² If a lawsuit is file, enforcement of the decision of SIPO is stayed.¹³

4.3 MEDIATION BY THE SIPO

4.3.1 The parties in a patent infringement dispute may also request the SIPO to conduct mediation between the two parties.¹⁴ In the course of an investigation of infringement, SIPO will often seek to mediate a settlement between the parties. A mediated settlement can include the payment of damages. This can be a very effective way to resolve disputes as SIPO can serve as an effective mediator based on their specialist knowledge of patent law.

4.3.2 In the 2006 national report released by the SIPO, it was reported that, nationwide, the SIPO accepted a total of 1,227 patent infringement cases for mediation, of which 200 cases involved invention patents, 459 involved

---

9. 2011 Administrative Patent Measures Rules, Article 14.
10. 2011 Administrative Patent Measures, Article 15.
11. Patent Law, Article 60.
12. Patent Law, Article 60.
13. 2011 Administrative Patent Measures, Article 42.
14. Patent Law, Article 60, 2011 Administrative Patent Measures, Chapter 3.

utility models, and 568 involved external design patents. Of the 1,227 cases, the SIPO settled 953 through mediation between the parties involved.

The SIPO as a Mediator

4.3.3 Patent infringement disputes that the SIPO may act as a mediator in are:

(a) Disputes regarding patent application rights and patent rights;
(b) Disputes on the qualifications of inventors and designers;
(c) Disputes regarding the reward and remuneration for inventors and designers of service-invention creations;
(d) Disputes on failing to pay proper fees after the application for a patent for invention had been published, but before the patent right granted.
(e) Other patent disputes.[15]

An Example of a Mediation Case

4.3.4 An example of a patent infringement dispute that was successfully mediated by the SIPO was a case involving the Hubei Provincial SIPO, Wuhan Municipal SIPO, and the Huangshi Municipal SIPO. The case involved a patent infringement dispute concerning the Infant Tricycle (231-B) external design patent. The Wuhan Municipal SIPO handled the dispute and the respondent paid compensation as well as undertaking to immediately cease selling the infringing products. However, in late 2007, the claimant discovered that the suspected infringing products were still being sold.

4.3.5 As a result, the claimant complained to the Hubei Provincial SIPO, who then sent enforcement personnel from the Wuhan Municipal SIPO to conduct on-site inspections. Following the on-site inspections, it was discovered that the suspected infringing products were being manufactured in Huangshi City by a third party. Thereafter, the Wuhan Municipal SIPO assisted the claimant, respondent, and third party in settling the dispute through a mediation agreement.

4.3.6 The mediation agreement required the claimant to be compensated 20 thousand renminbi; the molds used to manufacture the infringing products to be destroyed under the supervision of the SIPO, and the respondent

---

15. Patent Law Implementing Regulations, Article 85.

and third party receive training conducted by the SIPO to strengthen their understanding of intellectual property. On January 11, 2008, according to the mediation agreement, the Hubei Provincial SIPO, Wuhan Municipal SIPO, and Huangshi Municipal SIPO attended the on-site destruction of the molds and underwent intellectual property training.

4.4 GENERAL ADMINISTRATION FOR CUSTOMS

4.4.1 Under the Regulations for IP Customs Protection (IP Customs Regulations), an owner may record his trademarks, copyright, or patents with the General Administration of Customs (GAC) in Beijing.[16]

4.4.2 The recordal process is simple and can be done using GAC's online filing system. The GAC is required to make a decision to record the IP right within thirty days.[17] The recordal is effective for ten years unless the remaining validity of the recorded IP right is less than ten years and can be renewed within six months of expiry if the IP right remains valid. If an IP right expires or is invalidated, the record automatically expires.[18]

4.4.3 After registration with customs, Chinese Customs can seize infringing products being imported into or exported from China either at the request of the right holder or on its own volition.

4.4.4 Customs seizures are principally used for trademark and design patent cases where the customs officers at border control points can easily identify infringing items. Customs are also usually able to finalize a trademark or design case with an administrative decision.

4.4.5 Customs seizures can be made for products that infringe utility models or invention patent. However, it is very likely the patentee will be required to take court action in the jurisdiction the seizure occurs following a seizure. If there is no other way of obtaining samples of a product, a customs seizure can be a good way to obtain evidence for use in litigation.

Seizures

4.4.6 Local customs are responsible for seizing infringing goods at Chinese borders. A local customs may detain the infringing goods on its own volition,

---

16. IP Customs Protection Regulations, Article 7.
17. IP Customs Protection Regulations, Article 8.
18. IP Customs Protection Regulations, Article 10.

in which case it sends a notice to the IP owner. The IP owner has three days to file a request for seizure of the goods.[19]

4.4.7 The IP owner may bring an action in court against the consignor or the infringer.[20] This will be necessary if the local customs cannot determine whether the seized goods are infringing, which is very likely in utility model or design patent cases. If customs does not receive a request from the court to assist in the case, it is required to release the goods within fifty days after seizure.[21]

4.4.8 Alternatively, if the IP owner becomes aware of infringing goods crossing the Chinese border, he may request the local customs to seize the goods. In this case, the IP owner will be required to provide information about the goods such as evidence of infringement and shipping information.[22] If a seizure is made at the request of the IP owner, they are required to bring an action in court for infringement. If customs does not receive a request from the court to assist in the case, customs are required to release the goods within twenty days after seizure.[23]

4.4.9 In patent cases, the Intermediate People's Court in the location of the seizure will have jurisdiction over the case.[24]

Posting a Bond

4.4.10 If the goods are seized, for each seizure, the IP owner is required to post a bond based on the declared value of the goods[25] to cover any damages to the consignor or consignee and customs expenses, such as storage fees. For seizures up to 20 thousand renminbi, the bond shall be the full value of the goods; between 20 thousand and 200 thousand renminbi, the bond shall be 50 percent of the value but not less than 20 thousand renminbi; and over 200 thousand renminbi, the maximum bond is 100 thousand renminbi.[26]

---

19. IP Customs Regulations, Articles 12–13.
20. IP Customs Regulations, Article 23.
21. IP Customs Regulations, Article 24(2).
22. IP Customs Regulations, Article 16.
23. IP Customs Regulations, Article 24(1).
24. Administrative Litigation Law, Article 14(1).
25. IP Customs Regulations Article 14.
26. IP Customs Regulations Implementing Provisions Article 23. For trademark cases, a general bond may also be given to the GAC. See IP Customs Regulations, Implementing Provisions Article 24.

4.4.11 For the sake of completeness it is worth mentioning that for trademarks but not for patents, the trademark owner may also post a general bond to the GAC to cover all seizures in China, and will not be required to post bonds for every seizure. The general bond can be paid in the form of a bank guarantee letter.

Counterbond in Patent Cases

4.4.12 In patent cases, the shipper or consignee can post a counterbond in the same amount as the bond to have products seized released.[27]

---

27. IP Customs Regulations, Article 19.

CHAPTER 5
Patents

5.1 INTRODUCTION

5.1.1 This chapter provides an overview of the types of patents that can be obtained in the People's Republic of China (PRC or China) and then describes, as far as is relevant to patent litigation, the procedures for the examination and granting of patents.

5.2 TYPES OF PATENTS

5.2.1 Under the Chinese Patent Law, there are three types of patents, or *invention-creations,* as they are called, which are:

(a) Invention patents,
(b) Utility models, and
(c) External design patents.

5.2.2 There is no separate legislation covering external designs.

5.2.3 Article 2 of the Patent Law provides the following definitions of the three types of patents.

Invention Patents

5.2.4 *Invention* refers to a new technical solution put forward for a product, method, or the improvement thereof.

Utility Models

5.2.5 *Utility model* refers to a new practical technical solution for a product's form, structure, or the combination thereof.

Design Patents

5.2.6 *Design* means a new design of a product's shape, pattern, or the combination thereof; or the combination of its color and shape, and/or pattern, that is aesthetically pleasing and fit for industrial application.

Nonpatentable Subject Matter

5.2.7 Under Article 25 of the Patent Law, the following are not patentable:

   (a) Scientific discoveries;
   (b) Rules and methods for mental activities;
   (c) Methods for the diagnosis or the treatment of diseases;
   (d) Animal and plant varieties;
   (e) Substances obtained by means of nuclear transformation;
   (f) Designs that serve mainly as indicators of two-dimensional printing goods' pattern, the color, or the combination of the two.

5.2.8 Processes used to produce animal and plant varieties may, however, be granted patent rights.[1]

5.3 FILING REQUIREMENTS

5.3.1 All patent applications must be filed with the State Intellectual Property Office (SIPO) located in Beijing.

Inventions and Utility Models

5.3.2 The Patent Law provides that an applicant for a patent invention or utility model must submit to the SIPO the following documents, which must all be completed in Chinese and filed in duplicate:

   (a) Application;
   (b) Description of the invention (drawings where necessary);

---

1. Patent Law, Article 25.

(c) Abstract; and
(d) Claims.[2]

5.3.3 The description must be sufficient to enable a person skilled in the art to reconstruct the invention. The claims must state the extent of protection requested for the patents.

Design Patent

5.3.4 An application for a design patent requires the following:

(a) Application;
(b) Figures or photographs of the design;
(c) Product incorporating that design; and
(d) The class to which that product belongs must be indicated.[3]

5.4 TERM OF PROTECTION

5.4.1 The term of legal protection for patent rights for inventions is twenty years, and ten for utility models and design patents.[4] The period of protection is calculated from when the relevant application is first filed with the SIPO.

5.4.2 For priority applications, the date of filing for the purposes of calculating the term of protection is the date of filing in China and not the original filing date.[5]

Priority Claims

5.4.3 Under Article 30 of the Patent Law, if the applicant claims a priority right, the applicant must submit a declaration with the application and, within three months, submit a copy of the first-filed patent application. If the applicant fails to submit the declaration of priority application, the claim of priority shall be deemed not to have been made.

5.4.4 Priority can be claimed if a patent is filed in any country that is a signatory to a multilateral (such as the Paris Convention) or bilateral treaty

---

2. Patent Law, Article 26; Patent Law Implementing Regulations, Article 15.
3. Patent Law, Article 27.
4. Patent Law, Article 42.
5. Patent Law Implementing Regulations, Article 11.

with China.[6] The applicant may claim priority for an invention patent within twelve months of first filing, and within six months of first filing for utility models as well as external design patents.

5.5 GRACE PERIODS

5.5.1 There are certain narrow grace periods where novelty is not lost, if, within a period of six months before filing, the technology is made public in the following circumstances:

(a) An exhibition held or recognized by the Chinese government;
(b) A prescribed academic or technical meeting; or
(c) Any disclosure by any person without the consent of the applicant.[7]

5.6 PATENT EXAMINATION GUIDELINES

5.6.1 When examining a patent, the SIPO examiner will be guided by the Guidelines for Patent Examination (Examination Guidelines)[8] issued by SIPO, which sets out the principles to be used during patent examination.

5.6.2 The guidelines are divided into five parts covering the following:

Part I: Preliminary Examination
Part II: Substantive Examination
Part III: Examination of International Applications Entering the National Phase
Part IV: Examination of Requests for Re-Examination and for Invalidation
Part V: Processing of Patent Applications and Procedural Matters.

5.6.3 Each part is divided into chapters and sections that address specific topics and subtopics. These are cited in this book as, for example, Part IV, Chapter 3, Section 4.2.

5.6.4 The parts of the Examination Guidelines that are relevant to patent litigation are Part II that sets out the criteria for patentability applied by the Patent Office and Patent Review and Adjudication Board (PRAB) (also called in English the Patent Re-examination Board); and Part IV that addresses re-examination.

---

6. Patent Law, Article 29.
7. Patent Law, Article 24.
8. Examination Guidelines, Part II, Chapter 3.

5.6.5 The Examination Guidelines are referred to by the PRAB when considering invalidation requests and by the courts when hearing appeals on invalidation decisions. The courts will generally follow the Examination Guidelines, even though they do not consider that the guidelines are binding on them.

5.7 PRELIMINARY EXAMINATION

5.7.1 Examination of patent applications is divided into two stages: preliminary examination and substantive examination.

Preliminary Examination: Designs and Utility Models

5.7.2 Utility models and external design patent applications only undergo preliminary examination. Preliminary examination only examines form and for obvious substantive defects. Once the SIPO has conducted a preliminary examination, and no reasons for rejection have been established, the SIPO will issue a patent certificate for the utility model or external design patent as well as publish this in the *Utility Model Gazette* or the *Design Gazette*.[9]

5.7.3 The date on which the utility model or external design patent is published in their respective gazettes is the effective date for the utility model or external design patent.[10]

Preliminary Examination: Invention Patents

5.7.4 The Patent Law provides that, after receiving an application for an invention patent, the SIPO shall conduct a preliminary examination of the application. If the application conforms to the requirements of the law, the SIPO publishes the application after a period of eighteen months from the date of application, unless the applicant does not request this beforehand.[11]

5.7.5 Invention patents that have passed preliminary examination are published in the *Invention Patent Gazette*. The applicant is then required to apply for substantive examination with the SIPO within three years of filing

---

9. Patent Law, Article 40.
10. Patent Law, Article 40.
11. Patent Law, Article 34.

the application.[12] The SIPO may *ex officio* decide to conduct a substantive examination. If the applicant does not request a substantive application or fails to provide legitimate reasons for not doing so, the application will be regarded as having been withdrawn.

5.7.6 Article 44 of the Implementing Regulations of the Patent Law (Patent Law Implementing Regulations) provides that preliminary examination of an application for an invention patent shall include an examination of whether the application contains the necessary documentation; complies with the formal requirements; if filed by a foreign applicant, complies with the filing requirements for foreign applicants; seeks protection for a prohibited subject matter; or violates the single invention rule, i.e., the rule that only one invention can be claimed for one patent.

5.7.7 If, during the examination, SIPO determines the application does not comply with the legal requirements, it shall invite the applicant to comment on and/or correct the problems. If the response does not correct the defects, the application will be rejected.

5.8 SUBSTANTIVE EXAMINATION

5.8.1 Under Article 53 of the Patent Law Implementing Regulations, the grounds on which an invention patent can be rejected in substantive examination are the following:

(a) The application falls under Article 5 or 25 of the Patent Law, or the applicant is not entitled to a patent right in accordance with the provisions of Article 9 of the Patent Law.

(b) The application does not comply with the provisions of Article 2, paragraph two; Article 20, paragraph one; Article 22; Article 26, paragraphs three, four, or five; or Article 31, paragraph one of the Patent Law; or of Article 20, paragraph two of the Patent Law Implementing Regulations.

(c) The amendment to the application does not comply with the provisions of Article 33 of the Patent Law, or the divisional application does not comply with the provisions of Article 43, paragraph one of the Patent Law Implementing Regulations.

5.8.2 These are the same grounds for which a request for re-examination of patent under Article 65 of the Patent Law Implementing Rules can be made, except for two grounds, namely, Article 26(5) and Article 31(1) of the Patent Law.

---

12. Patent Law, Article 35.

5.8.3 The following chapter sets out the detailed grounds (as well as a summary table) under which a request for re-examination can be made and the analysis is not repeated here.

5.8.4 In essence, a patent will be examined to ensure that it complies with the Patent Law and, in particular, that the patent does not include subject matter that cannot be patented and that an invention or utility model possesses novelty, inventiveness, or practical applicability. The examiner will also examine to see if the patent makes sufficient disclosure so as to enable a person skilled in the art to carry out the invention or utility model; that the claims are supported by the description and that the independent claim outlines the technical solution.

5.8.5 The two grounds for which substantive examination is conducted but which are not grounds for invalidation are the following.

Article 26(5)

> Where an invention-creation is developed relying on the genetic resources, the applicant shall indicate, in the patent application documents, the direct and original source of such genetic resources; where the applicant is unable to indicate the original source, he or it shall state the reasons thereof.

Article 31(1)

> A patent application for invention or utility model shall be limited to one invention or utility model. Two or more inventions or utility models belonging to a single general inventive concept may be filed as one application.

5.8.6 These two items are not grounds for invalidation because, presumably, they are matters that SIPO consider should be considered by the examiner in examination alone and should not be a ground for a third party to seek to invalidate the patent.

5.9 REJECTION

5.9.1 SIPO may reject a patent application for a number of reasons relating to form or substance.

5.9.2 SIPO must notify the applicant of its opinion regarding the examination of the application and will then require the applicant to state their opinion or to rectify the application within a specified time limit. If the applicant has not given any response at the expiry of the time limit, the application shall be deemed to have been withdrawn.[13] If, after the applicant has stated opinions or made rectifications, the patent administrative department still considers the application not in conformity with the requirements, the application shall be rejected.[14]

5.10 RE-EXAMINATION

5.10.1 If the SIPO rejects the patent application, the applicant has three months from receipt of the application in which to file for re-examination with the PRAB.[15]

5.10.2 The Examination Guidelines specify that only the applicant of the rejected patent application has a right to file for patent re-examination. In the event that there are joint applicants, then all the applicants must file for re-examination. If not all applicants file for re-examination, the Patent Office will issue a notice to correct the defect. If all applicants then do not file for re-examination, the request re-examination will be deemed not to have been made.[16]

5.10.3 Re-examination may take place after preliminary examination or substantive examination of a patent on a number of grounds. When filing a re-examination application, an applicant may also file amendments to his application addressed to the defects notified by the Patent Office.[17]

5.10.4 When re-examining a patent, the PRAB will first remit the patent under re-examination to the patent office for reconsideration. If they agree to revoke their decision, the PRAB will issue a decision revoking the original decision, and the examination will proceed.[18]

5.10.5 For the re-examination of a patent application rejected during examination, the PRAB can revoke the decision of the Patent Office and restore the patent application or accept that amendments filed in re-examination have corrected defects found by the Patent Office, and remit the application

---

13. Patent Law, Article 37.
14. Patent Law, Article 38.
15. Patent Law, Article 41.
16. Patent Law, Article 25.
17. Patent Law Implementing Regulations, Article 61.
18. Patent Law Implementing Regulations, Article 62.

back to the patent for further examination.[19] The PRAB may also uphold the decision of the Patent Office rejecting the patent application.

5.10.6 If the PRAB revokes the decision of the Patent Office rejecting the application, the Patent Office must implement the decision of the PRAB and complete the substantive examination.

5.11 APPEAL OF THE RE-EXAMINATION DECISIONS TO THE COURT

5.11.1 Decisions of the PRAB on re-examinations may be appealed to the court by the applicant within three months of receiving the decision.[20] The procedures for doing so are discussed below when considering appeals against invalidation decisions.

---

19. Patent Law Implementing Regulations, Article 63(2).
20. Patent Law, Article 41(2).

CHAPTER 6

Grounds for Invalidating a Patent

6.1 INTRODUCTION

6.1.1 This chapter addresses the grounds upon which a party can challenge the validity of a patent in the People's Republic of China (PRC or China).

6.2 STATUTORY GROUNDS

6.2.1 The grounds for invalidating a patent are set out in Article 65(2) of the Implementing Regulations of the Patent Law (Patent Law Implementing Regulations), which is set out below in full, followed by a table setting out the main effect of each article. After the table, each ground is discussed other than those relating to design rights. The grounds relating to design rights are discussed in Chapter 13, "Design Patents."

6.2.2 Article 65(2) of the Patent Law Implementing Regulations provides:

> The grounds on which the request for invalidation is based, referred to in the preceding paragraph, mean that the invention-creation for which the patent right is granted does not comply with the provisions of Article 2, Article 20, paragraph one, Article 22, Article 23, Article 26, paragraph three or four, Article 27, paragraph two, or Article 33 of the Patent Law, or of Article 20, paragraph two or Article 43, paragraph one of these Implementing Regulations; or the invention-creation falls under the provisions of Article 5 or 25 of the Patent Law; or the applicant is not entitled to be granted the patent right in accordance with the provisions of Article 9 of the Patent Law.

6.2.3 The following table summarizes these provisions:

Patent Law	Summary of Provision
Article 2(1)	*Invention-creation*, referred to in this law, means invention, utility model, and design.
Article 2(2)	*Invention* refers to a new technical solution proposed for a product, method, or the improvement thereof.
Article 2(3)	*Utility model* refers to a new technical solution proposed for a product's form, structure, or the combination thereof, that is suitable for utility.
Article 2(4)	*Design* means a new design proposed for a product's shape, pattern, or the combination thereof; or the combination of its color and shape and/or pattern, that creates an aesthetic feeling and is suitable for industrial application.
Article 20(1)	A patent application should undergo confidentiality examination before being filed overseas.
Article 22	The patent should possess novelty [Article 22(2)], inventiveness [Article 22(3)] and practical applicability [Article 22(3)].
Article 23	Design rights shall be granted for a design that is the same as an existing design.
Article 26(3)	The patent does not make sufficient disclosure so as to enable a person skilled in the art to carry out the invention or utility model.
Article 26(4)	The claims should be supported by the description.
Article 27(2)	The design drawings should clearly identify the design.
Article 33	Amendments to the patent application have gone beyond the scope of the initial application.
Implementing Regulations	
Article 20(2)	The independent claim shall outline the technical solution and state the essential technical features.
Article 43(1)	A divisional application is entitled to the filing (and priority) date of the initial application, provided it does not go beyond the scope of initial application.
Prohibitions in the Patent Law	
Article 5(1)	The subject matter of the patent is contrary to law or social morality or detrimental to the public interest.
Article 5(2)	A patent is not to be granted to a patent that breaches laws or regulations relating to the use of genetic resources.
Article 25	A patent cannot be granted for subject matter that cannot be patented.
Article 9	A patent should be granted to the earlier applicant if two or more patents are filed for same invention.

6.3 DEFINITIONS OF INVENTION AND UTILITY MODEL

6.3.1 The Guidelines for Patent Examination (Examination Guidelines) provide that the definition of an invention in Article 2(2) of the Patent Law is "a general definition to the subject matters for which patent protection may be sought, rather than a specific examination criteria."[1]

6.3.2 The Examination Guidelines then provide:

> A technical solution is an aggregation of technical means applying the laws of nature to solve a technical problem.
>
> A solution that does not adopt technical means to solve a technical problem and thereby does not achieve a technical effect in compliance with the laws of nature does not constitute a subject matter defined in Article 2(2).
>
> Smell, signals such as sound, light, electricity, magnetism and waves or energy do not constitute subject matter as provided by Article 2.2.

6.3.3 As utility models use the same examination criteria, these provisions will apply to Article 2.3 as well.

6.4 CONFIDENTIALITY EXAMINATION

6.4.1 Article 20(1) of the Patent Law provides:

> Any entity or individual filing a patent application in a foreign country for an invention-creation made in China, shall apply in advance for the confidentiality examination conducted by the patent administrative department under the State Council. The procedures and duration of the confidentiality examination shall be enforced in accordance with the provisions of the State Council.

6.4.2 This provision was a cause for great concern for foreign companies who conduct research and development in China during the drafting of the third revisions to the Patent Law and while the Patent Law Implementing Regulations were being revised. The Patent Law Implementing Regulations have provided some further clarity and state that the invention or utility model referred to in Article 20 refers to:

> an invention or utility model of which the substantive contents of the technical solution were completed within the territory of China.[2]

---

1. Examination Guidelines, Part II, Chapter 1, Section 2.
2. Patent Law Implementing Regulations, Article 8.

6.4.3 The following three methods are provided in the Patent Law Implementing Regulations for applying for confidentiality examination:

1. File a request for confidentiality examination directly with the Patent Office in advance of filing overseas describing the technical solution in detail;[3]

2. If the applicant has filed an application in China, file a request for confidentiality examination with the Patent Office in advance of filing overseas;[4] or

3. File an international patent application with the Patent Office which shall be deemed to be a request for confidentiality examination.[5]

6.4.4 If the applicant does not receive a notification that the patent should be examined for confidentiality within four months of filing the application, they may proceed to apply for the patent overseas.[6]

6.4.5 Part V, Chapter 5, Section 6.1, of the Examination Guidelines provides more details of the procedures for requesting a confidentiality examination.

6.4.6 As these rules are new, there have not yet been any cases in which invalidation actions have been filed on the basis of a failure to request a confidentiality exam. However, there is a clear scope for numerous issues to arise. The test is whether the substantive content of an invention is made in China. This is a subjective test and not based on the nationality of the inventors or any other objective criteria. Foreigners could complete an invention in China. Chinese nationals could complete an invention outside China. An invention could be made by a team operating around the world.

6.4.7 The provisions open up the possibility to numerous challenges to patents. Applicants should err on the side of caution and seek confidentiality examination for any patents for which inventors are located in China and keep accurate records of inventors and their contribution to inventions.

6.5 NOVELTY

6.5.1 Article 22 of the Patent Law provides that:

> Any invention or utility model for which patent right may be granted must possess novelty, inventive step and practical applicability.

---

3. Patent Law Implementing Regulations, Article 8(1).
4. Patent Law Implementing Regulations, Article 8(2).
5. Patent Law Implementing Regulations, Article 8(3).
6. Patent Law Implementing Regulations, Article 9(1). Article 9(2) addresses the situation in which a confidentiality examination is conducted.

> Novelty means that the invention or utility model neither belongs to an existing technology, nor has any entity or individual previously filed before the date of filing with the patent administrative department under the State Council an application on an identical invention or utility model recorded in patent application documents published or patent documents announced after the said date of filing.[7]

Article 22(4) defines existing technology as the following:

> The existing technology referred to in this Law means any technology known to the public before the date of filing in China or abroad.

Examination Principles

6.5.2 The Examination Guidelines, Part II, Chapter 3, Section 3.1, provide that an examiner shall adhere to the following principles when examining for novelty:

(a) *Precondition.* Only inventions that possess practical applicability shall be examined for novelty.

(b) *Identical invention.* The invention in the application shall be deemed an identical invention to that in the prior art "if their technical fields, technical problems to be solved, technical solutions and their expected effects are substantially the same."

(c) *Independent comparison.* The examiner shall compare each claim of an application with the relevant technical content disclosed in a *single prior art reference*, rather than comparing it to a combination of references.

Disclosure

6.5.3 The Examination Guidelines provide in Part II, Chapter 3, Section 2.1.2, that:

> The means of disclosure of prior art includes disclosure by publications disclosure by use and disclosure by other means, without limitation on territory.

---

7. Article 22.2 of the Patent Law was revised by the third amendment to the Patent Law and changed the definition of novelty by adding the parts shows in bold: "**that the invention or utility model shall neither belong to an existing technology,** nor has any entity or individual previously filed before the date of filing with the patent administrative department under the State Council an application on an identical invention or utility model which was recorded in patent application documents or **other patent documents** published after the said date of filing" (changed parts bolded). Article 22.4 of the Revised Patent Law was added to define "existing technology." Therefore, under the Revised Patent Law, an invention or utility model publicly used or otherwise known to the public outside China before the filing date is no longer considered novel.

By Publication

6.5.4 Section 2.1.2.1 provides that publication refers to an independently existing tangible disseminating carrier containing contents of technology or design which shall indicate or have other evidence to prove the date of issue or publication.[8] Publications include printed and typed documents (such as patents, magazines, books, manuals, reports, newspapers, brochures, product catalogues) and tangible media made by other methods (such as microfiche, film, tape, and CD). They can also be materials from the Internet or in other online databases.

6.5.5 The language of the document is irrelevant. It is also irrelevant whether it has been read at all.

By Use

6.5.6 Section 2.1.2.2 provides that disclosure by use as "the technical solution is disclosed or placed in a state of being available to the public." Disclosure by use "includes disclosure through making, using, selling, importing, exchanging, presenting, demonstrating, exhibiting and the like that can make the technical content available to the public."

6.5.7 An exhibition or demonstration, if the technical contents is not explained so a man skilled in the art cannot know the structure, function, or composition of the product, is not treated as disclosure.

6.5.8 If the structure or function can be ascertained by taking a product apart, this is treated as disclosure.

By Other Means

6.5.9 Section 2.1.2.3 provides that disclosure by other methods includes "oral disclosure. Examples are talking, reporting, speaking at symposium, broadcasting or televising and cinematographing that make the technical contents known to the public."

---

8. Examination Guidelines, Part II, Chapter 3, Section 2.1.2.1.

Prior Art References

6.5.10 Part II, Chapter 3, Section 2.3, of the Examination Guidelines, states "generally speaking, because the examiner can not possibly know the technology disclosed by use or known by the public or by other methods in China or abroad, in the procedures of substantive examination, the reference documents cited at this stage are mainly publications."

6.5.11 When citing prior art references, the examiner should refer to the disclosed technical content of the reference. The disclosed technical content includes that which a person skilled in the art would understand to be obviously implicated in the reference. The disclosed technical content also includes the technical features that can be obviously discovered from the drawings. Technical content inferred from the drawings without further explanation is not within the disclosed technical content.

Criteria for Examination of Novelty

6.5.12 The Examination Guidelines (Part II, Chapter 3, Section 3.2) set out certain criteria for judging novelty. The primary criterion is whether the prior art discloses an "invention whose technical fields, technical problems seeking resolution, and technical solutions are the same in substance, and their prospective results are the same." The guidelines provide specific criteria for determining novelty in the following common situations:

(a) *Invention with identical contents.* If the subject matter of the application is completely identical to the technical content disclosed in the prior art, or there is only a simple change in wording, the invention does not possess novelty. The technical content disclosed in the prior art references includes that which can be derived directly from the references by a person skilled in the art.

(b) *Specific (lower level) concept and generic (upper level) concept.* If the only difference between the application's subject matter and the prior art is that the application discloses a generic concept (e.g., a product made of metal) and the prior art discloses a specific concept (e.g., a product made of copper) to limit the technical features, the prior disclosure of the specific concept will cause the invention to lose novelty. However, the prior disclosure of a generic concept will not destroy the novelty of an invention that discloses the specific concept.

(c) *Direct substitution of customary means.* There is no novelty if the technical solution disclosed in the application (e.g., using bolts for fixing) is merely a direct substitution of the customary means employed in the relevant field for the technical solution disclosed in the prior art (e.g., using screws for fixing).

(d) *Numerical value and range of values.* The guidelines provide detailed criteria for judging novelty in situations in which the claimed technical solution is defined by a numerical value or range of changing numerical values. Basically, the rules are as follows:

The value or range in reference document is entirely within the range of a claimed feature.	No novelty.
The value or range in the reference document overlaps with the range of a claimed feature.	No novelty.
The end points in the reference document are the same as the discrete numerical values of a claimed feature.	No novelty for numerical values that are the same as end points; novelty for other values.
The end points in the reference document are not the same as the values or range of a claimed feature.	Novelty.

Specific examples are provided in the Examination Guidelines and reference should be made to these if necessary.

6.6 INVENTIVENESS

6.6.1 Article 22(3) of the Patent Law defines *inventiveness* as:

> Inventiveness means that, as compared with the existing technology, the invention has prominent and substantive features and represents a notable progress, or the utility model possesses substantive features and represents progress.

6.6.2 Inventiveness can be likened to the requirement used in the United States and some other countries of *non-obviousness.* The lower threshold for inventiveness for utility models should be noted. It can be much harder to invalidate utility models because of this lower threshold.

Examination Guidelines

6.6.3 Part II, Chapter 4, Sections 2.2 and 2.3, of the Examination Guidelines further defines "has prominent substantive features" and "represents notable progress" as follows:

> That an invention has prominent substantive features means that, having regard to the prior art, it is non-obvious to a person skilled in the art. If the person skilled in the art can obtain the invention just by logical analysis, inference, or limited experimentation on the basis of the prior art, the invention is obvious and therefore has no prominent substantive features.

That an invention represents notable progress means that the invention can produce advantageous technical effect as compared with the prior art. For instance, the invention has overcome the defects and deficiencies in the existing technology, or has provided a different technical solution to solve a certain technical problem, or represents a certain new trend of technical development.

Examination Principles

6.6.4 The examiner shall adhere to the following principles when examining for inventiveness:[9]

(a) Only inventions that possess novelty shall be examined for inventiveness;

(b) When examining for inventiveness, the examiner shall consider not only the technical solution itself, but the technical field to which the invention pertains, the technical problem solved, and the technical effect produced by the invention;

(c) Unlike the principle of *independent comparison* for novelty, the examiner may combine different prior art references in evaluating inventiveness; and

(d) If an independent claim possesses inventiveness, the related dependent claims do not need to be examined for inventiveness.

Criteria for Examination of Inventiveness

6.6.5 Article 22(3) of the Patent Law is stated to be the governing criteria for examining for inventiveness.

6.6.6 "In order to facilitate understanding of the criteria," the Examination Guidelines provide a typical approach, as follows, for determining whether an invention has significant substantive features and represents notable progress.[10]

Significant Substantive Features

6.6.7 In Part II, Chapter 4, Section 3.2.1.1, the Examination Guidelines provide a three-step approach for determining whether an invention is obvious as compared with the prior art, as follows.

6.6.8 Determine the closest prior art. The closest prior art is usually in the same technical field as the invention, involves a related technical problem or effect, and discloses the greatest number of technical features of the invention.

---

9. Examination Guidelines, Part II, Chapter 4, Section 3.1.
10. Examination Guidelines, Part II, Chapter 4, Section 3.2.

6.6.9 Determine the distinctive features of the invention and technical problem resolved by the invention. The distinctive features of the invention are determined by comparison with the closest prior art. The technical problem resolved by the invention refers to the technical improvement over the prior art to achieve a better technical result, and is determined based on the technical effect achieved by the distinguishing features.

6.6.10 Determine whether the invention is obvious to a person skilled in the art. Obviousness is determined based on the examiner's judgment from the perspective of a person skilled in the art considering the closest prior art and the technical problem resolved by the invention. In the course of this judgment, the examiner shall determine whether there is technical motivation in the prior art, that is, whether the prior art provides the motivation to apply the distinctive features to the most relevant existing technology to resolve the technical problem. This motivation would allow a person skilled in the art to create the invention if he or she were facing the technical problem (the invention would be obvious). Technical motivation is usually regarded as existing in the prior art where:

(a) The distinctive feature is common knowledge, such as the habitual practice in the relevant field for resolving the technical problem;

(b) The technical means related to the closest prior art, such as a technical means disclosed in another part of the same reference document;

(c) The technical means disclosed in another reference, the function of which is the same as that of the distinguishing feature.

Notable Progress

6.6.11 In evaluating whether an invention represents notable progress, the primary consideration is whether it has a useful technical result.[11] An invention will usually be regarded as having a useful technical result if:

(a) The invention has a better technical effect than the most relevant existing technology (that is, is an improvement);

(b) The invention provides a technical solution of substantially the same level as the prior art using a different technical concept;

(c) The invention represents a new trend of technical development; or

(d) The invention, despite the negative effects in some respects, has positive effects in other respects.

---

11. Examination Guidelines, Part II, Chapter 5, Section 3.2.2.

Supplemental Criteria for Determining Inventiveness

6.6.12 Part II, Chapter 4, Section 5 of the Examination Guidelines, provides further criteria that may contribute to the determination of inventiveness:

(a) The invention resolves a technical problem, the resolution of which had been long awaited;
(b) The invention overcomes a technical prejudice held by people in the field and adopts the technical means abandoned by those people due to the technical prejudice;
(c) The invention has obtained an unexpected technical result as compared with the prior art; and
(d) The invention has achieved commercial success as the direct result of the technical feature of the invention.

6.7 PRACTICAL APPLICABILITY

6.7.1 Article 22(4) of the Patent Law defines practical applicability as:

> that the invention or utility model can be made or used and can produce positive results.

6.7.2 Practical applicability is examined before the examination of novelty and inventiveness.[12]

6.7.3 The Examination Guidelines provide that an invention has practical applicability if it can resolve a technical problem and can be made or used industrially.[13] The invention "shall not violate the laws of nature and shall be reproducible."[14] For most applications, the assessment as to practical applicability is the quickest of the three stages in the substantive examination.

Examination Principles

6.7.4 The examiner will use two principles to determine whether an invention possesses practical applicability:[15]

(a) The examination will not be constrained to an examination of the claims, but shall also include the entire subject matter contained in the description and drawings.

---

12. Examination Guidelines, Part II, Chapter 5, Section 3.
13. Examination Guidelines, Part II, Chapter 5, Section 3.2.
14. Examination Guidelines, Part II, Chapter 5, Section 3.2.
15. Examination Guidelines, Part II, Chapter 5, Section 3.2.

(b) The examiner, during the examination, will not consider the origin of the invention nor how it has been exploited.

6.8 SUFFICIENCY OF DISCLOSURE

6.8.1 Article 26(3) of the Patent Law provides that:

> The description shall describe the invention or utility model in a manner sufficiently clear and complete so as to enable a person skilled in the relevant field of technology to accurately produce it; where necessary, drawings shall be appended. The abstract shall state briefly the technical essentials of the invention or utility model.

The Examination Guidelines[16] further explain this requirement as containing the elements described in the following sections.

Clarity

6.8.2 A description shall meet the following clarity requirements:[17]

"*The subject matter shall be clear*: . . . the description shall disclose the technical problem the invention or utility model aims to solve and the technical solution adopted to solve the problem; and state, with reference to the background art, the advantageous effects of the invention or utility model. The said technical problem, technical solution and advantageous effects shall be adapted to one another and free of contradiction or irrelevancy."

"*Precise Expression*: A description . . . shall precisely express the technical contents of the invention or utility model without any ambiguity or equivocation which may prevent a person skilled in the art from understanding the invention or utility model clearly and properly."

Completeness

6.8.3 A complete description shall include "all the technical contents which are necessary for understanding and carrying out the invention or utility model,"[18] which means "all relevant contents that a person skilled in the art

---

16. Examination Guidelines, Part II Chapter 5, Section 3.1.
17. Examination Guidelines, Part II, Chapter 2, Section 2.1.
18. Examination Guidelines, Part II, Chapter 2, Section 2.1.1.

cannot obtain directly and solely from the prior art shall be described in the description."[19]

6.8.4 Specifically, Part II, Chapter 2, Section 2.1.2, of the Examination Guidelines states that a complete description shall include the following contents:

(1) contents which are indispensable for the understanding of the invention or utility model, such as the description of the relevant technical field and the state of the background art and the brief description of the drawings if any;

(2) contents that are needed for determining whether or not the invention or utility model possesses novelty, inventive step, and practical applicability, such as the technical problem to be solved by the invention or utility model, the technical solution adopted to solve the problem, and the advantageous effects of the invention or utility model; and

(3) contents that are needed for carrying out the invention or utility model, such as the mode for carrying out the technical solution adopted to solve the technical problem of the invention or utility model.

Enablement

6.8.5 Part II, Chapter 2, Section 2.1.3, of the Examination Guidelines provides in relation to enablement:

> The description shall enable a person skilled in the art to carry out the invention or utility model. It means that the person skilled in the art shall be able, in accordance with the contents of the description, to carry out the technical solution of the invention or utility model, solve the technical problem, and achieve the expected technical effects.

6.8.6 "A description shall . . . disclose all technical contents necessary for understanding and carrying out an invention or utility model, to the extend that a person skilled in the art may carry out the invention or utility model. . . ." In the following cases, the technical solution described in a description is regarded as "unable to be carried out due to lack of technical means to solve the technical problem:"

(a) The description sets forth only a task and/or assumption, or simply expresses a wish and/or result, providing no technical means that a person skilled in the art can implement;

---

19. Examination Guidelines Part II, Chapter 2, Section 2.1.2.

(b) The description sets forth a technical means, but the means is so ambiguous and vague that a person skilled in the art cannot concretely implement it according to the contents of the description;

(c) The description sets forth a technical means, but a person skilled in the art cannot solve the technical problem of the invention or utility model by adopting the said means;

(d) The subject matter of an application is a technical solution consisting of several technical means, but one of the means cannot be implemented by a person skilled in the art according to the contents of the description; and

(e) The description sets forth a concrete technical solution but without experimental evidence, while the solution can only be established upon confirmation by experimental result.[20]

6.9 CLAIMS MUST BE SUPPORTED BY THE DESCRIPTION

6.9.1 Article 26(4) of the Patent Law provides that:

> The claims shall, on the basis of the description, define the scope of the patent protection sought for in a clear and concise manner.

6.9.2 This is further clarified by the Examination Guidelines:[21]

> The claims "shall be supported by the description" means that the technical solution for which protection is sought in each of the claims shall be a solution that a person skilled in the art can reach directly or by generalization from the contents sufficiently disclosed in the description, and shall not go beyond the scope of the contents disclosed in the description.

Examination Criteria

6.9.3 Part II, Chapter 2, Section 3.2.1, of the Examination Guidelines provides detailed examination criteria.[22] The following sets out the key points:

(a) Claims are usually generalizations from one or more embodiments or examples as set forth in the description. The generalization of a claim shall not go beyond the scope of the contents disclosed in the description.

(b) For claims generalized in generic terms or by parallel options, . . . if the generalization of a claim is such that the person skilled in the art can reasonably doubt that one or more specific terms or options included

---

20. Examination Guidelines Part II, Chapter 2, Section 2.1.2, final paragraph.
21. Examination Guidelines, Part II Chapter 2, Section 2.1.3.
22. Examination Guidelines, Part II, Chapter 2, Section 3.2.1.

in the generic terms or parallel options cannot solve the technical problem aimed to be solved by the invention or utility model and achieve the same technical effects, then it shall be taken that the claim is not supported by the description.

(c) As for a broadly generalized claim relating to the whole class of materials or machines, if it is fairly supported by the description, and there is no reason to suppose that the invention or utility model cannot be worked through the whole of the field claimed, then the claim may be acceptable even if it is of broad scope.

(d) A technical feature defined by function in a claim shall be construed as embracing all the means which are capable of performing the function.

(e) If the description merely states in vague terms that other alternative means may be adopted, but the person skilled in the art cannot understand what they might be or how they might be used, then definition by function in the claims is not permitted.

(f) When determining whether a claim is supported by the description, the examiner shall take into account the whole contents of the description, rather than merely the contents in the part of specific mode for carrying out the invention or utility model.

(g) For the claims, including both independent and dependent claims or different kinds of claims, each of the claims shall be examined as to whether it is supported by the description.

Clarity of Claims

6.9.4 The Examination Guidelines further explain the clarity required for claims made in applications:[23]

(a) First, the category of each claim shall be clear. The title of the subject matter of a claim shall indicate clearly whether the claim is a product claim or a process claim.

> ... When parameters are used for the expression, the parameters used must be those which can be clearly and reliably determined by a person skilled in the art according to the teachings of the description or by customary means of the relevant art.

---

23. Examination Guidelines, Part II, Chapter 2, Section 3.2.1.

(b) Second, the scope of protection as defined by each claim shall be clear.

The scope of protection of a claim shall be construed according to the meaning of the words used in the claim. Generally, the words used in a claim shall be understood as having the meaning which they normally have in the relevant art.

Any term which meaning is indefinite, such as "thick," "thin," "strong," "weak," "high temperature," "high pressure," "very broad scope," shall not be used in a claim, unless the term has well-recognized definite meaning in the particular art. . . .

Such expressions as "for example," "such as," "had better," "especially," "where necessary," shall not be used in a claim, as they will define different scopes of protection in a single claim and make the scope of protection unclear. . . .

Generally, such terms as "about," "approximately," "etc.," "or the like," shall not be used in a claim, as they are likely to make the scope of the claim unclear. . . ."

6.10 AMENDMENTS

6.10.1 Article 33 of the Patent Law provides:

An applicant may amend his or its application documents for a patent, but the amendment to the application documents for a patent for invention or utility model must not go beyond the scope of the disclosure contained in the original specification and the claims, and the amendment to the application documents for a patent for design must not go beyond the scope of the disclosure as shown in the original drawings or photographs.

6.10.2 Patent applications may be amended in the following circumstances:[24]

(a) *At the request of the applicant:* The applicant may amend the patent application at its own volition within three months of the date of notification of substantial examination of an invention patent or within two months from the application date of a utility model.

(b) *At the request of the Patent Office:* At any time during the application, the applicant may amend the application at the request of the Patent Office to correct defects notified by the patent office.

(c) *By the Patent Office:* The Patent Office may amend obvious clerical and symbolic mistakes at their own volition.

---

24. Examination Guidelines, Part II, Chapter, 2, Section 3.2.2.

Utility Models and Design Patents

6.10.3 As no substantive examination of utility models or external design patents is conducted, the Patent Law Implementing Regulations only allow for applicants to make amendments to the utility model and external design patent within two months of filing the application with the SIPO.[25]

Methods of Making Amendments

6.10.4 Part II, Chapter 8, Section 5.2, of the Examination Guidelines sets out the methods for making amendments.

Permitted Amendments

6.10.5 The following amendments are permitted under the Examination Guidelines:[26]

(a) Adding technical features to an independent claim to further define the independent claim, in order to overcome defects in the initial claim;

(b) Changing one or more of the technical features of the independent claim to eliminate defects in the initial claim, such as lacking support in the description;

(c) Changing the category, title of the subject matter, and the corresponding technical features of an independent claim;

(d) Deleting one or more claims;

(e) Delimiting an independent claim from the closest prior art;

(f) Amending the reference portion of dependent claim so as to correct a mistaken reference and accurately reflect the specific mode for carrying out the invention or embodiment described in the original description;

(g) Amending the characterizing portion of a dependent claim so as to accurately reflect the scope of protection of the dependent claim.

Specific Requirement on Amendments to Numerical Ranges

6.10.6 Part II, Chapter 8, Section 5.2.2.1, of the Examination Guidelines provides specific rules for amendments to numerical ranges:

> As for the amendment to the numerical range of the claim which contains the technical feature defined by such range, it is allowable only when the two extreme values of the

---

25. Patent Law Implementing Regulations, Article 51.
26. Patent Law Implementing Regulations, Article 51.

revised numerical range are actually described in the initial description and/or claims and the revised numerical range is within the initial numerical range.

Prohibited Amendments

6.10.7 Part II, Chapter 8, Section 5.2.3, of the Examination Guidelines provides a detailed list of disallowable amendments, including disallowable additions (Section 5.2.3.1), disallowable changes (Section 5.2.3.2), and disallowable deletions (Section 5.2.3.3).

6.10.8 The overriding general principle described in Section 5.2.3 is:

> As a principle, any amendment to the description (and the drawings) and the claims that is not in conformity with the Provisions of Article 33 of the Patent Law is not allowable.
>
> Specifically, if, after the addition, change, and/or deletion of part of the contents of the application, the information as seen by a person skilled in the art is different from those described in the initial application and such information cannot be directly or unambiguously derived from those described in the initial application, such amendment such not be allowable.

6.10.9 The following amendments are examples of key amendments that are prohibited under the Examination Guidelines:

(a) Deleting or amending technical features in an independent claim, which exceeds what is described in the original specification and claims;[27]

(b) Adding experimental data to illustrate the advantageous effects of the invention;[28]

(c) Changing indefinite contents into definite and specific contents,[29] for example by changing "higher temperature" to "temperature higher than 40°C";

(d) Deleting contents from the description that makes the amended description go beyond the original scope of disclosure.[30]

6.11 CLAIMS MUST CONTAIN THE ESSENTIAL TECHNICAL FEATURES

6.11.1 Under Article 20(2) of Patent Law Implementing Regulations, independent claims should state the technical solution and include all the technical features necessary to solve the technical problem.[31]

---

27. Examination Guidelines, Part II, Chapter 8, Sections 5.2.1 and 5.2.2.
28. Examination Guidelines, Part II, Chapter 8, Sections 5.2.3.2(1) and Section 5.2.3.3(1).
29. Examination Guidelines, Part II, Chapter 8, Section 5.2.3.1(6).
30. Examination Guidelines, Part II, Chapter 8, Section 5.2.3.2(2).
31. Examination Guidelines, Part II, Chapter 8, Section 5.2.3.3(2).

6.11.2 The Examination Guidelines defines an *essential technical feature* as follows:[32]

> "Essential technical features" refers to the technical features of an invention or utility model that are indispensable in solving the technical problem and the aggregation of which is sufficient to constitute the technical solution of the invention or utility model and distinguish the same over the technical solutions disclosed in the background art.

6.11.3 In determining whether a technical feature is essential, the examiner shall "start from the technical problem to be solved and take account of the whole contents of the description, rather than simply take the technical features of an embodiment as the essential technical features."[33]

6.12 DIVISIONAL APPLICATIONS MUST NOT GO BEYOND SCOPE OF ORIGINAL APPLICATION

6.12.1 Article 43 of the Patent Law Implementing Regulations provides

A divisional application filed in accordance with the provisions of Article 42 of these Implementing Regulations shall be entitled to the filing date and, if priority is claimed, the priority date of the initial application, provided that the divisional application does not go beyond the scope of disclosure contained in the initial application.

6.12.2 The Examination Guidelines in Part II, Chapter 6, and, in Section 3.3, in which the examination of divisional applications is discussed, repeat the rule that the divisional application shall not go beyond the scope of disclosures without giving any further guidance.

6.13 LAW, MORALITY, OR PUBLIC INTEREST

6.13.1 Article 5(1) of the Patent Law provides:

> Patent right is not granted for any invention-creation that violates the laws of the State or social morality or that is detrimental to the public interest.

---

32. Patent Law Implementing Regulations, Article 20(2).
33. Examination Guidelines, Part II, Chapter 2, Section 3.1.2.

6.13.2 Article 10 of the Patent Law Implementing Regulations, however, makes it clear that the provisions of Article 5 of the Patent Law do not apply "merely because exploitation of the patent is prohibited by law."

6.13.3 If an application partially contravenes Section 5(1) of the Patent Law, it may be amended to remove the offending part.[34]

Prohibited by Law

6.13.4 The Examination Guidelines provide that the relevant laws are only laws passed by the National People's Congress or its Standing Committee and not any other lower regulations. Examples of the products prohibited by laws are gambling facilities, drug-taking appliances, and apparatuses for counterfeiting banknotes and other documents. However, products such as sedatives and playing cards are not excluded from protection even though they may be abused in unlawful ways. Products such as guns, the use of which is prohibited or regulated but the manufacture of which is not, are not excluded from protection.[35]

Contrary to Social Morality

6.13.5 The Examination Guidelines provide for exclusion based on *social morality*, meaning ethical or moral norms commonly accepted by society and note that these change from time to time. Examples of inventions that would be contrary to social morality are artificial sexual organs not for medical use, processes for the genetic modification of human beings, processes for cloning human beings, and methods of bestiality.[36]

Detrimental to the Public Interest

6.13.6 The Examination Guidelines provide that "detrimental to the public interest" refers to exploitation that is to the detriment of society or disrupts the normal order of the state and society. Examples given are devices for

---

34. Examination Guidelines, Part II, Chapter 2 Section 3.1.2.
35. Examination Guidelines, Part II, Chapter 1, Section 3.1.4.
36. Examination Guidelines, Part II, Chapter 1, Section 3.1.1. (As an aside, because SIPO examines patents on behalf of Macau, SIPO will, for example, examine patents relating to gambling, solely for registration in Macau.)

injuring a person; devices that will cause serious pollution; words or pictures in an application concerning an important political event or disparaging religious or ethnic groups. However, if an invention has certain defects despite positive effects, such as side effects for a pharmaceutical, this is not detrimental to the public interest.[37]

6.14 BREACH OF LAW OR REGULATIONS RELATING TO GENETIC RESOURCES

6.14.1 Article 5(2) of the Patent Law provides:

> Patent right is not granted for any invention-creation which violates the laws and administrative regulations to acquire or use genetic resources, and relies on the said genetic resources for completion.

6.14.2 The Examination Guidelines provide that this provision will be breached if laws requiring prior approval to acquire or use genetic resources are breached, such as, the Animal Husbandry Law of China.[38]

6.15 PROHIBITED INVENTIONS

6.15.1 Article 25 of the Patent Law Provides:

> For any of the following, no patent right is granted:
>
> (1) Scientific discoveries;
> (2) Rules and methods for mental activities;
> (3) Methods for the diagnosis or for the treatment of diseases;
> (4) Animal and plant varieties;
> (5) Substances obtained by means of nuclear transformation;
> (6) Designs that serve mainly as indicators of two-dimensional printing goods' pattern, the colour or the combination of the two.

6.15.2 These are standard exceptions. The Examination Guidelines provide detailed guidelines on whether the first five of these provisions are breached in Part II, Chapter 1, Section 4. Reference should be made to these if necessary.

---

37. Examination Guidelines, Part II, Chapter 1, Section 3.1.2.
38. Examination Guidelines, Part II, Chapter 1, Section 3.1.3.

6.16 EARLIER APPLICATION

6.16.1 Article 9 of the Patent Law provides

> For the same invention-creation, only one patent right can be granted. However, when the same applicant applied for both a utility model patent and an invention patent on the same day, the invention patent may be granted if the utility model patent right that is obtained first is not yet terminated, and the applicant declares to renounce the said utility model patent right.
>
> If two or more applicants apply separately for a patent on the same invention-creation, the patent right is granted to the person who applies first.

6.16.2 Effectively, this provision is a requirement that a patent be novel and that an application filed for the same invention, second in time, should not be granted.

CHAPTER 7

Patent Revocation Proceedings

7.1 INTRODUCTION

7.1.1 This chapter addresses the procedure for invalidating invention patents and utility models. Design patent revocation proceedings are considered in Chapter 13, "Design Patents."

7.2 APPLICATION FOR REVOCATION

7.2.1 Article 45 of the Patent Law provides:

> Where, starting from the date of the announcement of the grant of the patent right by the patent administrative department under the State Council, any unit or individual considers that the grant of the said patent right is not in conformity with the relevant provisions of this Law, it or he may request the Patent Reexamination Board to declare the patent right invalid.[1]

7.2.2 Two points come from this. First, a patent may only be revoked after grant. There are no opposition proceedings.[2] Second, anyone (including the patentee) may apply to revoke a patent.

Pre-Grant Third-Party Submissions

7.2.3 Although there are no opposition proceedings, under the Implementing Regulations of the Patent Law (Patent Law Implementing

---

1. Patent Law, Article 45.
2. The Patent Law prior to the 2002 amendments did provide for opposition proceedings.

Regulations), any party may submit their opinions to the State Intellectual Property Office (SIPO) as to why they consider the patent is not in conformity with the Patent Law.[3] Such submissions are regularly filed. SIPO has no obligation to consider or give a formal response to such submissions. Tactically, whether to file such submissions needs to be considered carefully. Unless the submissions are strong and are likely to stop a patent from grant, the submissions may help the applicant to strengthen their patent by allowing them to amend their claims to overcome the cited prior art.

No Revocation in Patent Litigation

7.2.4 Only the Patent Review and Adjudication Board (PRAB, also called, in English, the Patent Re-examination Board) has the power to consider the validity of patents. Courts do not have the power to consider the validity of patents other than when hearing appeals of a PRAB decision.

7.2.5 The 2009 Patent Law does, however, include a "prior art defence," under which, if a defendant shows that their allegedly infringing product or process derives from or is based on prior art, it is therefore non-infringing.[4] This effectively allows a defendant to challenge the novelty of a patent in court, although the court does not have the power to invalidate the patent. The prior art defense is discussed further in Chapter 12, "Defenses."

7.3 INVALIDATION PROCEDURES

7.3.1 The procedure for seeking to have a patent declared invalid based on the Patent Law, Patent Law Implementing Regulations, and the Guidelines for Patent Examination (Examination Guidelines) are set out below. Part IV, Chapters 1 and 3, of the Examination Guidelines provide comprehensive rules of procedure.

Filing of Request

7.3.2 The party seeking to have a patent declared invalid shall submit a request for declaration of invalidity and supporting evidence to the PRAB.[5]

---

3. Patent Law Implementing Regulations, Article 48.
4. Patent Law, Article 62.
5. Patent Law, Article 45; Patent Law Implementing Regulations, Article 65.

The request should clearly state each of the grounds for which invalidation is sought and the evidence that supports each ground.

Formal Examination

7.3.3 After accepting a request for invalidation, the PRAB shall first conduct a formal examination of the request. Under Article 66 of the Patent Law Implementing Regulations, the formal examination will consider the following and if the grounds are not satisfied, the request for invalidation will be rejected:

(a) If the request is filed by a foreigner or foreign entity, whether it has been filed by a Chinese patent agent;[6]

(b) Whether the grounds for invalidation are one or more of those provided in Article 65 of the Patent Law Implementing Regulations;[7]

(c) Whether the grounds for invalidation are the same as those in a prior request for invalidation upon which the PRAB has already made a decision;[8]

(d) Whether the request for invalidation has stated the grounds in detail and indicated the supporting proof.[9]

7.3.4 In addition, the PRAB will examine whether the request for invalidation complies with the formal requirements for filing an invalidation action. If it does not, the PRAB may issue notice to rectify the request.[10]

Filing of Additional Grounds and Evidence

7.3.5 Once the PRAB accepts the request for a declaration of invalidity, the applicant has one month within which to supplement the request with additional grounds and evidence.[11]

Response by Patentee

7.3.6 The PRAB shall send a copy of the request for invalidation of the patent right and copies of the relevant documents to the patentee and invite

---

6. Patent Law Implementing Regulations, Article 66(1).
7. Patent Law Implementing Regulations, Article 66(1); Examination Guidelines, Part IV, Chapter 3, Section 3.3(2).
8. Patent Law Implementing Regulations, Article 66(2); Examination Guidelines, Part IV, Chapter 3, Section 3.3(3).
9. Examination Guidelines, Part IV, Chapter 3, Section 3.3(5).
10. Patent Law Implementing Regulations, Article 66(4).
11. Patent Law Implementing Regulations, Article 67.

it or him to present its or his observations within a specified time limit.[12] This time limit is usually one month.

7.3.7 If the patentee does not respond within the time limit, the PRAB will proceed with the case.[13]

Amendment to Patent

7.3.8 During the PRAB's review of a request for a declaration of invalidity, the patentee "may make alterations in his/her claims, but the scope of protection of the original patent must not be extended."[14]

7.3.9 The patentee is not allowed to amend the description or drawings.[15]

No Obligation to Comprehensively Examine Validity of the Patent

7.3.10 The PRAB is not obliged to examine comprehensively the validity of the patent. The PRAB usually determines invalidity based only on the grounds and evidence raised in the request. The applicant is entitled to abandon grounds and evidence and the PRAB will not consider these grounds or evidence.[16]

7.3.11 However, the PRAB may conduct a review *ex officio* rather than confined by scope, grounds, or evidence raised by the parties.[17] Part IV, Chapter 3, Section 4.1, Paragraph 5, sets out specific grounds under which the PRAB may conduct *ex officio* examination. These include that the patent has the following:

(a) An obvious defect that excludes it from patent protection;[18] and
(b) A defect not raised by the petitioner that precludes making a finding on the grounds raised by the petitioner, for example, a claim is challenged

---

12. Patent Law Implementing Regulations, Article 68.
13. Patent Law Implementing Regulations, Article 68(2).
14. Patent Law Implementing Regulations, Article 69(1).
15. Patent Law Implementing Regulations, Article 69(1).
16. Examination Guidelines, Part IV, Chapter 3, Section 2.2.
17. Examination Guidelines, Part IV, Chapter 1, Section 2.4.
18. Examination Guidlines, Part IV, Chapter 2, Section 4.1, Para 5(2).

for lack of inventive step, but is found by the PRAB to lack clarity so they cannot analyze whether there is an inventive step.[19]

Parties' Right to Make Submissions

7.3.12 The PRAB shall, before making a decision, give a party who will be adversely affected by the decision an opportunity to provide observations on the grounds, evidence, and affirmed facts adopted in the decision.[20]

Oral Proceedings

(a) The Patent Law Implementing Regulations provides the PRAB may "decide to hold an oral hearing in respect of a request for invalidation."[21]

7.3.13 The parties may request an oral hearing on the following grounds:[22]

(a) One party requests face-to-face cross-examination of the evidence.
(b) There is a need to explain the facts to the panel.
(c) There is a need to demonstrate a material object.
(d) There is a need to call a witness.

7.3.14 Part IV, Chapter 3, Section 4.4.4, of the Examination Guidelines sets out the circumstances under which the PRAB will decide to hold an oral hearing. These are summarized in the following table.

1	There is no request for an oral hearing from the patentee and the evidence is sufficient to invalidate in whole or in part.	No oral hearing and the patent may be invalidated in whole or in part.
2	PRAB considers petitioner's case may succeed in whole or in part.	There may be an oral hearing.
3	The response from the patentee appears well founded.	Whether to hold oral hearing depends on the specific circumstances of the case.
4	The patentee has not responded, but it appears that the evidence submitted by the petitioner is insufficient and a decision to uphold the patent can be made.	There will be no oral hearing.
5	The oral hearing did not proceed due to fault of parties.	The PRAB may decide not to hold new oral hearing.

19. Examination Guidlines, Part IV, Chapter 2, Section 4.1, paragraph 5(2).
20. Examination Guidelines, Part IV, Chapter 1, Section 2.5.
21. Patent Law Implementing Regulations, Article 70.
22. Examination Guidelines, Part IV, Chapter 4, Section 2.

7.3.15 If the PRAB decides to hold an oral hearing, the hearing should be in public, and the PRAB should publish and circulate the decision of the invalidation proceedings, except in confidential cases.[23]

7.3.16 Generally, the panel will be a three-person panel. A five-person panel shall be formed for cases that have a significant impact in China and abroad, involve important and complex legal issues, and involve significant economic interests.[24] Simple cases may be examined by a single examiner.[25]

Recusal of Panel Members

7.3.17 A panel member shall be excluded from serving on the panel if he or she:

(a) Is a close relative or an agent of a party involved in the invalidation procedures;
(b) Has an interest in the patent application or the patent;
(c) Has any other kind of relationship with a party or its agent that may influence impartial examination and hearing; or
(d) Has taken part in the examination or re-examination of the patent application.[26]

Withdrawal of Invalidation Action

7.3.18 If the requestor withdraws his request before the PRAB makes a decision concerning the invalidation, the invalidation procedures shall terminate. However, if, based on the examination work it has done, the PRAB finds that it is able to make a decision invalidating the patent in whole or in part, the examination procedure shall not be terminated.[27]

7.4 GROUNDS FOR INVALIDATION

7.4.1 Under the Patent Law, the grounds on which the request for invalidation is based are "that the grant of the said patent right is not in conformity with the relevant provisions of this Law."[28]

---

23. Examination Guidelines, Part IV, Chapter 1, Section 2.6.
24. Examination Guidelines, Part IV, Chapter 1, Section 3.2.
25. Examination Guidelines, Part IV, Chapter 1, Section 4.
26. Patent Law Implementing Regulations, Article 37. Further definitions and procedures are provided in the Examination Guidelines, Part IV, Chapter 1, Section 5.
27. Article 72, Patent Law Implementing Regulations; Examination Guidelines, Part IV, Chapter 1, Section 2.3.
28. Patent Law, Article 45.

Invention Patents

7.4.2 For invention patents, this means the patent may be invalidated on most of the grounds for which a patent can be invalidated during the examination, which were discussed in detail in Chapter 6, "Grounds for Invalidating a Patent."

Utility models

7.4.3 For utility models, as they are unexamined, Part IV, Chapter 6, of the Examination Guidelines provides special provisions covering the grounds for invalidation of a utility model.

7.4.4 Essentially, the grounds on which a utility model can be invalidated for not being patentable[29] or lacking novelty are the same as for invention patents.

7.4.5 For inventiveness, because the test for inventiveness is that the invention has prominent features and represents progress (rather than prominent substantive features and the notable progress required for an invention patent), in determining whether there is a technical teaching in the prior art the examination differs in two aspects:[30]

(a) *Field of art references*: These are generally limited to the technical field to which the invention belongs (as opposed to proximate or relevant fields and those fields a person skilled in the art would consider).

(b) *Number of prior art references*: These are normally limited to one or two references in examining a utility model.

7.5 EVIDENCE

Burden of Proof

7.5.1 The party requesting invalidation bears the burden of proof and shall provide evidence to support the request.[31]

---

29. Examination Guidelines, Part IV, Chapter 6, Sections 2 and 3.
30. Examination Guidelines, Part IV, Chapter 6, Section 4.
31. Patent Law Implementing Regulations, Article 65(1); Examination Guidelines, Part IV, Chapter 8, Section 2.1.

Admissible Evidence

7.5.2 Part IV, Chapter 8, of the Examination Guidelines addresses the evidence that can be used before the PRAB. Where they do not make provision for evidence, "the relevant provisions applied by the People's Court in civil procedures may be referred to."[32]

7.5.3 The evidence accepted by the PRAB includes the following:

(a) Documentary evidence
(b) Material evidence
(c) Audio-visual materials
(d) Oral evidence of witnesses
(e) Statements of the parties
(f) Conclusions of experts
(g) Records of on-site investigation and examination

7.5.4 This is the same evidence that is admissible before the courts under the Civil Procedure Law. Generally, the main evidence filed to the PRAB are patent documents from China or other countries, scientific publications, and manuals or product catalogues.

Original Evidence Admissible

7.5.5 Original evidence originating from mainland China is admissible. This could include books or magazines published in China or tax receipts to prove sale.

7.5.6 Copies of documents kept by mainland Chinese entities can also be used if they are stamped with the official chop of the entity that has possession of the original to confirm it is a true copy.

Physical Evidence

7.5.7 Physical evidence can be submitted within the time limits for submitting evidence. Photographs and written descriptions can also be submitted to support the physical evidence. If the physical evidence has been notarized,

---

32. Examination Guidelines, Part IV, Chapter 8, Section 1.

the notary report only has to be submitted as part of the evidence submitted and the physical evidence can be submitted no later than the oral hearing.[33]

Notarized Evidence

7.5.8 However, in order to increase the admissibility of evidence, parties will often engage notaries to verify evidence, even if this is not strictly necessary. This is sometimes necessary, for example, if the party wished to prove a third party has made certain statements or is using certain equipment. Notarized evidence is discussed in detail in Chapter 10—"Evidence".

7.5.9 The Examination Guidelines provide that a notary report shall be deemed to prove the facts stated unless disproved by counter evidence or there are serious defects in the document, such as the lack of a notary seal.[34]

Non-Mainland Chinese Evidence—Notarization and Legalization

7.5.10 Subject to the exceptions discussed below, evidence from overseas must be notarized and legalized. Evidence from Hong Kong, Taiwan, and Macao is required to be verified in accordance with the special procedures established for each jurisdiction.[35]

7.5.11 Depending on the jurisdiction, these procedures can be time-consuming and cumbersome. Sufficient time should be allowed to comply with these formalities.

Non-Mainland PRC Evidence—Exceptions to the Requirements for Notarization and Legalization

7.5.12 There are three exceptions to the requirement for notarization and legalization for foreign evidence. They are evidence:[36]

(a) That can be obtained from domestic official channels, for example, patent documents and foreign literature from a public library;
(b) The authenticity of which can be supported by other evidence;
(c) The authenticity of which is acknowledged by the opposite party.

---

33. Examination Guidelines, Part IV, Chapter 8, Section 2.2.3.
34. Examination Guidelines, Part IV, Chapter 8, Section 4.3.4.
35. Examination Guidelines, Part IV, Chapter 8, Section 2.2.2.
36. Examination Guidelines, Part IV, Chapter 8, Section 2.2.2.

7.5.13 For evidence from Hong Kong, Macao, and Taiwan, the first exception does not apply. The other two exceptions do apply to these jurisdictions.

7.5.14 The main practical effect of these exceptions is that foreign patent documents can be used without notarization and legalization. The fact that the exception does not apply to Hong Kong is of no practical significance in relation to invention patents because Hong Kong operates a re-registration system of Chinese or United Kingdom patents (including European patents designating Britain).[37] A party can rely on the underlying Chinese, United Kingdom, or European patent designating the UK patent publication.

7.5.15 For other public documents, parties will still often notarize and legalize them to ensure their admissibility.

7.5.16 The other exceptions are rarely relied upon. A party may admit the evidence filed by the other party if they also wish to rely upon it. However, it is not good practice to file evidence in the expectation that the other party will admit it.

Translations

7.5.17 Chinese translations of foreign documents are required to be submitted within the time limit for filing evidence.[38] Partial translations are acceptable; however, the PRAB will only accept as evidence that part for which a translation has been provided. If the PRAB requires further translation of a document to be submitted, these will be accepted as evidence.[39]

7.5.18 If the other party objects to a translation, they must submit their own translation. If a translation cannot be agreed, a translation agency will be appointed to provide a translation with each party bearing 50 percent of the costs.[40]

7.5.19 Many examiners can read English and other foreign languages, so there are usually limited disputes concerning the translation of a document that is submitted.

---

37. See Section 3 Patents (Designation of Patents Offices) Notice, made pursuant to Section 8 of the Hong Kong Patents Ordinance.
38. Examination Guidelines, Part IV, Chapter 8, Section 2.2.1 (1).
39. Examination Guidelines, Part IV, Chapter 8, Section1 (3).
40. Examination Guidelines, Part IV, Chapter 8, Section 2.2, 1, Paragraphs 4 and 5.

Publication on the Internet

7.5.20 The date a publication is issued on the Internet is deemed to be the date of publication.[41] It can, however, often be hard to prove the date of publication on the Internet from a website. The best practice is to notarize printouts from a website as soon as the publication is available.

Public Use or Oral Disclosure Proven by Documents

7.5.21 Evidence of public use proven by documents (such as a newspaper article) is considered the best evidence. Documentary evidence post-dating the application date can be used; however, it will be given less probative value.[42]

7.5.22 For example, this type of evidence can be used if a product has been publicly announced on one date and reported on in a magazine some time later. If any application is filed between the public announcement and publication in the magazine, the magazine article can be used as evidence of prior use.

Common Knowledge

7.5.23 Common knowledge may be proved by citing technical contents of reference books, such as textbooks, technical dictionaries, and technical manuals. The burden of proof in asserting common knowledge is on the party alleging that a technical means is common knowledge.[43]

7.5.24 The PRAB may also *ex officio* determine whether a technical means is common knowledge and introduce technical dictionaries, technical manuals, or textbooks into the examination.[44]

Witnesses

7.5.25 Chinese courts and tribunals prefer not to rely on the testimony of witnesses. They would rather rely on documentary evidence and treat oral testimony as unreliable.

---

41. Examination Guidelines, Part IV, Chapter 8, Section 5.2.
42. Examination Guidelines, Part IV, Chapter 8, Section 5.2.
43. Examination Guidelines, Part IV, Chapter 8, Section 4.3.3.
44. Examination Guidelines, Part IV, Chapter 3, Section 4.1, Paragraph 5(7).

7.5.26 This bias is reflected in the Examination Guidelines which, while making provision for witnesses, limits the value of a witness's evidence significantly, as follows, in that witnesses are:

(a) Limited to the evidence of the specific facts they have experienced. Inference, conjecture, and observations based on experience are not admissible.[45]

(b) Required to appear to be examined by the PRAB and the other party unless physically unable to appear.[46]

7.5.27 The examination of the witness is not cross-examination. The other party may be allowed to ask questions, but will not be able to cross-examine the witness. The questioning is required to be "impartial, objective, specific, and clear."[47]

Expert Evidence

7.5.28 Given the above rules on witnesses, the PRAB will not accept opinions or expert evidence from a witness of the parties.

7.5.29 The PRAB may invite experts to give consultation opinions or expert if necessary. The cost is borne by the PRAB or the relevant party.[48]

7.6 ORAL HEARING

7.6.1 The oral hearing is divided into four stages:[49]

(a) Stage 1: Formalities
(b) Stage 2: Investigation
(c) Stage 3: Debate
(d) Stage 4: Deliberation by the panel and conclusion of oral proceedings

Formalities

7.6.2 The formalities, including confirmation of the parties and their agents, introduction of the panel; asking if there are objections to the panel;

---

45. Examination Guidelines, Part IV, Chapter 8, Section 4.3.1(1).
46. Examination Guidelines, Part IV, Chapter 8, Section 4.3(3).
47. Examination Guidelines Part IV, Chapter 4, Section 5.2, Paragraph 4.
48. Examination Guidelines, Part IV, Chapter 8, Section 5.3.
49. Examination Guidelines, Part IV, Chapter 4, Section 5.

whether witnesses will be called; and the parties will be asked if they wish to compromise.[50]

Investigation

7.6.3 In the investigation stage, the PRAB will review the case and confirm the evidence to support the grounds of invalidation and address any requests to amend the patent by the patentee. Witnesses will be questioned in this stage.[51]

Debate

7.6.4 In the debate stage, the parties make submissions regarding the facts shown by evidence, applicable law, and issues in dispute and answer questions from the panel. The submissions on law usually follow each ground of opposition. After the debate, the parties can make final submissions. The petitioner can, at this time, renounce some claims or narrow the scope for invalidation. The patentee can seek to narrow the scope of the claims or renounce part of the claims.[52]

7.6.5 After investigation, the panel may also make observations as to their view of the case and hear further submissions.[53]

Deliberation by the Panel

7.6.6 The panel will then deliberate and either announce their decision, or state the decision is to be made at a later date.[54] If the decision will be made at a later date in writing, the PRAB may allow the parties to file written submissions to support their statements at the oral hearing. The PRAB will almost invariably announce their decision in writing at a later date.

7.7 APPEAL OF PRAB'S INVALIDATION DECISION

7.7.1 Any party not satisfied with the PRAB's decision may, within three months of the date of receipt of notification, appeal to the People's Court.[55]

---

50. Examination Guidelines, Part IV, Chapter 4, Section 5.1.
51. Examination Guidelines, Part IV, Chapter 4, Section 5.2.
52. Examination Guidelines, Part IV, Chapter 4, Section 5.3, Paragraphs 1 and 2.
53. Examination Guidelines, Part IV, Chapter 4, Section 5.3, Paragraph 3.
54. Examination Guidelines, Part IV, Chapter 4, Sections 5.4 and 7.
55. Patent Law, Article 46.

7.7.2 The appeal will be heard by the Beijing First Intermediate People's Court. The proceeding between the party and the PRAB is considered to be an administrative proceeding, and thus the Chinese Administrative Litigation Law is applicable. Appeals of the PRAB's invalidation decisions were previously handled by the Administrative Litigation Branch of the People's Courts rather than the Intellectual Property Branch of the People's Courts. In Beijing, they have now created a unified IP tribunal to handle all IP cases and appeals are generally heard by this tribunal.

The Court's Role

7.7.3 The People's Court shall examine whether the PRAB has:[56]

(a) Affirmed that the facts are correct and supported by solid evidence.
(b) Applied the laws or regulations correctly.
(c) Complied with relevant procedural rules.

Decision

7.7.4 After hearing a case, the People's Court:[57]

(a) Shall make a judgment upholding the PRAB's decision, if it finds the facts determined by the PRAB to be supported by the evidence, correct application of the law and regulations, and compliance with procedural rules.

(b) May cancel the decision in whole or in part, or order the PRAB to re-decide the case, if it finds insufficient evidence, an erroneous application of the law or regulations, or a violation of legal procedure.

Applicable Laws

7.7.5 When reviewing the PRAB's decisions, the People's Court shall employ the criteria set forth in the Patent Law and Patent Law Implementation Regulations. As for the Examination Guidelines, the People's Court may "refer to" them,[58] which means that the People's Court may refuse to employ the criteria set forth in the Examination Guidelines if it finds them in conflict with higher laws or regulations.

---

56. Administrative Litigation Law, Article 54.
57. Administrative Litigation Law, Article 54.
58. Administrative Litigation Law, Article 53.

7.7.6 That said, the People's Court normally employs the criteria set forth in the Examination Guidelines.

Appeals and Re-examination of a People's Court Decision

7.7.7 The judgment of the People's Court, at the first instance, may be challenged by an appeal to the People's Court at a higher level. In the case of appeals against invalidation decisions, the appellate court is the Beijing Higher People's Court. Generally, any decision by the Beijing Higher People's Court will be a final decision, unless the Supreme People's Court of China (Supreme Court or Supreme People's Court) accepts a request for review.

7.8 EFFECT OF A FINAL INVALIDATION DECISION

7.8.1 Patents which are declared invalid are deemed not to have existed from the beginning. There is no retroactive effect on any decision on infringement that has been complied with or compulsorily executed. However, damages caused by a patentee acting in bad faith will be compensated.[59]

7.8.2 Article 47 of the Patent Law provides the following specific examples of circumstances in which the PRAB's decision will have no retroactive effect:

(a) Any judgment or ruling relating to patent infringement that has been made and enforced by the People's Court;

(b) Any decision concerning a patent infringement dispute that has been complied with or compulsorily executed; and

(c) Any patent licensing contract or patent assignment contract that has been performed prior to the declaration of invalidation.

7.8.3 This means that if a judgment is entered against a party for patent infringement and damages ordered by the court have been paid and the patent is subsequently invalidated, the court order continues to be effective even though the patent has been declared invalid. The only option available for the Defendant is to appeal the decision to a higher

---

59. Patent Law, Article 47.

people's court, whereby the evidence that the patent has been invalidated can be adduced.

7.8.4 If a final decision has been made, or a patentee is out of time to appeal, then the original judgment will stand unless the patentee can show bad faith.

CHAPTER 8

Civil Litigation in China

8.1 INTRODUCTION

8.1.1 This chapter provides a summary of the People' Republic of China (PRC or China) civil litigation system. Chapter 9, "Preliminary and Interlocutory Issues," addresses issues to be considered prior to bringing action, Chapter 10, "Evidence" addresses issues relating to the collection and admissibility of evidence. Chapter 11, "Patent Infringement Litigation," addresses issues specific to patent litigation for patents and utility models.

8.2 SUMMARY OF CIVIL PROCEEDINGS

8.2.1 The figure on the following page summarizes the main steps in civil litigation in China. The People's Courts have broad discretion on how to conduct cases, so there are many procedural variations. Additionally, although regulations provide filing and service deadlines, in practice, these deadlines are often not met.

8.3 JUDGING PANEL

8.3.1 Panels hearing patent infringement cases will usually consist of three judges.[1]

8.4 FILING FEES

8.4.1 The plaintiff must pay a fee when it files the claim, which is calculated as a percentage of the damages claimed in the case. The official court fees

---

1. People's Court Administration Law, Article 10.

Summary of main steps in civil litigation

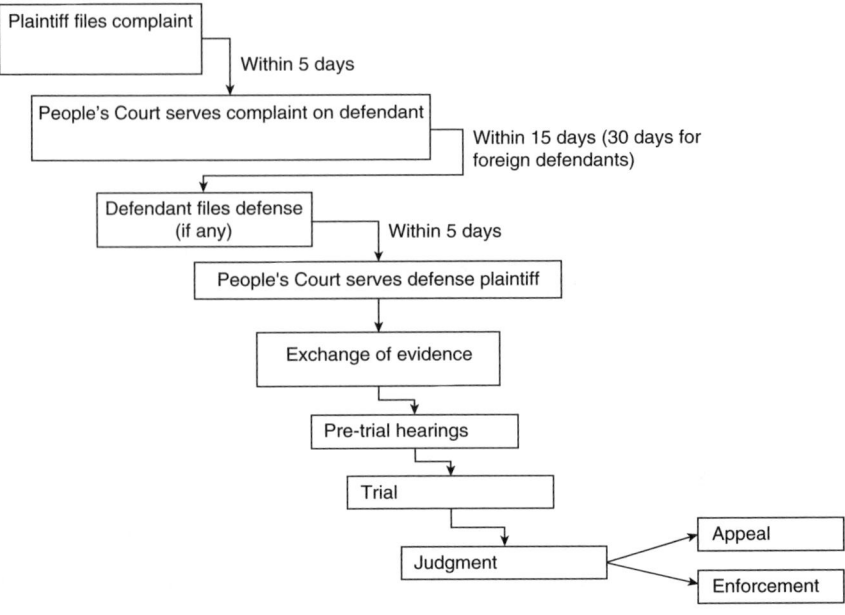

that must be paid to the court are determined by the *Methods for the Payment of Litigation Fees* and may be a fixed sum.[2] Detailed information can be found in Table 3.

8.5 THE COMPLAINT

8.5.1 To file a case, the plaintiff must submit a complaint to the court together with one copy of the complaint for each defendant. The complaint must contain the following information:[3]

(a) Plaintiff's name, nationality, occupation, address, and the name and position of the legal representative or principal responsible person if the plaintiff is an organization;

(b) Defendant's name and address, and the name and position of the legal representative or principal responsible person if the defendant is an organization;

(c) Plaintiff's request for relief and the facts and reasons on which the request is based; and

(d) Evidence and its source, and the name and address of the intended witness(es).

---

2. Methods for the Payment of Litigation Fees, Article 13.
3. Civil Procedure Law, Article 110.

8.5.2 Complaints in China are generally very short documents that set out the bare bones of the plaintiff's case. The plaintiff has an opportunity at the trial to set out in full their case. It is generally better to do so at that time once the plaintiff knows what evidence is before the court.

8.5.3 Many courts will require the complaint to be chopped or personally signed by the plaintiff or its authorized representative rather than by their appointed lawyers or agents. In intellectual property (IP) cases, the Supreme People's Court of China (Supreme Court or Supreme People's Court), in its 2009 Economic Condition Opinion, said that courts should waive this requirement for foreign companies.[4]

8.6 ACCEPTANCE OF THE COMPLAINT

8.6.1 The complaint will be filed to the acceptance chamber of the court. There, an acceptance judge will review the complaint to ensure that the complaint is in the jurisdiction of the court, and that plaintiff has complied with the other requirement for filing a suit as set out above.[5]

8.6.2 The court should issue a notice of acceptance or nonacceptance of the case within seven days for filing of the complaint.[6]

8.7 SERVICE OF THE COMPLAINT

8.7.1 The court is required to serve the complaint within five days of acceptance and establishment of the case.

8.7.2 Court documents must also be served personally on a party in China. If the party refuses to accept service, substituted service may be permitted by the People's Courts. Chinese law also provides for service by post when it is difficult to effect personal service. Service may also be affected through the offices of another People's Court or through public announcement, in which case, service is deemed effective sixty days after publication of the announcement.[7]

8.7.3 If a defendant is overseas, the People's Courts may serve through diplomatic channels or through other procedures acceptable in the jurisdiction in which the defendant is located.[8]

---

4. 2009 Economic Condition Opinion, Article 12.
5. Civil Procedure Law, Article 112.
6. Civil Procedure Law, Article 112.
7. Civil Procedure Law, Articles 77 to 84 provide specific rules for domestic service.
8. Civil Procedure Law, Article 245 provides the methods of overseas service.

8.8 DEFENSE

8.8.1 The time limit for the defendant(s) to file a defense is within fifteen days of receipt of the complaint.[9] For foreign defendants, the period for filing a defense is thirty days after receipt of the complaint.[10]

8.8.2 It is not necessary to file a defense and, in most cases, a defendant does not. This is because the burden of proof of proving almost all elements of a case falls on the plaintiff. A defense may admit facts that the plaintiff is not able to prove. Defendants will, therefore, prefer to see the plaintiffs' evidence before making any admissions. If the defendant has a positive defense, such as a license, then a defense may be filed to plead the point.[11]

8.9 PROCEEDINGS IN THE ABSENCE OF A PARTY

8.9.1 If a party fails to appear, the court will still proceed with the case without the other party being represented.[12]

8.10 MEDIATION

8.10.1 Under the Civil Procedure Law, if the parties are willing, the People's Court may conduct mediation for the parties.[13] However, even though both parties may voluntarily submit to the court for mediation, they may at anytime be withdrawn if one of the parties does not sign and exchange the mediation agreement with the other side.[14] Once the mediation agreement is signed and exchanged by both parties, it becomes legally binding. If the parties do settle the matter through court-assisted mediation, they will only have to pay half the amount of case acceptance fees required by the court.[15]

8.10.2 Mediation can be a useful way to settle a case if the parties are both willing to reach a settlement. One problem with mediation in the Chinese courts is that the judges trying the case will be involved in the mediation, making it difficult for a party to concede weak points in the mediation.

---

9. Civil Procedure Law, Article 113.
10. Civil Procedure Law, Article 246.
11. In over ten years of handling IP cases in court in China, the author has seen a defense filed only once. This occurred because the author's client had a claim to be licensed.
12. Civil Procedure Law, Article 130.
13. Civil Procedure Law, Article 85.
14. Civil Procedure Law, Article 89.
15. Methods for the Payment of Litigation Fees, Article 15.

8.11 EVIDENCE COLLECTION AND ADMISSIBILITY

8.11.1 The collection and submission of admissible evidence is the most important part of civil litigation in China. Given its importance, this is addressed in detail in Chapter 10, "Evidence."

8.12 EVIDENCE EXCHANGE

8.12.1 Under the Supreme Court Evidence Rules, parties are required to produce their evidence to the court and the other side before the start of trial. The time for submitting evidence shall be longer than thirty days after the parties receive a notice of acceptance. The parties may agree a time period for evidence exchange.[16]

8.12.2 The parties are required to categorize and number evidential material, provide a brief description of the source and facts of the case in which the evidence is produced.[17]

8.12.3 Any one of the parties may request a pre-trial evidence exchange hearing.[18] This is common in patent cases. At the hearing, the parties exchange the evidence they intend to rely on and explain its relevance to the court. The other side can object to the evidence.[19]

8.12.4 Parties may apply to file rebuttal evidence. As a general rule, evidence should only be exchanged a maximum of two times, except for significant, complex, or difficult cases.[20]

8.12.5 The goal of evidence exchange is explained in Article 39 of the Supreme Court Evidence Rules, as follows:

> "Through the exchange of evidence, the major disputes between the parties shall be determined."

8.12.6 Evidence exchange is a very important part of patent litigation in China. It is vital that evidence is well prepared and properly explained, and that any possible objections by the other side thought through in advance. Objections should be made to the other side's evidence so as to reduce the admissible evidence they have to argue the case. At the evidence-exchange

---

16. Supreme Court Evidence Rules, Article 33.
17. Supreme Court Evidence Rules, Article 14.
18. Supreme Court Evidence Rules, Article 37.
19. Supreme Court Evidence Rules, Article 39.
20. Supreme Court Evidence Rules, Article 39.

hearing, the principal judge handling the case will have his first chance to consider the case in detail, and parties must be on top of their case at this stage.

8.12.7 After evidence exchange, only new evidence may be produced at the trial.[21] The Supreme Court Evidence Rules provide that new evidence includes evidence:

(a) Newly discovered by one of the parties after the expiration of the time period for producing evidence in the hearing of first instance;

(b) That any party was not reasonably able to provide within the time period for producing evidence and was still unable to provide within any extended time period approved by the people's court.[22]

8.13 TRIAL

8.13.1 Once the People's Court has finished the investigation stage and evidence exchange, it will order a trial hearing. In complex patent cases, it can take a year or more from when the case was commenced before the first trial hearing. All patent cases, whether at first instance or on appeal, are open to the public. The court may be closed if trade secrets are to be disclosed.[23]

8.13.2 The court will decide the issue of infringement and, if this is proved, it will also decide on damages in the same decision.

Trial Format

8.13.3 The format of the Chinese civil trial is set out in the Civil Procedure Law as follows:[24]

(a) Opening statements are given by both sides.
(b) Oral evidence is given (in practice, oral evidence is unusual).
(c) Documentary evidence (including audio and video evidence) is presented.
(d) Judicial Appraisal (or expert statements) is read.
(e) The written record of evidence (that is, inspection by the court or another People's Court) is read.
(f) With the court's permission, new evidence may be presented and witnesses questioned (in practice, this rarely happens).

---

21. Civil Procedure Law, Article 125.
22. Supreme Court Evidence Rules, Article 41.
23. Civil Procedure Law, Article 66.
24. Civil Procedure Law, Articles 124–127.

(g) The parties' lawyers debate and make submissions on the evidence and the law.

8.13.4 Lawyers will usually prepare a "representative's statement," which will either be presented to the court at the hearing or within a short period after the hearing. This statement will summarize the case, by reference to the evidence and legal arguments. This is the most important document to be submitted in a case and needs to be well prepared.

8.14 JUDGMENT

8.14.1 The court will issue a written judgment,[25] usually within a few months of trial, depending on the complexity of the case. In important cases, the adjudication committee[26] may review a judgment before it is issued by the court.

8.14.2 Chinese judgments are required to be a specific form by Article 138 of the Civil Procedure Law, which requires the judgment set out:

(1) The cause of action, claims, and the facts and reasons of disputes;

(2) The facts and reasons on which the judgment is based and the laws to which are applied;

(3) The consequences of a judgment and the liability for litigation costs; and

(4) The time limit for filing an appeal and the appellate court with which the appeal shall be filed.

8.15 APPEALS

8.15.1 A party can appeal the judgment to the next higher level court within fifteen days of delivery of the decision from a People's Court.[27] In the case of a foreign party, the appeal period is thirty days from delivery of the decision.[28] The appeal should be filed to the court that made the original decision. If it is filed to the appeal court, the appeal court should within five days send the appeal to the original court.[29]

---

25. Civil Procedure Law, Article 138.
26. See Chapter 3, "Introduction to China's Administrative and Judicial Patent Systems," for a discussion of the role of the adjudication committee.
27. Civil Procedure Law, Article 147.
28. Civil Procedure Law, Article 247
29. Civil Procedure Law, Article 149.

Notice of Appeal

8.15.2 A notice of appeal is required to include the:

(a) Names of all parties;
(b) Names of legal persons and their legal representatives, or the names of other organizations and their principal leading personnel;
(c) Name of the people's court where the case was originally tried;
(d) Docket number, and the cause of action; and
(e) Claims and reasons of appeal.

Procedure

8.15.3 The appellate courts apply the same procedure as first instance cases unless special provisions are made otherwise.[30]

Decision that Can Be Made by the Appellate Court

8.15.4 Under Article 153 of the Civil Procedure Law, the appellate court can make any of the following decisions:

(1) If the facts were clearly found and the law was correctly applied in the original judgment, the appeal shall be rejected by a judgment and the original judgment shall be sustained;

(2) If the law was incorrectly applied in the original judgment, the judgment shall be amended according to law;

(3) If in the original judgment the facts were incorrectly found or were not clearly found and the evidence was inconclusive, the judgment shall be rescinded and the case remanded by an order to the original People's Court for a retrial, or the People's Court of second instance may amend the judgment after investigating and clarifying the facts; or

(4) If, in the original judgment, a violation of the prescribed procedure may have affected the correctness of the judgment, the judgment shall be rescinded and the case remanded by an order to the original people's court for a retrial.

8.15.5 The judgment of the appeal court is final.[31]

---

30. Civil Procedure Law, Article 157.
31. Civil Procedure Law, Article 158.

8.16 EFFECT OF AN APPEAL

8.16.1 An appeal of a first instance decision automatically stops a first instance decision become effective and it cannot be enforced.[32] Applying for a review by the Supreme Court of People's Procuratorate does not stay the coming into force of a second instance decision. (The review procedure is discussed below).

8.17 NEW EVIDENCE ON APPEAL

8.17.1 New evidence which is admissible on appeal includes the following evidence:

(a) Newly discovered after the hearing of first instance has been completed;
(b) For which any party unsuccessfully applied to the people's court for an order for the investigation and collection of the relevant evidence prior to the expiration of the time period for producing evidence in the court of first instance but was collected by the court of second instance on the basis that such an order was necessary following the application of one of the parties.[33]

8.18 REVIEW OF THE DECISION BY THE SUPREME COURT OR PROCURATORATE

8.18.1 Even though decisions of appellate courts are final, if the appellate court was not the Supreme Court, the parties can seek a review by the Supreme Court[34] within two years of the judgment becoming effective.

8.18.2 Under Article 179(1) of the Civil Procedure Law, the grounds for seeking a review are any of the following:

(1) There is new evidence which is conclusive enough to overrule the original judgment or ruling;
(2) The main evidence used in the original judgment or ruling to find the facts was insufficient;

---

32. Civil Procedure Law, Article 141.
33. Supreme Court Evidence Rules, Article 41(2).
34. Civil Procedure Law, Article 177.

(3) The main evidence used in the original judgment or ruling to find the facts was forged;

(4) The main evidence used in the original judgment or ruling to find the facts was not cross-examined;

(5) Any party to a lawsuit was unable to obtain the evidence necessary for adjudicating the case because of some realistic reasons and has applied to the people's court for investigation and collection of such evidence in writing, but the people's court fails to investigate and collect such evidence;

(6) There was an error in the application of the law in the original judgment or ruling;

(7) The court exercised jurisdiction was in violation of legal provisions;

(8) The trial panel was unlawfully formed or the judges that should withdraw have not done so;

(9) A party under on incapacity was not represented by a legal agent, or the party that should participate in the litigation failed to do so because of the reasons not attributable to himself or his legal agent;

(10) The party's right to debate was deprived of in violation of the law;

(11) The default judgment in the absence of the party was made whereas that party was not served with summons;

(12) Some claims were omitted or exceeded in the original judgment or ruling; or

(13) The legal document on which the original judgment or ruling was made is canceled or revised.

8.18.3 In addition, Article 179(2) of the Civil Procedure Law provides:

> With respect to a violation of the legal procedure by a people's court that may have affected the correctness of the judgment or ruling in the case or the situation that adjudicating personnel involved themselves in any conduct of embezzlement, bribery, practicing favoritism for himself or relatives, or twisting the law in rendering judgment, the people's court shall retry the case.

8.18.4 The Supreme Court has recently expanded the number of judges and is accepting a greater number of review applications.

8.18.5 Parties can also seek a re-trial by applying to the People's Procuratorate[35] on the same grounds that a review application can be made to the Supreme Court. Such applications are rare in patent cases, as the People's Procuratorate has limited knowledge of patent law.

---

35. Civil Procedure Law, Article 187.

CHAPTER 9
Preliminary and Interlocutory Issues

9.1 INTRODUCTION

9.1.1 This chapter deals with eight preliminary issues that need to be addressed or considered prior to bringing action under the Patent Law of the People's Republic of China (PRC or China). These are:

(a) Powers of attorney
(b) Limitation periods
(c) Obtaining jurisdiction (forum shopping)
(d) Search reports for utility models and design patents
(e) Pre-trial or interim relief
(f) Asset preservation orders
(g) Declaration of non-infringement
(h) Stay of proceedings for invalidation

9.1.2 Gathering appropriate evidence to ensure that an action is not statute barred and to obtain appropriate jurisdiction is very important. These issues are therefore addressed in a separate chapter before considering evidence gathering and specific infringement issues.

9.1.3 Evidence Collection and Evidence Preservation Orders are also discussed in Chapter 10, "Evidence."

9.2 POWERS OF ATTORNEY

9.2.1 In order to instruct lawyers or other agents to appear before the courts, it is necessary to submit a power of attorney to the court granting the agent the power to appear on behalf of the party.[1] In the case of a company, the power of attorney should be signed by the legal representative (or equivalent) of the company or chopped with the company's seal.[2] If foreigners wish to instruct lawyers, they are required to instruct Chinese lawyers to appear on their behalf.[3]

9.2.2 For powers of attorney from a foreign party, it is necessary to have the power of attorney notarized by a domestic notary and legalized by the Chinese embassy or consulate[4] that handles matters for the jurisdiction in which the company is incorporated. If there is no Chinese embassy or consulate, such as in countries that do not have diplomatic relations with China, a Chinese consulate in a third country can perform the legalization.[5] In Hong Kong, the notarization is done by China-appointed attesting offices. In Taiwan, a special organization will verify documents.

9.2.3 In addition, it is necessary to produce evidence that the person signing the power of attorney has the power to bind the company. For companies in civil law countries, this can be relatively easy because the company records will often indicate who has power to bind the company. For companies in common law jurisdictions, this can be more difficult because there is often no official record of who can bind the company. In such circumstances, the person signing the power of attorney can also sign a certificate of legal representative confirming that they have the power to bind the company.

9.2.4 The process can take a number of weeks, and it is necessary to arrange to have a power of attorney signed and notarized and legalized as soon as possible.

9.2.5 One solution that is used to ensure that powers of attorneys can be prepared quickly is grant a general power of attorney to a domestic Chinese subsidiary or an individual allowing them to sign powers of attorney for specific cases. Most courts will accept specific powers of attorney granted under a general power in this way.

---

1. Civil Procedure Law, Article 59(1).
2. Civil Procedure Law, Articles 49 and 50, proscribe the power of legal representatives to conduct proceedings and the powers of agents. Article 58 deals with the power of litigation representatives.
3. Civil Procedure Law, Article 239.
4. Civil Procedure Law, Article 59(3), if the party overseas is Chinese; Article 246, if the party is a foreigner or foreign company.
5. Civil Procedure Law, Article 59(3), if the party overseas is Chinese; Article 246, if the party is a foreigner or foreign company.

9.3 LIMITATION PERIODS

9.3.1 Limitation periods are governed by the General Principles of Civil Law; Patent Law, Article 69(1); and the Provisions of the Supreme People's Court on Certain Issues Concerning the Application of the Statute of Limitations to Civil Case Trials (2008 Limitation Provisions).

9.3.2 The general limitation rules are:

(a) The limitation period is two years.[6] The limitation period starts to run from the date the patentee knows or should know his rights have been infringed.[7]

(b) If the intellectual property (IP) right owner files infringement claims after the expiry of the two-year period, his claims will be dismissed unless the infringer voluntarily consents to the claims.[8]

Continuous Infringement

9.3.3 In repeat or continuous infringement cases, which consist of more than one independent action (e.g., the manufacture of infringing goods), the limitation period runs from each act of infringement and claims may be made for any acts within the two-year limitation period. In such cases, the damages will be calculated, at the earliest, from the date two years before the filing of the infringement action.[9]

Stopping the Running of the Limitation Period

9.3.4 The patentee or other interested party can stop the running of the limitation period by giving notice to the infringer of its claims.[10] The notice can be given in the following ways:[11]

(a) Hand delivering documents to the infringer;
(b) Sending mails or emails to the infringer; or
(c) Publishing announcements in media[12] if the infringer cannot be located.

---

6. Patent Law, Article 68(1); General Principles of Civil Law, Article 135.
7. Patent Law, Article 68(1); General Principles of Civil Law, Article 137.
8. General Principles of Civil Law, Article 138.
9. 2001 Patent Trial Guidelines, Article 23.
10. General Principles of Civil Law, Article 140.
11. 2008 Limitation Provisions, Article 10.
12. The media should be (1) the national media; or (2) the provincial-level media in the place where the claimee has domicile. *See* 2008 Limitation Provisions, Article 10.

9.3.5 In order to overcome a limitation defense, the plaintiff will need to prove (e.g., with the signature of the legal representative or other senior employee, seal, or other means) that the infringer has received the document,[13] or that the document reached or should have reached the infringer.

9.3.6 As a best practice, a patentee or interested party should either receive direct confirmation from the potential defendant that they have received the notice or use a notary to send the notice so as to have third-party proof the notice was sent.

Making Claims to the People's Court, People's Procuratorate, or Public Security Bureau

9.3.7 The limitation period can also be tolled by making claims to the People's Court, People's Procuratorate, or Public Security Bureau. The claims can be made in the following ways:[14]

(a) Filing of a civil or criminal complaint or report requesting protection of rights;

(b) Applying for a pre-litigation assert preservation order, preliminary injunction, or other pre-litigation reliefs;

(c) Applying for compulsory enforcement;

(d) Applying to join a co-defendant or other parties to a litigation;

(e) Making a counterclaim;

(f) Making claims by filing an arbitration;

(g) Asserting rights through a third party.

9.3.8 If the patentee or interested party sends a request for protection of its rights to a government agency, a public institution, or a social group that has the power to resolve the relevant IP dispute according to the law, such a request can also stop the running of the limitations period.[15]

Asserting Defense Based on the Limitation Period

9.3.9 If a party to a lawsuit does not assert a defense based on the limitation period, the court is required not to bring the limitation period to the attention of the party on its own volition or make a ruling based on the limitation period.[16]

---

13. 2008 Limitation Provisions, Article 10.
14. 2008 Limitation Provisions, Articles 13 and 15.
15. 2008 Limitation Provisions, Articles 14 and 15.
16. 2008 Limitation Provisions, Article 3.

9.3.10 This requirement was imposed under the 2008 Limitation Provisions. Before these provisions were issued, the courts would often check whether the statute of limitations had expired of their own volition and dismiss cases for being outside the limitation period.

9.3.11 If a party fails to raise the defense of limitation during the first-instance trial, then it is barred from asserting such a defense on appeal, unless the defense is based on new evidence.[17]

Waiving Limitation Periods by Agreement

9.3.12 The limitation period cannot be extended or shortened by any agreement between the parties.[18] Nevertheless, as the limitation period may be restarted by giving notice of a claim, parties who wish to extend a limitation period could do so if one party gives notice of the claim, the receipt of which the other party confirms in writing.

9.3.13 The court also does not accept agreements in which one party waives to make defense based on the statute of limitations.[19]

9.4 JURISDICTION

Generally

9.4.1 Articles 22 to 35 of the the Civil Procedure Law of the People's Republic of China (PRC or China) make provision for the jurisdiction of the different People's Courts in China. In general, whether a court has the jurisdiction to hear a case depends on whether the defendant's domicile or residence[20] or the infringing act occurred in the territorial jurisdiction of the court.[21]

9.4.2 If an action involves several defendants that fall within the jurisdiction of two or more courts, all such courts have the jurisdiction.[22] In the event that more than one court has jurisdiction, then the plaintiff may select a court to file suit or, if they have filed in several courts, the court in which they first filed proceedings alone will have jurisdiction.[23]

---

17. 2008 Limitation Provisions, Article 4.
18. 2008 Limitation Provisions, Article 2.
19. 2008 Limitation Provisions, Article 2.
20. Civil Procedure Law, Article 22.
21. Civil Procedure Law, Article 29; Patent Trial Guidelines, Article 5.
22. Civil Procedure Law, Article 35.
23. Civil Procedure Law, Article 35.

Patent Cases

9.4.3 Under the 2001 Patent Trial Guidelines issued by the Supreme People's Court, jurisdiction for first instance patent disputes is limited to certain Intermediate People's Courts and Higher People's Courts.[24]

9.4.4 At the time of writing, seventy-six Intermediate People's Courts had been designated to handle patent cases. These are Intermediate Courts based in the capitals of provinces and major cities in each province and certain other intermediate courts designated by the Supreme Court. The number of courts with the jurisdiction to try patent cases is limited so as to ensure that the courts that handle patent cases have the technical ability to do so. As a result, the courts are given broader territorial jurisdiction than their normal jurisdiction to try patent cases. A list of courts currently able to try patent cases is provided as Appendix Seven. One Primary People's Court in Yiwu Zhejiang has been given jurisdiction to try utility model and design cases on a trial basis.

Objection to Jurisdiction

9.4.5 Any party may raise an objection over the jurisdiction of the court after a case has been accepted within the time limited for filing the defense.[25] If an objection is not filed within the time limited for filing a defense, the defendant is deemed to have accepted the jurisdiction of the court.

9.4.6 If an objection is filed, the court is then required to examine the objection and, if accepted, to transfer the case to a court which does have jurisdiction over the case.[26]

Forum Shopping

9.4.7 Despite the fact that the number of courts that have jurisdiction to try patent cases is limited, plaintiffs will prefer to obtain jurisdiction in a court that will be favorable to them.

9.4.8 In the case of foreign plaintiffs, this will generally be larger cities such as Beijing and Shanghai, which have better developed court systems

---

24. 2001 Patent Trial Guidelines, Article 2. First instance patent disputes are under the jurisdiction of the intermediate people's courts located in the provinces, autonomous regions, and cities directly under the Central Government, and those intermediate people's courts appointed by the Supreme People's Courts.
25. Civil Procedure Law, Article 38.
26. Civil Procedure Law, Article 38.

and large economies, so that there is less scope for local protectionism. For companies that have made large investments in a certain area, they will also consider taking action in the courts of that area as these investments are likely to assist in ensuring a neutral hearing.

9.4.9 In the case of Chinese plaintiffs, they will often seek to sue in their hometown so as to take advantage of playing in their "home court."

9.4.10 Obtaining jurisdiction in a preferred court can be difficult, because the defendant will often not be domiciled in that jurisdiction and it can often be hard to find an act infringement in that jurisdiction.

Joining a Defendant

9.4.11 The best course is to identify a party in the preferred jurisdiction to join as a defendant to the action who is involved in infringement. Article 6 of the Several Regulations of the Supreme People's Court Concerning the Applicable Law for Hearing Patent Disputes, which determines that the court in the jurisdiction in which the sale of the infringing products takes place, is the court that will hear the case if the manufacturer and the seller are sued as joint defendants.

9.4.12 The case of retail sales can be relatively easy; often, a retail store is joined as a defendant for selling infringing products in a case brought against the infringer or manufacturer.

9.4.13 In the case of wholesaler or trade sales, this can be more difficult because it can be difficult to identify a wholesaler or trader within the preferred jurisdiction from which to purchase an infringing product. It is often necessary to rely on investigations to ascertain whether a wholesaler or trader is dealing in the infringing product and make a notarized purchase from that entity.

Relying on Place of Infringement

9.4.14 It can difficult to rely on the place of infringement to obtain jurisdiction. In cases in which the plaintiff only files suit against the manufacturer of the infringing products, but not the seller, and the parties are unrelated, then the court in the location of the manufacturer has jurisdiction.[27]

---

27. 2001 Patent Trial Guidelines, Article 6.1.

However, if the seller is a subsidiary of the manufacturer and the plaintiff takes action against the act of the manufacturer for manufacturing selling the product, the People's Court of the place where the products are sold has the jurisdiction.[28]

9.4.15 If action is taken against both the manufacturer and seller accused as the co-defendants, the people's court of the place where the infringing products were sold has the jurisdiction.[29]

Trade Fairs

9.4.16 Parties will sometimes try to rely on sales or offers for sales made at trade fairs in a preferred jurisdiction. Some courts will accept such cases. The author, however, has had the experience of the Shanghai No. 2 Intermediate Court refusing to accept a case based on an offer to sell at a trade fair in Shanghai on the basis the trade fair had finished.[30]

9.5 SEARCH REPORTS FOR UTILITY MODEL AND DESIGN CASES

9.5.1 Under Article 61(2) of the Patent Law, the court can require the patentee of a utility model or design to file a search report issued by the State Intellectual Property Office (SIPO) after SIPO has conducted a search, analysis, and evaluation of the patent.[31] The search report will provide SIPO's view of the validity of the patent. The search report may be used as evidence in infringement disputes.

9.5.2 Patentees of utility models and designs will often obtain such search reports prior to bringing proceedings, so as to seek to avoid a stay of proceedings. If the search report finds that the patent is partially valid, the patentee may seek to proceed in relation to the claims that have been found in the search report to be valid.

9.5.3 Defendants or potential defendants may also obtain a search report from the SIPO Search and Consulting Center. This is a non-profit organization established by SIPO, and the search reports are not considered to be official search reports. The search reports are issued in the same form as the

---

28. 2001 Patent Trial Guidelines, Article 6.2.
29. 2001 Patent Trial Guidelines, Article 6.1.
30. The court refused to issue a written decision.
31. Patent Law, Article 61.

official search reports and will cite prior art found and give an opinion as to the validity of the claims of the patent. A party requesting a search report may also provide prior art to the consulting center when requesting the search.

9.5.4 An alternative to obtaining a search report from the SIPO Search and Consulting Center is to obtain a judicial appraisal from a judicial appraisal center as to the validity of the patent. This would most likely be combined with an analysis of infringement.

9.5.5 If the patentee is seeking any type of preliminary relief for utility models or design patents, the plaintiff must file a search report before the court will grant any such relief.[32]

9.6 PRETRIAL OR INTERIM INJUNCTIONS

9.6.1 A People's Court has the power to order pre-trial or interim injunctions before an act of infringement takes place or while the infringing act is occurring:

9.6.2 Article 66(1) of the Patent Law provides:

> Where any patentee or interested party has evidence to prove that another person is infringing or will soon infringe its or his patent right and that if such infringing act is not stopped from occurring in time, it is likely to cause irreparable harm to it or him, it or he may, before legal proceedings are instituted, petition the people's court to adopt measures to stop the relevant acts.

9.6.3 Upon the filing of an application for a preliminary injunction, a court has an obligation to make a ruling within forty-eight hours if all the criteria are satisfied and, if satisfied, the injunction will be immediately enforced.[33] Courts very often do not comply with the obligation to make a ruling within 48 hours and it can often take several weeks for a court to issue a ruling.

9.6.4 The criteria include the applicant providing the following evidence detailed in Article 4 of the Several Provisions of the 2001 Interim Measure Rules:

(a) Patent owners must provide proof of the authenticity and validity of the patent rights, including the patent certificate, patent claims, description, patent annuity payment certificate, as well as a search report issued by the SIPO if it is a utility model patent;

---

32. 2001 Patent Interim Measures Rules, Article 4(1).
33. Patent Law, Article 66(3); 2001 Patent Interim Measures Rules, Article 9.

(b) Related injured parties (generally sole or exclusive licensees[34]) must provide proof of their standing to bring action, such as in the case of licensees, their license to the patent and proof that it has been recorded with the SIPO, or if it has not been recorded, confirmation of the license from of the patent owner;

(c) Proof that the alleged infringer is infringing or about to infringe the patent rights, together with a sample of the accused infringing product and material to compare the technical characteristics of the accused infringing product with the the patented product.

9.6.5 When considering whether to issue a preliminary injunction, the court will consider whether:

(a) Patent infringement is occurring or about to occur;

(b) The patent rights holder will suffer irreparable harm that damages will be difficult to remedy by payment of damages;

(c) Appropriate security has been provided by the applicant; and

(d) The public interest would be harmed if an injunction was issued ordering the respondent to cease the acts.[35]

9.6.6 In practice, preliminary injunctions are rarely granted in patent cases, other than for mechanical patents, given the complexity of most cases. In Article 14 of the 2009 Economic Situation Opinion, the Supreme Court provided further guidance which restricted the scope of pre-trial injunctions. Article 14 of the Economic Situation Opinion specifically stated that in cases of applications for preliminary injunctions in patent cases, if there was not a direct infringement read and the court would need to consider complex issues, it should not granted a preliminary injunctions.[36] Additionally, if the Respondent had filed for a declaratory judgment of non-infringement or for invalidation of the patent, the courts should be cautious in issuing interim injunctions.

Security Required

9.6.7 At the time of filing the above-mentioned evidence, the applicant must also provide the court with a security, generally in the form of a bond,[37] to cover any losses caused to the defendant from the granting of the injunction. The bond is usually provided in cash, but other security, such as a mortgage,

---

34. The definition of "related injured parties" is discussed in the following chapter.
35. 2001 Patent Interim Measure Rues, Article 11.
36. 2009 Economic Situation Opinion, Article 14.
37. Article 66(2), Patent Law; 2001 Patent Interim Measures Rules, Article 6.

can be offered. In Article 14 of the 2009 Economic Situation Opionion, the Supreme Court provided that in calculating the bond, the main consideration was the potential loss to the Respondent from being injuncted, but the compensation claimed by the Applicant could also be considered.

9.6.8 The court can require the applicant to increase this security if there is a risk that the injunction will cause a significant loss to the respondent.[38] In one case brought by Eli Lilly in Shanghai, the court required the bond for a preliminary injunction to be increased on two occasions as the case progressed.[39] The 2009 Economic Situation Opinion also encourages courts to consider whether to lift an injunction after considering how the case is progressing.[40]

Compensation If Preliminary Injunction Wrongly Granted

9.6.9 If the preliminary injunction is later found to be wrongly granted, the applicant is liable to pay damages to the defendant. The compensation is not limited to the amount of the bond and is the actual loss caused to the defendant. In the Eli Lilly case mentioned above, after the Shanghai Higher People's Court found that the patent was not infringed, the defendant brought a lawsuit against Eli Lilly claiming eight million United States dollars in damages.[41] Article 14 of the 2009 Economic Situation Opinion encourages courts to give proper compensation to defendants where a pre-trial injunction has been improperly applied for or the main infringement action is ultimately unsuccessful.

Pretrial Injunction—Suit Must Be Filed in Fifteen Days

9.6.10 The party in whose favor a pre-trial injunction has been filed, must file suit in the People's Court within fifteen days, otherwise the injunction will be withdrawn by the People's Court.[42]

---

38. 2001 Patent Interim Measures Rules, Article 7.
39. Presentation by a Judge of the Shanghai No. 1 Intermediate Court to the EU Chamber of Commerce in China in 2008.
40. 2009 Economic Situation Opinion, Article 14.
41. Presentation by a Judge of the Shanghai No. 1 Intermediate Court to the EU Chamber of Commerce in China in 2008.
42. Article 66(4), Patent Law, 2001 Patent Interim Measures Rules, Article 12.

Review of the Decision to Grant or Not Grant Injunction

9.6.11 The plaintiff may seek a review of a decision not to grant a preliminary injunction. The defendant may also seek a review of a decision to grant a preliminary injunction.[43] The review application should be made within ten days of receipt of the order.[44] In the event that a defendant does seek a review of the preliminary injunction, the injunction will be enforceable throughout the reconsideration proceedings.[45]

9.6.12 A preliminary injunction remains in force until final judgment is issued, or another specific date determined by the People's Court.[46]

9.7 ASSET-FREEZING ORDERS

9.7.1 A party to any action in China may make an application to freeze the assets of the defendant so as to ensure that there will be assets to satisfy any judgment that is ultimately granted.[47]

9.7.2 Such orders are regularly sought and obtained in China. The party seeking the order is required to put up a bond equal to the amount to be frozen,[48] but the court does have discretion to accept a lower bond or other guarantee.

9.8 DECLARATION OF NON-INFRINGEMENT

9.8.1 Declarations of non-infringement are not provided for in the Patent Law. However, Article 18 of the 2010 Judicial Interpretation provides:[49]

> If a right-holder issues a warning against another party regarding the infringement of patent rights, if the party which has been warned or an interested party has urged in writing that the right-holder exercises its right to sue, and if within one month after receiving said notice in writing, or within two month after such request in writing is sent, the right-holder fails to withdraw the warning or to file a lawsuit, if the party which has been warned or the interested party files a suit at the People's Court to request a determination that its conduct does not infringe the patent rights, the People's Court shall accept the case.

---

43. Patent Law, Article 66(3).
44. 2001 Patent Interim Measures Rules, Article 10.
45. Patent Law, Article 66(3).
46. 2001 Patent Interim Measures Rules, Article 10 and Article 14.
47. Civil Procedure Law, Article 93.
48. Supreme People's Court Opinions on Several Issues regarding the Application of the PRC Civil Procedure Law, Article 98.
49. 2010 Judicial Interpretation, Article 18.

9.8.2 The 2009 Economic Situation Opinion, which, arguably, is now superseded on this point by the 2010 Judicial Interpretation, also stated that declaratory action could be brought where:

> a party, who is implementing or preparing to implement investment and construct factories and other such business activities and receives from the intellectual property right holder in some other way a related patent infringement etc warning or threat, and takes the initiative to request the right holder confirm that its behavior does not constitute infringement, and provides in a reasonable manner the information required and materials to make such a confirmation and the right holder does not within a reasonable period reply or refuses to provide confirmation.[50]

9.8.3 Prior to the enactment of these provisions, the Supreme Court had approved the bringing of declaratory judgment actions in the cases *Suzhou Longbao v. Suzhou Langli*,[51] *Changzhou Huasheng v. Eli Lilly*,[52] and *Honda v. Shijiazhuang Shuanhuan*.[53] Importantly, in these decisions, the Supreme Court held that the recipient of a warning letter or other threat of action could bring a declaratory action in their home court on the basis that harm had been done to them in their home jurisdiction under Article 29 of the Civil Procedure Law. As discussed above, this could make winning a case hard for the patentee.

9.8.4 Given the provisions of Article 18 of the 2010 Judicial Interpretation and the possibility that recipients may bring a declaratory judgment in their home court, patentees should take great care not to send warning letters or make other threats of action unless they are ready to sue.

9.9 STAY OF INFRINGEMENT PROCEEDINGS

9.9.1 In most patent cases, a defendant will file an application to the Patent Review and Adjudication Board (PRAB) to invalidate the patent and apply to stay the infringement action pending a decision on validity.

---

50. 2009 Economic Situation Opinion, Paragraph 13.
51. Supreme Court Notice Concerning Suzhou Longbao Bioengineering Industry Co. v. Suzhou Langli Health Care Co. Request for Confirmation of Non-Infringement in the Patent Dispute.
52. Supreme Court Notice concerning jurisdiction in a patent dispute between Eli Lilly and Changzhou Huasheng Pharmaceutical Co. Ltd.
53. Supreme Court Notice Concerning Honda Technology Co. Ltd. v. Shijazhuan Shuanhuang Automobile Co. Ltd., concerning jurisdiction in a patent dispute (2004).

Articles 8 to 11 of the 2001 Patent Trial Guidelines address how a court should handle and application for a stay.

Stay in Invention Patent Cases

9.9.2 Under Article 11 of the 2001 Patent Trial Guidelines, for invention patents (or utility models or design patents that have already been declared valid in invalidation proceedings), the courts are allowed to not stay the infringement action. Generally, a court will not stay an action in these cases. However, if the plaintiff can produce a search report or other evidence showing that there is a good chance the patent will be invalidated, the court does have the discretion to stay the action.

9.9.3 As a general practice, courts will not make a decision on infringement until validity had been decided, but there is no hard and fast rule on this. Generally, courts will time decisions on infringement to be issued after a decision on validity. However, there are no written rules concerning this.

Stay of Utility Model and Design Cases

9.9.4 Because they are unexamined, the 2001 Patent Trial Guidelines treat utility model and design patents (except those that have already been held to be valid) differently from invention patents, and the general rule is that such actions should be stayed.

9.9.5 Article 9 of the 2001 Patent Trial Guidelines provides that the court shall stay the infringement action pending a defendant's request for a declaration of invalidity of a utility model or design except under any of the following circumstances:

(a) No technical documentation is found in the search report produced by the plaintiff that results in the loss of novelty or inventiveness of the patent for utility model.

(b) The defendant's evidence is sufficient to prove that its or his used technology has been known to the public.

(c) The proof or basis the defendant has furnished for requesting the invalidation of the patent right in question is obviously insufficient.

(d) The People's Court finds that the legal proceedings should not be stayed under any other circumstances.

9.9.6 In actual practice, many courts will not stay the infringement proceedings until at least the first trial hearing when they will consider all the evidence.

If the case can be dismissed because of lack of evidence or because the court determines there is no infringement, the courts will do so. If they consider the infringement claim is strong, they will then likely stay the action pending a decision on validity.

Time Limit for Applying for a Stay

9.9.7 If a defendant requests to stay proceedings in a patent case, they must file an application to invalidate the patent within deadline for filing the defense.[54] This is fifteen days after service of the complaint for domestic parties (including foreign-invested enterprise incorporated in China) and thirty days if the defendant is a foreign party.

9.9.8 After that, the court will not grant a stay unless after consideration of the evidence the court considers granting a stay to be necessary.[55]

---

54. 2001 Patent Trial Guidelines, Article 8(2).
55. 2001 Patent Trial Guidelines, Article 10.

CHAPTER 10
Evidence

10.1 THE IMPORTANCE OF EVIDENCE

10.1.1 The major issue in patent litigation in the People's Republic of China (PRC or China) is obtaining evidence to prove infringement. This can be very difficult as the Chinese court system only provides for very limited discovery. There is no obligation on the parties involved in the litigation to disclose any information to the other party, unless the court actually takes evidence preservation measures.

10.1.2 Article 64 of the Civil Procedure Law provides:

> Parties in relation to matters they have asserted themselves have the responsibility to submit evidence.

10.1.3 The effect of this is that the burden of proving a case remains on the plaintiff throughout the trial, and this continues even if the defendant files no evidence. The courts are very reluctant to draw any inferences from evidence. Essentially, the burden of proof on a party who has to prove something is "beyond reasonable doubt."

10.1.4 This rule that "whoever asserts must prove" also applies to damages and makes it very difficult for a plaintiff to prove substantial damages.

10.1.5 The collection of admissible evidence takes up substantial time in a case and can be very frustrating for foreign plaintiffs.

10.1.6 This section discusses the permitted evidence and ways in which such evidence can be made admissible, followed by a discussion of how evidence can be obtained during court proceedings. Finally, private investigations and the admissibility of evidence obtained through private investigations are discussed. Generally, any patent case will require private investigations to obtain evidence.

10.2 PERMITTED EVIDENCE

10.2.1 These are the seven types of evidence admissible in Chinese courts;

(a) Documentary evidence;
(b) Material evidence;
(c) Audio-visual material;
(d) Testimony of witnesses;
(e) Statements of the parties;
(f) Conclusions from judicial appraisals;
(g) Records of inspection and on-site records.[1]

10.2.2 These types of evidence are subject to different requirements before they can be used as evidence in a case and must be examined by the court. For example, the court must authenticate and compare audio-visual material and statements of the parties with other evidence in the same case before it can be used as evidence.[2]

(a) Official documents are given the most weight.

In China, documents prepared by state organs or social bodies in compliance with their respective functions are usually given more weight than other types of documentary evidence.[3] This type of evidence includes records such as file extracts, investigation reports, and interview records from interviews by the government. Courts tend to give the most weight to this type of evidence. Therefore, in an IP dispute, if a government agency [for example, the State Intellectual Property Office (SIPO) for patents, State Administration of Industry and Commerce (SAIC) for trademarks, and National Copyright Administration (NCA) for copyright] has investigated the case before and has issued an investigation report, that report will likely be given much weight in the court and can be decisive to the outcome of the case.

(b) Evidence of witnesses is given little weight.

Evidence of witnesses, especially if the testimony is given by a party to a case, is given very little weight by a court unless it is a statement

---

1. Civil Procedure Law, Article 63; Administrative Litigation Law, Article 31.
2. Civil Procedure Law, Article 69 and Article 71.
3. Supreme Court Evidence Rules, Article 77(1).

against interest. Where a party makes a statement to the court, the court is required to examine if the statement is consistent with other evidence in the case before accepting it.[4]

10.2.3 Only after the courts have verified the truth of the evidence can the evidence be used to establish facts in the case.[5] Each of the seven categories of evidence must comply with the provisions of the Supreme Court Evidence Rules to be accepted as evidence by the courts.

10.3 BEST EVIDENCE RULE

10.3.1 China adopts a best evidence rule for litigation. Original evidence needs to be submitted if available.[6]

10.3.2 If original evidence is not available, other evidence such as copies, photographs, duplicates, or extracts can be submitted. But the court will give much higher evidentiary weight to the original evidence if one party's original evidence conflicts with the other party's copies or photographs.[7] If one party's allegation is only supported by copies without the support of any original evidence and the copies cannot be verified in any way, the court will generally find the allegation has not been proved.

10.4 NOTARIZED EVIDENCE

10.4.1 The Supreme Court Evidence Rules provide that if facts are proved by a valid notary report this creates a rebuttable presumption that the facts are true.[8]

10.4.2 For original evidence obtained from one party by the other, such as an infringing sample purchased by the intellectual property (IP) rightholder from the infringer, notarization is recommended. This is because the infringer would likely argue that the sample is not what the infringer sold. (Notarized purchases are discussed below.)

10.4.3 Original evidence originating from within China is not required to be notarized to be relied upon by the court; examples are a magazine published in China or the statements of third parties. Nevertheless, for

---

4. Civil Procedure Law, Article 71.
5. Civil Procedure Law, Article 63.
6. Civil Procedure Law, Article 68.
7. Supreme Court Evidence Rules, Article 77.
8. Supreme Court Evidence Rules, Article 9(6).

non-original documentary evidence, a notarized document also has more evidentiary weight than a document that is not notarized.[9] For instance, it is a good practice to notarize the printouts of website pages to be submitted to the court.

10.5 FOREIGN EVIDENCE: NOTARIZATION AND LEGALIZATION

10.5.1 The collection of international evidence, and the admission of this evidence to Chinese courts, is regulated by Article 11 of the Supreme Court Evidence Rules. If evidence has been obtained from overseas, the source must be stated; it must be certified by a public notary from that country; and legalized by the Chinese consulate in the country, or in accordance with the related verification procedures in a treaty signed between China and that country. Evidence from Hong Kong, Macao, and Taiwan is required to be verified according to special procedures.

10.5.2 The process of notarization and legalization can sometimes be lengthy and, therefore, it should be completed as soon as possible to comply with any limitation periods or other deadlines.

10.5.3 The litigant should also review the documents in advance to look for any issues, such as political issues, that will slow down the notarization or legalization. The author handled one case in which the Chinese consulate refused to legalize a document because the document stated that Taiwan is a country. (The Chinese government regards Taiwan as part of China.) In another case a Chinese Embassy refused to legalize a foreign judgment because it referred to China as "China" and not the People's Republic of China.

10.6 FOREIGN LANGUAGE EVIDENCE

10.6.1 Non-Chinese language evidence must be translated into Chinese in order for it to be admissible.[10] Partial translation of the relevant part of a document is acceptable.

10.7 EXPERT EVIDENCE

10.7.1 Article 72 of the Civil Procedure Law provides that when the People's Court faces a problem that requires expert analysis, it should be passed to

---

9. Supreme Court Evidence Rules, Article 77.
10. Civil Procedure Law, Article 68(2); Supreme Court Evidence Rules, Article 12.

a Judicial Appraisal Centre for appraisal. A Judicial Appraisal Center representative is permitted to speak to the parties and witnesses to understand the case and to issue a written report.

10.7.2 In patent cases involving pharmaceuticals, chemicals, and high technology, evidence on technical issues will usually be required by the People's Court.

10.7.3 The common practice is for a plaintiff to engage a Judicial Appraisal Center or other expert to provide report to prove infringement. In certain cases, it is acceptable to rely on an internal report prepared by a party. If the other side objects to the contents of the report, the court will then appoint a third-party expert under Article 72 of the Civil Procedure Law.[11]

10.7.4 A party may challenge a judicial appraisal report obtained by the court and request a new report from a different entity on any of the following grounds:

(a) The authentication institution or expert does not hold the requisite qualifications.

(b) The authentication process used involves a serious breach of law.

(c) The evidence relied on to reach the authentication conclusions is clearly inadequate.

(d) Any other circumstances indicate that the conclusions, if subject to cross-examination, cannot be used in evidence.[12]

10.7.5 No defective judicial appraisal report that can be rectified by way of supplementary judicial appraisal, fresh cross-examination, or supplementary cross-examination shall be re-authenticated.[13]

10.8 EVIDENCE PRESERVATION ORDERS

10.8.1 A party may also apply to a court for an Evidence Preservation Order, asking the court to preserve (seal on site) or seize documentary or physical evidence, pursuant to Article 67 of the Patent Law,[14] which provides for pre-action preservation of evidence and Article 74 of the Civil Procedure Law which provides for evidence preservation generally. Articles 23 and 24

---

11. Supreme Court Evidence Rules, Article 28.
12. Supreme Court Evidence Rules, Article 27.
13. Supreme Court Evidence Rules, Article 27(2).
14. 2001 Patent Interim Measures Rules. Article 16 also provides for pre-action evidence preservation when seeking a pre-action injunction.

of the Supreme Court Evidence Rules provide further rules regarding evidence preservation.

10.8.2 The applicant for an Evidence Preservation Order should specify in the application what evidence he wishes the court to preserve. Courts may also require the applicant to post security for an Evidence Preservation Order, but in most cases they do not.[15]

10.8.3 The deadline to apply for an Evidence Preservation Order is the seventh day before the evidence submission deadline.[16] The evidence submission deadline is set by the court, and it is normally the thirtieth day after the court accepts the case.

10.8.4 The preconditions for obtaining an Evidence Preservation Order are:[17]

(a) It is possible that the evidence will be lost or it will be difficult to obtain the evidence in the future.
(b) The petitioner is not able to collect the evidence.

For patent infringement cases, depending on the court, it can be easy to obtain an Evidence Preservation Order as it is not difficult to convince the court that the infringer could destroy evidence.

10.8.5 The court may or may not allow the applicant to be present when the court executes the Evidence Preservation Order.[18] The applicant may request to be present when the court executes the Evidence Preservation Order, but the opposing party often objects by arguing that such presence may compromise trade secrets or other confidential information. In those cases, the court normally asks the applicant not to attend execution of the Evidence Preservation Order.

10.8.6 When the court is investigating and collecting evidence, a party should not refuse a request to provide such evidence.[19]

10.8.7 In practice, many parties do not actively cooperate with evidence preservation orders and refuse to disclose documents or give documents that are not relevant. A party cannot rely on evidence preservation obtaining evidence to prove a case and should only seek to rely on evidence preservation obtaining supplement evidence.

---

15. Patent Law, Article 67; Supreme Court Evidence Rules, Article 23(2).
16. Supreme Court Evidence Rules, Article 23.
17. Civil Procedure Law, Article 74.
18. Supreme Court Evidence Rules, Article 24(2).
19. Civil Procedure Law, Article 65(1).

10.9 EVIDENCE COLLECTION BY THE COURT

10.9.1 Under Article 64 of the Civil Procedure Law and Article 17 of the Supreme Court Evidence Rules, a party may also apply for collection of evidence under any of the following circumstances:

(a) The evidence that the party concerned requests be investigated and collected is stored in archive files maintained by the relevant organ of the state and can only be accessed on the basis of an order made by the people's court.

(b) The materials concern state secrets, commercial secrets, or private personal information.

(c) Any other materials that, on objective grounds, cannot be collected by the party concerned or the representative thereof.

10.9.2 The deadline for making an application is seven days before the deadline for evidence submission.[20]

10.10 THE BURDEN OF PROOF DOES NOT SHIFT IF THE OTHER PARTY DOES NOT COMPLY WITH AN EVIDENCE REQUEST

10.10.1 Under Article 64 of the Civil Procedure Law, the party asserting a fact has the burden of proving it. Even if a court orders a party to produce evidence and they do not comply, the burden of proof does not shift.

10.10.2 There is, however, an exception if one party can prove that the other party has evidence. If there is evidence to prove that a party has evidence, but the party refuses to provide it without reasonable grounds, then the other party can claim that the evidence is not favorable to the first party, and that claim will be regarded as established by the court hearing the dispute.[21]

10.11 PENALTIES FOR DESTROYING EVIDENCE

10.11.1 If the court orders a party to produce some given evidence and that party subsequently destroys the said evidence, the court can either fine or detain the party.[22] For organizations, the main person responsible or the person directly responsible can be fined or detained by the court. An individual can be fined no more than 10 thousand renminbi and an

---

20. Supreme Court Evidence Rules, Article 19.
21. Supreme Court Evidence Rules, Article 75.
22. Civil Procedure Law, Article 102.

organization can be fined between 10 thousand and 300 thousand renminbi.[23] A period of detention can be no longer than fifteen days and can be enforced by the Public Security Bureau.[24] A fine or detention must be approved by the president of the responsible court and issued as a written decision.[25]

10.12 INVESTIGATIONS BY THE PARTIES

10.12.1 The evidence gathered by a party is generally collected by private investigators but can be collected by employers. Relevant evidence includes samples of products, invoices, receipts, and details/maps of the premises. It is critical, during the collection of evidence, to obtain evidence directly linking the infringing party with the infringing products. Receipts are the best evidence of such links. However, when obtaining significant evidence it is advisable to have notaries witness the purchase or other method of obtaining evidence to ensure that it will be accepted by the court when a law suit is filed.

10.12.2 A lawyer entrusted by a party can investigate and collect evidence legally.[26]

Private Investigators

10.12.3 It is common practice in China to hire investigators to gather evidence. However, regulations issued in 1993 by the Ministry of Public Security (MPS) prohibit companies from being registered with a business scope including private investigation. Many "market research" and "consulting companies" therefore operate as private investigation agencies. Though the MPS regulations seem to forbid this, many of these companies work regularly with the Public Security Bureau and, indeed, are asked to conduct investigations by them.[27]

10.12.4 Investigators should use legal means to obtain evidence. If an investigator's acts involve obtaining state secrets, infringing personal privacy, committing a crime, etc., the evidence cannot be used in court, and the

---

23. Civil Procedure Law, Article 104(1).
24. Civil Procedure Law, Article 104(2)–(3).
25. Civil Procedure Law, Article 105.
26. Civil Procedure Law, Article 61; Guo Jinlian v. Li Xincai, (2008) Gan Intermediate People's Court Civil Fourth Division No. 31, Jiangxi Province Ganzhou City Intermediate People's Court.
27. It should also be noted that strictly speaking, the 1993 regulations are only administrative regulations and not law.

party who hired the investigator may become civilly or criminally liable. It is important that only consulting companies with extensive experience, networks with the various government agencies, and integrity are retained to collect evidence and conduct other litigation support roles.

Notarized Purchases

10.12.5 The best strategy to prove infringement is to make a purchase of the alleged infringing product when accompanied by a notary public (notarized purchase). Investigators will therefore work with notaries public to make purchases.

10.12.6 Courts will accept evidence of a notarized purchase as evidence of sale and notarized purchases are rarely challenged. The other party will need to file compelling evidence to challenge a notarized purchase.[28]

10.12.7 Should a notary make any mistakes, a party may apply for these to be corrected without affecting the validity of the notarization, unless they are mistakes concerning illegality or authenticity.[29]

10.12.8 Many notaries are reluctant to notarize a purchase. They will state that they must identify themselves as a notary at the time of the purchase, which defeats the purpose of making a notarized purchase. It can take some time to find notaries who are willing to notarize purchases in intellectual property cases. Investigators and law firms will generally work with notaries who are experienced at this work.

10.13 INADMISSIBILITY OF ILLEGALLY OBTAINED EVIDENCE

10.13.1 Evidence that is obtained by a party that infringes upon the lawful rights and interests of others or is prohibited by law cannot be used as evidence in litigation.[30] In China, the courts will determine whether

---

28. Civil Procedure Law, Article 67; Notarization Law of the People's Republic of China, Article 36.
29. Notarization Law of the People's Republic of China, Article 39; Reply of the Ministry of Justice Concerning the Issue of How to Handle Notarization Administrative Complaints After the Implementation of the Notarization Law of the People's Republic of China, Ministry of Justice, Judicial Reply No. [2006] 8.
30. Supreme Court Evidence Rules, Article 68; Shanghai Zhongti Real-Estate Co., Ltd. v. Shanghai Guangchuan Construction Design Consulting Co., Ltd., (2006) Shanghai No. 2 Intermediate Civil Fourth (Commercial) Division No. 521, Shanghai No. 2 Intermediate People's Court.

evidence has infringed a party's rights in balance with the nature and collection methods that are used to obtain the evidence in question.[31] Unless the collection of the evidence breaches any civil procedure rules, or a crime has been committed in obtaining the evidence, then the courts will generally not rule that evidence is inadmissible.

10.14 ADMISSIBILITY OF PRETEXT OR TRAP PURCHASES

10.14.1 Given the limitations on obtaining evidence from the other side and the strong burden of proof on a plaintiff, using pretexts to conduct investigations is an accepted practice, and the evidence obtained can be used in court. The investigator and the notary do not have to disclose their identities when making the purchase.

10.14.2 Article 8 of the Interpretations of the People's Supreme Court Concerning the Application of Laws to the Trial of Civil Disputes of Copyright provides that

> Where any party concerned purchases infringing reproductions by ordering or on-the-spot dealing by himself or authorizing any other person, the physical objects and invoices, etc. obtained thereby may be used as evidence.
>
> The notary reports issued by any notary public, without disclosing his own identity to the party that is suspected of infringement, concerning the evidence obtained by the party concerned in the ways as mentioned in the preceding paragraph or concerning the process of obtaining the evidence shall be used as evidence unless there is evidence that can prove the opposite.

10.14.3 Although this applies to copyright infringement cases, it can be used for reference in other IP cases.

10.14.4 In a civil lawsuit in China, People's Courts will admit notarized trap purchases by the plaintiff as evidence. This was confirmed by Supreme People's Court in a judgment, *Beijing University Founder (Group) Co., Ltd. v. Beijing Gaoshu Technology Co., Ltd.* The Supreme People's Court stated in the judgment that

> Beijing University Founder (Group) Co., Ltd relies on a notarised purchase to obtain the evidence that Gaoshu Company installed pirated Founder software as well as evidence

---

31. Nantong Jiangong Group Co., Ltd. Hainan Subsidiary v. He Xiaoming, (2007) Hainan Intermediate Civil First Instance No. 444, Hainan Province Haikou City Intermediate People's Court; Jialun Industry (Shenzhen) Co., Ltd. v. Roman Tam, (2004) Guangdong Higher Civil Fourth Division No. 31, Guangdong Province Higher People's Court.

or clues of evidence that Gaoshu conducted similar infringing acts. The notarised purchase has a justified purpose and did not harm the interests of social public or other people. In addition, since it is very hard to obtain the evidence of the infringing acts in relation to computer software copyright infringement and such evidence is usually deeply hidden, notarised purchases can help solve such issue in evidence collection, so as to deter and inhibit the similar infringing acts, which is also in accordance with the spirit of intensifying IP right protection.

CHAPTER 11

Patent Infringement Litigation—Invention Patents and Utility Models

11.1 INTRODUCTION

11.1.1 In order to prove infringement of its patent, the plaintiff will need to prove the following:

(a) The plaintiff has a right to bring action under the patent.
(b) The defendant has committed at least one act in the People's Republic of China (PRC or China) that is considered to be infringement.
(c) The product the infringer dealt with or the process used is covered by at least one of the claims of the patent.

11.1.2 This chapter will discuss the key legal aspects of patent infringement litigation in China and covers the following topics:

(a) Right to bring action of patentee and other injured parties
(b) Acts of direct infringement
(c) Indirect infringement
(d) Joint infringement
(e) Reverse burden of proof for process claims for new products
(f) Claim interpretation
(g) Doctrine of equivalents
(h) File wrapper estoppel
(i) Rectification of claims
(j) Proving infringement

11.2 THE RIGHTS OF PATENTEES AND RELATED INJURED PARTIES TO BRING ACTION

11.2.1 Article 60 of the Patent Law provides (in part):

> Where a dispute arises as a result of the exploitation of a patent without the authorization of the patentee, that is, the infringement of the patent right of the patentee, it shall be settled through consultation by the parties. Where the parties are not willing to consult with each other or where the consultation fails, the patentee or any related injured party may institute legal proceedings in the people's court, or request the administrative authority for patent affairs to handle the matter.

11.2.2 It is clear from this that a patentee has the right to bring action.

11.2.3 The Patent Law and the two judicial interpretations on patent infringement trials do not, however, define a *related injured party*.

11.2.4 However, Article 1(2) of the 2001 Interim Measures, provides:[1]

> The related injured party that files an application includes the licensee of a licensing contract for exploitation of the patent, and the legal successor to the property right of the patent, etc. Among the licensees of the licensing contract for exploitation of the patent, the licensee of an exclusive patent licensing contract may file an application with the people's court; the licensee of a sole licensing contract in the circumstances where the patentee does not apply, may file an application.

11.2.5 As the applicant for pretrial measures is required to bring action within fifteen days, it is clear that the rules apply to a main action as well. Therefore, the related injured parties who can bring a patent infringement lawsuit are the following:

(a) An exclusive licensee
(b) A sole licensee where the patentee does not bring action
(c) The legal successor to patent rights

11.2.6 A licensee who has been granted a right to bring action in their patent license may also be able to bring action.

---

1. Article 8(2) of the Administrative Patent Enforcement Measures has a similar provision.

11.3 ACTS OF INFRINGEMENT

11.3.1 Article 11 of the Patent Law provides in relation to invention patents and utility models, as follows:

> After the grant of the invention or utility model patent right, except where otherwise provided for in this Law, any unit or individual must not, without the authorization of the patentee, exploit the patent, that is, for production or business purposes, to make, use, offer to sell, sell or import the patented product, or use the patented method, or use, offer to sell, sell or import the product directly obtained through the patented method.[2]

11.3.2 The acts of infringement in relation to a patented product are for production or business purposes to:

(a) Make
(b) Use
(c) Offer to sell
(d) Sell
(e) Import

11.3.3 The acts of infringement in relation to a patented process are for production or business purposes:

(a) Use the patented method, or
(b) Use, offer to sell, sell, or import the product directly obtained through the patented method.

11.3.4 Export of a patented product or a product directly obtained through a patented method is also a breach of the Articles 2 and 3 of the Regulations for IP Customs Protection (IP Customs Regulations).

11.3.5 Most of these acts of infringement are self-explanatory. Interpretations have been issued with regard to (1) use if products use an infringing component; (2) what constitutes an offer to sell; and (3) processing a product obtained through a patented process. These are discussed below.

Use: Products that Use an Infringing Component

11.3.6 The Supreme People's Court of the People's Republic of China (Supreme People's Court or Supreme Court) Interpretation on Several Issues Regarding Legal Application in the Adjudication of Patent Infringement Cases (2010 Judicial Interpretation) provides that if a

---

2. Patent Law, Article 11.

product is made from a component that infringes a patent, the acts of making and selling the product are infringing acts.[3] This provision clarifies an issue that was argued in some patent infringement cases in China. With this clarification, downstream manufacturers will be found liable for using patent infringing components to build their products.

Offer to Sell

11.3.7 The 2001 Patent Trial Guidelines provides that offering to sell includes an intention to sell by way of advertisement, shop window display, or exhibition.[4]

Processing a Product Obtained Through a Patented Process

11.3.8 Using a product "directly obtained" through a patented process constitutes patent infringement.[5] Moreover, the act of further processing a product obtained through a patented process is considered using a product directly obtained through the patented process and, therefore, constitutes patent infringement.[6]

11.3.9 In practice, this allows companies, such as pharmaceutical companies, to sue if a process patent covers an intermediary that was used in making the final product.

11.4 INDIRECT INFRINGEMENT

11.4.1 No provisions of the Patent Law, Patent Law Implementing Regulations or Judicial Interpretations address indirect infringement. The Beijing Higher People's Court Opinion (Beijing Opinion) on the handling of patent cases provides detailed provisions on indirect infringement. Essentially, this provides that there must be the provision of an essential component with knowledge.[7] Given that the amendments to the Patent Law have not followed this opinion, it is possible that the Beijing Opinion will not be followed by courts.

---

3. 2010 Judicial Interpretation, Article 12.
4. 2010 Judicial Interpretation, Article 24.
5. Patent Law, Article 11.
6. 2010 Judicial Interpretation, Article 13.
7. Beijing Higher People's Court Opinion on Several Provisions Relating to Patent Infringement Establishment, Articles 73–80.

11.4.2 In the first draft of the 2010 Judicial Interpretation, the following provision was included as Article 16:

> If an acting person knows that a relevant product can only be used as the raw material, intermediate product, part, equipment etc, for embodying a certain invention or utility model patent, but still provides it to a third party to carry out a patent infringing act, and if the right-holder contends that said acting person and said third party shall be jointly liable, the People's Court shall support that position. If said third party's implementation is not for the purpose of manufacturing of commerce, and if the right-holder contends that said acting person bears civil liability, the People's Court shall support that position.

11.4.3 This was a very broad definition of indirect infringement that included that even if the end-use was non infringing because it was not commercial use, the acts before this constituted infringement. In appropriate cases, a court may apply this test; however, at present, it cannot be considered part of the law. It is therefore best to rely on the concept of joint infringement in situations in which there are allegations of indirect infringement.

11.5 JOINT INFRINGEMENT

11.5.1 Article 130 of the General Principles of Civil Law provides:

> If two or more persons jointly infringe upon another person's rights and cause him damages, they shall bear joint liability.

11.5.2 Article 148(1) of the Supreme People's Court's Interpretation of the General Principles of Civil Law, which interprets Article 130 of the General Principles of Civil Law, provides that a party conspiring or assisting another party to carry out infringement of rights will be held jointly liable.

11.5.3 The 2010 Judicial Interpretation provides that the situation in which an infringing component is used in a product constituting infringement and two or more people have "cooperated and divided their labor," will be considered joint infringement.[8]

---

8. 2010 Judicial Interpretation, Article 12(3).

11.6 REVERSE BURDEN OF PROOF IF THE PATENT RELATES TO A METHOD OF MAKING A *NEW PRODUCT*

11.6.1 Article 61 of the Patent Law provides:

> Where any infringement dispute involves a invention patent for a process for the manufacture of a new product, any entity or individual manufacturing the identical product shall furnish proof to show that the process used in the course of producing its or his product is different from the patented process.

11.6.2 This provision shifts the burden of proof onto the defendant that, if a patent relates to a method of making a new product, to prove that it uses a method different from the patented method for making the product. Until 2010, some courts had interpreted the phrase *new product* as a product that is not known in China before the patent application.

11.6.3 The 2010 Judicial Interpretation, however, interprets the phrase *new product* more narrowly. A product is new if "the product or the technical scheme of the product is not known to the domestic *or overseas* public before the application date of a patent." [Emphasis added.][9] This interpretation limits the situations in which the reverse burden of proof provision can be applied to products that are new anywhere in the world.

11.7 CLAIM INTERPRETATION

11.7.1 The general principles to be used in claim interpretation are included in Article 59 (formerly Article 56) of the Patent Law, which provides that:

> The extent of protection of a patent for an invention shall be determined by the terms of the claims. The description and appended drawings may be used to interpret the claims.

2001 Patent Trial Guidelines

11.7.2 Article 17 of the Guidelines on the Application of the Law Regarding Trials of Patent Infringement Cases (2001 Patent Trial Guidelines) provides that:

> This provision of Article 56 [now Article 59] of the Patent Law means that the extent of protection of patent right should be determined by the necessary technical features

---

9. 2010 Judicial Interpretation, Article 17.

expressly stated in the claims, including the extent as determined by the features equivalent to the necessary technical features.

The equivalent features refer to the features which uses substantially the same means, perform substantially the same function and produce substantially the same as the stated technical features and which can be contemplated by an ordinarily skilled artisan in the art without inventive labor.

2010 Judicial Interpretation

11.7.3 The 2010 Judicial Interpretation introduced a number of further rules for interpreting claims, as described below:

Claims to Be Interpreted Based on Understanding of Person of Ordinary Skill

11.7.4 Article 2 of the 2010 Judicial Interpretation provides that the People's Court should determine the content of the claims based on the claim language itself and the understanding of the claims by a person of ordinary skill in the art after he/she reads the patent specification and the figures.[10]

11.7.5 Article 3 of the 2010 Judicial Interpretation further specifies:

> The People's Court may use the specification, figures, relevant claims of the patent, and the patent prosecution file to interpret a claim. If the specification contains a specific definition regarding certain terminology in the claim, the specific definition shall control the meaning of the terminology in the claim. If the meaning of the terminology in the claim still cannot be determined using the above methods, the claim can be interpreted using a combination of literature available to the public including reference books and textbooks etc, as well as the ordinary meaning understood by a person of ordinary skill in the art.

11.7.6 Therefore, intrinsic evidence should be used first in claim interpretation, and if the meaning of the relevant claim language cannot be determined by use of intrinsic evidence, extrinsic evidence can be used.

11.7.7 A patentee may also be his own lexicographer in redefining claim terms in the patent specification.

---

10. 2010 Judicial Interpretation, Article 2.

Technical Limitation Through Functions or Effects

11.7.8 Article 4 of the 2010 Judicial Interpretation specifies that:

> when the claim describes a technical limitation though functions or effects, the People's Court shall determine the contents of the technical limitation according to the specific embodiments and the equivalent embodiments of the technical limitation described by the specification and figures.

11.7.9 This provision limits the scope of protection for means-plus-function claims to the embodiments that are described in the patent specification and their equivalents.

Inventions Disclosed But Not Included in the Claims

11.7.10 Article 5 of the 2010 Judicial Interpretation provides that inventions that have only been disclosed in the specification or figures but not claimed are not protected. Though this may seem obvious, some courts, over the years, had been willing to extend protection to inventions that had not been properly claimed.

No Redundant Designation Principle

11.7.11 Article 7 of the Judicial Interpretation provides that

> when the accused technical scheme lacks one or more technical features recited by the patent claim, or if one or more technical features is not identical or equivalent, the People's Court shall determine that the accused technical scheme does not fall into the scope of protection of patent rights.

11.7.12 This overrides the Beijing Opinion, which only required comparison of all essential technical elements in a patent claim and states that "obviously unnecessary (or redundant)" technical claim elements should be ignored in determining patent scope.[11] This so-called *redundant designation doctrine* was applied by some Chinese courts because, in many earlier patents, unskilled patent agents made the mistake of unnecessarily including various claim elements in patent claims, making the patent unenforceable if the all elements rule is applied. Over the years, the overall skill level of Chinese patent agents has improved, and the redundant designation doctrine has fallen out of favor.

---

11. Beijing Higher People's Court Opinion on Several Provisions Relating to Patent Infringement Establishment, Article 47.

The 2010 Judicial Interpretation, therefore, abandons the redundant designation doctrine.

11.8 DOCTRINE OF EQUIVALENTS

11.8.1 Infringement under the doctrine of equivalents is recognized in China for invention patents and utility model patents.

11.8.2 Article 17 of the 2001 Patent Trial Guidelines, provides that patent protection extends not just to "the necessary technical features expressly stated in the claims," but also to "features equivalent to the necessary technical features."

11.8.3 Equivalent features are defined in Article 17 as "features that use basically the same means, perform basically the same function, and produce basically the same result as the stated technical features, which can be contemplated by an ordinarily skilled person in the art without inventive labor."

11.8.4 The only other guidance on application of the doctrine of equivalents can be found in Article 4 of the 2009 Economic Situation Opinion, which provide that courts should "strictly apply the provisions of the doctrine of equivalents, explore and improve the application of equivalent infringement rules to prevent inappropriate expansion of the scope of protection."[12]

11.8.5 The Beijing Opinion also dealt with the doctrine of equivalents in Articles 31 to 42 and may still be followed by other courts. The Beijing Opinion can be summarized as follows:

(a) This doctrine applies if one or more elements of the accused product are literally different from but equivalent to the elements of the claim. For a feature in an accused product to be the equivalent of a claim element, it must meet two conditions:

(i) If compared to the claim element, the technical feature of the accused product must use basically the same means to perform basically the same function, and achieve basically the same result.

(ii) A person of ordinary skill in the art, having read the patent, would have arrived at the features in the accused product without using any inventive labor.

(b) The doctrine of equivalents allows the substitution of specific claim elements, but not the substitution of the entire technical solution. The

---

12. Article 4 of the 2009 Economic Situation Opinion.

court must determine whether the specific features that fall outside the literal meaning of the claim are equivalent to the claim elements, and not whether the overall technical solution is equivalent. The issue of whether the technical features of the accused product are equivalent to those in the claim is determined as of the date of the alleged infringement.

(c) If a defendant intentionally omits a technical element of the claim from its product, resulting in an inferior technical solution to that described in the patent, and it is obvious that the altered inferior technical solution results from the omission of the element, the product can nevertheless infringe the patent.

(d) The doctrine of equivalents will not apply if the technical features of the accused product are part of the prior art or are contained in a prior filed application.

Supreme Court Case on Doctrine of Equivalents

11.8.6 The Supreme People's Court has considered the doctrine of equivalents in a number of cases. One case, *Dalian Xinyi Jiancai Co., Ltd. v. Dalian Renda Xinxing Qiangti Building Material Factory*,[13] is worth considering.

11.8.7 This case was a retrial case from the Liaoning Higher People's Court that was heard by the Supreme People's Court. The case involved a utility model patent, patent number ZL98231113.3, that had been granted for concrete thin walled components.

11.8.8 In early 2001, Dalian Renda Xinxing Qiangti Building Material Factory (Renda) and Benmiao Wang signed a patent license contract with Hunan Province Lixin Building Material Co., Ltd. (Lixin) to use that patent in Liaoning Province, for which the royalty fees were 200 thousand renminbi. In September, a supplementary agreement was signed between the parties specifying that the patent license was an exclusive and not an ordinary license.

11.8.9 In 2002, Renda discovered that Dalian Xinyi Jiancai Co., Ltd. (Xinyi) was manufacturing a similar product and placing this on the market. Although the product looked similar, on comparison, the accused infringing products bobbin section had one less layer of glass fiber, and the bottom section had no glass fiber.

11.8.10 The Dalian Intermediate People's Court found that the accused infringing product's method, function, and effect constituted infringement

---

13. 2005 Civil Third Division No. 1.

under the doctrine of equivalents. This case was appealed to the Liaoning Higher People's Court, who found both the accused infringing product and the patented product to be identical in technical construction. The Liaoning Higher People's Court stated that although there was a difference existing in the written essential technical claims regarding the number of layers of the glass, however, these differences and the chemical compound, as well as the combination of the compound and scope, were only a shift in quantity. As a result of these factors, the nature of the product itself did not change and the Dalian Intermediate People's Court was correct in their first instance judgment that infringement under the docitrine of equivalents had been established. Xinyi disagreed with the decision of the Liaoning Higher People's Court, and filed for a retrial with the Supreme People's Court in Beijing on the following three grounds:

(a) *Ground 1:* The original court wrongly determined the scope of protection for the patent.

(b) *Ground 2:* The original court mistakenly used the doctrine of equivalents in their determination.

(c) *Ground 3:* The original court's decision to order a public apology be made lacked a legal basis.

11.8.11 Xinyi argued on Ground 2 that the relevant judicial interpretation issued by the Supreme People's Court, stated that *equivalent* referred to equivalence in individual technical characteristics, not equivalence in the entire technical solution. The accused infringing product had clear differences with the patented product, having two layers less of cement and one layer less of glass cloth. The original courts' judgments that it was "basically the same in method, function, and effect" clearly breached the judicial interpretation issued by the Supreme People's Court.

11.8.12 In relation to Renda's claims that, as a result of technical progress, only one layer of fiberglass could achieve the purpose of the patent, Xinyi stated that, before the application for the patent had been filed, alkali-resistant fiberglass had been used in China. Moreover, the protection for a utility design model patent was the structure, shape, or combination of both, and not the related characteristics of the material. So, the claims of Renda that the technical progress of the fiberglass amounted to equivalence could not be established.

11.8.13 In reply, Renda argued that the technical characteristics of the bobbin section of the accused infringing product and the corresponding technical characteristics of the patent were equivalent. The difference in one layer and two layers of fiberglass was only a difference in quantity, not in nature, so the methods were basically identical. Second, the adding of the fiberglass was for the function of increasing the strength of the thin wall and, in both, these were equivalent. Third, creative labor was not required to select the number of layers of fiberglass.

11.8.14 The Supreme People's Court addressed the issue of equivalence in the second point of their judgment. The question to be answered was whether the insertion of one layer of fiberglass in the inorganic cement material of the bobbin section could be regarded as an equivalent characteristic of the corresponding technical characteristic of the patent.

11.8.15 The court stated that the scope of protection for invention and utility model patents was governed by Article 56 [now Article 59] of the Patent Law, i.e., that the claims and could be interpreted reference to the description and figures.

11.8.16 In the claims of the patent, the phrase "at least two layers" was used, and the court regarded this as an extremely clear limitation. When looking at the description in the patent, it was also written that it was possible to have "at least two layers."

11.8.17 The court emphasized that this obvious limiting factor could not be disregarded in determining equivalence. The first point made by the court was that overlooking the phrase *at least two layers* would be like removing part of the independent claim and cause an unreasonable expansion of the protection scope of the patent.

11.8.18 The second point the court considered was that the difference in the levels of fiberglass could not simply be regarded as difference in quantity. The court held that the resistance, inner volume, and floor weight possessed had distinct mechanical effects in the accused infringing product and the patented product. There was a difference in effect with regard to "at least two layers" and having only "one layer" of fiberglass so, for this reason, the one layer of fiberglass inserted in between the organic cement material could not be classified as an equivalent characteristic or an identical characteristic. Therefore, the accused infringing product did not fall into the scope of protection for the patent, and the Xinyi's acts did not constitute patent infringement.

11.9 FILE WRAPPER ESTOPPEL

11.9.1 Article 6 of the 2010 Judicial Interpretation provides:

> If a patent applicant or a patent right holder in the course of grant or invalidation, abandoned a technical scheme through amendments to the claims or specifications or in a statement of opinion, and the right holder in a patent infringement suit seeks to include it in the scope of protection of patent rights, the people's court will not support it.

11.9.2 This provides for wide-ranging estoppel if the patentee has either during prosecution or invalidation proceedings given up a claim to a certain technical solution.

11.9.3 It does mean that, in all cases of patent infringement, the parties need to inspect the full prosecution and invalidation files (if any) to see whether there are any possible file wrapper estoppel arguments.

11.10 INTERPRETATION OF CLAIMS TO RECTIFY MISTAKES

11.10.1 A patentee may find an error in their claims before filing action. According to Article 57 of the Patent Law Implementation Rules, the State Intellectual Property Office (SIPO) shall rectify errors that appear in patent documents immediately upon discovery and publish the rectifications thereafter in the Patent Gazette. The term *errors* is not defined. In practice, the SIPO will amend "clerical errors" such as typing errors.[14]

11.10.2 If it is not possible to amend the patent under Article 57, the patentee will need to convince the court to interpret the claim to rectify the mistake.

11.10.3 There is no provision in the Patent Law or any effective Supreme Court judicial interpretations or opinions regarding rectification of claims. Article 21 of the Beijing Higher Court Opinion, however, provides:

> obvious clerical errors in patent claims or description shall be given proper construction according to circumstances.

11.10.4 In one infringement case, *Hu Yunping v. Chongqing Sanlida Electronics Co. Ltd.*, the Chongqing No. 1 Intermediate People's Court interpreted a claim to overcome an error and stated that, by considering the patent description and figures together, it can be determined whether there is a clerical error.

11.11 PROVING INFRINGEMENT

11.11.1 As set out at the beginning of this chapter, in order to prove infringement of its patent the plaintiff will need to prove the following:

(a) Plaintiff has a right to bring action under the patent.
(b) Defendant has committed at least one act in China that is considered to be infringement.

---

14. SIPO has accepted applications to amend whether the mistake was on its part, but generally refuses applications where the patentee has made a mistake.

(c) The product the infringer dealt with or the process used applies to at least one of the claims of the patent.

11.11.2 The evidence needed to prove that the plaintiff has a right to bring action has been dealt with above. This should be relatively easy to produce.

11.11.3 The chapter on evidence has described the procedures to be followed to gather evidence of infringement. In cases involving the sale of a product that infringes a patent, the actual act of infringement will be relatively easily proved in court. The evidence necessary to prove that a process patent has been infringed can be hard to gather as this will generally be in the hands of the infringer. How the claims are interpreted will assist in making a decision as to whether there is sufficient evidence to support an infringing claim interpretation.

Proving Defendant's Product or Process Is Covered by the Claims

11.11.4 As a first step, the plaintiff is required to state which of the claims of the patent they allege are infringed. For each claim asserted, the plaintiff is then required to produce evidence to show that each of the technical features of the claim, or an equivalent, is present.[15]

11.11.5 In the case of dependent claims, the plaintiff needs to show that the technical features of the dependent claim and all claims it is dependent on are present.[16]

11.11.6 This process is generally done by the preparation of a claim chart that breaks the claims of the patent down into each technical feature and then identifies the evidence that shows that the feature is present in the alleged infringing product or used in the alleged infringing process.

11.11.7 In preparing the chart, the plaintiff needs to bear in mind the rules of claim interpretation and, in particular, any limitations in the specification or drawings or any statement on the file wrapper that will narrow the scope of the claim. If the plaintiff is relying on the doctrine of equivalents, this needs to be identified.

11.11.8 This process should be commenced as soon as litigation is contemplated so that evidence can be gathered to match the claim interpretation that the plaintiff intends to assert.

---

15. 2010 Judicial Interpretation, Article 1(1).
16. 2010 Judicial Interpretation, Article 7(1).

CHAPTER 12
Defenses

12.1 TYPES OF DEFENSE

12.1.1 The primary defenses in a patent case are that the patent is invalid or that it is not infringed on the grounds that the evidence does not show the defendant has committed an infringing act or the alleged infringing product or process is not covered by the claims asserted by the plaintiff.

12.1.2 In addition, there are certain other defenses in either the law or interpretations or opinions, including:

(a) Prior art defense
(b) Innocence as defense to damages

Statutory Defenses

12.1.3 Certain statutory defenses are also provided for under Article 69 of the Patent Law of the People's Republic of China (PRC or China). These are:

(a) Exhaustion of rights
(b) Prior use
(c) Temporary entry into China
(d) Scientific research and experiments
(e) Clinical trials

12.1.4 Finally two other possible defenses are the following:

(a) Breach of the anti-monopoly law
(b) Non-infringement because the patent has been incorporated in a standard

12.1.5 These defenses are discussed in order, in the following sections.

12.2 INVALIDITY

12.2.1 The process and grounds for seeking to invalidate have been addressed in detail in the chapters dealing with invalidity proceedings.

12.2.2 In China, because of the bifurcated system for trying infringement and validity, invalidity is not strictly a defense in a patent infringement case. The court will not hear arguments on validity other than to consider whether to grant a stay. If the patent is invalidated during the course of the trial or an appeal, the case will be dismissed.

12.3 NON-INFRINGEMENT

Insufficient Evidence

12.3.1 Defendants will normally put plaintiffs to strict proof of all the evidence they seek to adduce to prove infringement. Technical points are regularly taken, such as whether notarized evidence has been properly notarized or whether documents are original or not. The courts accept this as part of the procedure and there is no embarrassment for parties in challenging evidence that they could easily admit themselves. For example, it is common for a defendant not to admit that they themselves produced or sold a product, even though they clearly did. It is also common for defendants not to admit documents are true copies if originals cannot be found, even if the documents originated from them.

12.3.2 By not admitting evidence, defendants will seek to poke holes into the plaintiff's cases so the court will ultimately not be able to find infringement based on there being insufficient evidence.

Irrelevance to Claims

12.3.3 The defendant will argue that the alleged infringing product or process is not covered by claims relying on the provisions of the patent law cited in Chapter 11, "Patent Infringement Litigation—Invention Patents and Utility Models," which address infringement. These provisions are not repeated here.

12.3.4 In summary, they can argue that an element is not present or, on a proper reading of the patent, the words in the claim have a different meaning than those asserted by the plaintiff. If the defendant is asserting the doctrine of equivalents, they can argue that the technical element is not equivalent. The defendant may also seek to rely on file wrapper estoppel.

12.4 PRIOR ART DEFENSE

12.4.1 Article 62 of the Patent Law provides:

> During a patent infringement dispute, if the suspected infringer has evidence proving its or his technology or design belongs to existing technology or existing design, no patent infringement shall be found.

12.4.2 Further clarification of the prior art defense can be found in the Supreme People's Court of the People's Republic of China (Supreme People's Court or Supreme Court) Interpretation on Several Issues Regarding Legal Application in the Adjudication of Patent Infringement Cases (2010 Judicial Interpretation), which provides that the requirements of the prior art defense are satisfied if "all the technical characteristics alleged to fall within the scope of protection of a patent right are identical *or without substantial differences* to corresponding technical characteristics of a prior art technical scheme." (Emphasis added.) Regarding design patents, the provision requires the court to determine whether the accused design is identical to *or has no substantive differences* with the prior art design.[1]

12.4.3 According to 2010 Judicial Interpretation, when considering a prior art defense, a court should compare the allegedly infringing technical scheme with the prior art with respect to the elements of the patent claim being asserted. Also, the allegedly infringing technical scheme does not have to be exactly the same as the prior art; the prior art defense can succeed if the two are considered equivalent. It should be noted that the defendant will generally not be allowed to combine prior art references to make out a prior art defense; however, it is likely that the defendant will be allowed to use evidence of common knowledge to show that the prior art technical scheme is equivalent to the infringing technical scheme.

12.4.4 This interpretation of the prior art defense is reasonable. As an example, consider a patent that covers a tricycle that has a special braking mechanism on the front wheel. A prior art reference discloses a bicycle that has the same braking mechanism. If the patent owner asserts the patent against a tricycle manufacturer, the manufacturer can use the prior art defense and argue that a tricycle should be considered an equivalent to the bicycle in the prior art reference. This is reasonable because the invention is really about

---

1. 2010 Judicial Interpretation, Article 14.

the braking mechanism, and a person of ordinary skill, reading the prior art reference, would certainly know how to use the braking mechanism on a tricycle. The patent is, in essence, obvious in view of the prior art and should not be enforceable.

12.5 EXHAUSTION OF RIGHTS

12.5.1 Article 69(1) of the Patent Law provides that the following shall not be deemed as infringement of a patent:

> Where, after the sale of a patented product or products directly obtained by using the patented process, which was made by the patentee or an entity/individual authorized by the patentee, any other person uses, offers to sell, sells or imports that product;

12.5.2 This is a very broad exhaustion of rights defense and by the use of the word *imports* makes it clear that it intends to provide for the international exhaustion of rights. The reference to products being made by anyone authorized by the patentee, which broadly covers licensees and anyone else who has consent from the patentee to work the patent.

12.6 PRIOR USE DEFENSE

12.6.1 The prior use defense is provided for in Article 69(2) of the Patent Law. It states that identical products manufactured prior to patent application date, that have used an identical method or already been manufactured, or necessary preparations for their use have been made, and will only continue to be manufactured and used only within the original scope, will not be regarded as an infringement of patent rights.[2]

12.6.2 Article 15 of the 2010 Judicial Interpretation provides further guidance as to the meaning of the prior use defense.

12.6.3 First, the 2010 Judicial Interpretation makes it clear that the prior use defense only applies to technology that has been obtained legally.

12.6.4 Second, "already made the necessary preparations for manufacturing or using" is defined as occurring in the either the following situations:

(a) The main technical drawings or technical documents needed for implementing the invention-creation have been completed.

---

2. *Shanghai Meijia Industrial Co., Ltd. v. Shanghai Zhongling Daily Use Articles Co., Ltd.—Patent Infringement Dispute*, (2007) Shanghai No.1 Intermediate People's Court (Intellectual Property Division) First Instance Judgment No. 311, p. 4.

(b) The main equipments or raw materials needed for implementing the invention-creation have been manufactured or purchased.

12.6.5 Third, the *original scope* is defined to include:

the existing manufacturing scale as well as the manufacturing scale which can be reached using the existing manufacturing equipment or based on the existing preparations for manufacturing before the date of application for the patent.

12.6.6 Fourth, the prior use defense is not available to an assignee or licensee. However, if the original company that made the prior use is transferred simultaneously with the technology or design, the transferee can rely on the prior use defense.

Case Example

12.6.7 In the case of *Shanghai Meijia Industrial Co., Ltd. v. Shanghai Zhongling Daily Use Articles Co., Ltd.*, the plaintiff sued the defendant for infringing their external design patent by manufacturing and selling a product that was identical to the plaintiff's external design patent. The plaintiff claimed that the product fell into the scope of protection for the plaintiff's external design product, which was a clothes rack. During the court hearing, the defendant admitted that the product they sold was similar to the plaintiff's external design; however, they argued that before the application date of the plaintiff's external design; patent, they had already manufactured and sold the infringing goods. In this particular case, the defendant provided sufficient evidence to rebut the plaintiff's claims. The plaintiff had shown that they were the patent rights-holder, that the defendant had sold products similar to their external design patent, yet they had not provided evidence to refute the defendant's claims that the product was manufactured and sold before the plaintiff's patent application date. More important, they had not shown that the defendant after the grant of the plaintiff's patent that the defendant had exceeded the original scope of manufacture of the accused infringing product.[3] The court confirmed that the defendant had prior rights to the product, had not infringed the plaintiff's external design, and the plaintiff's claims could not be upheld.

---

3. Shanghai Meijia Industrial Co., Ltd. v. Shanghai Zhongling Daily Use Articles Co., Ltd.— Patent Infringement Dispute, (2007) Shanghai No.1 Intermediate People's Court (Intellectual Property Division) First Instance Judgment No. 311, p. 4.

Prior Use Defense Compared with Prior Art Defense

12.6.8 To assert the prior use defense, the defendant needs to prove that he has been using or has made plans to use the patented technology before the patent application date. This is different from a prior art defense, in which the defendant shows that he is using a prior art technology, but does not need to show that he is using the technology prior to the patent application date.

12.7 TEMPORARY ENTRY INTO CHINA

12.7.1 Article 69(3) provides that the following is not infringement:

> Where any foreign means of transport which temporarily passes through the territory, territorial waters or territorial airspace of China uses the patent concerned, in accordance with any agreement concluded between the country to which the foreign means of transport belongs and China, or in accordance with any international treaty to which both countries are party, or on the basis of the principle of reciprocity, for its own needs, in its devices and installations.

12.7.2 This exception primarily applies to ships and aircrafts that pass through China. It does not apply to ships or aircrafts that are registered in China. It does not apply to goods that are loaded on aircraft, ships or trucks that are in transit through China. However, in such a case there may not be infringement because there is no importation into China.

12.8 RESEARCH AND DEVELOPMENT

12.8.1 Under Article 69(4) of the Patent Law, use of a patent solely for scientific research and experimentation is not regarded as patent infringement.

12.8.2 The word *solely* is important, and research and experimentation that has a business purpose could infringe.

12.9 CLINICAL TRIALS

12.9.1 Article 69(5) of the Patent Law provides that the following is not infringement:

> For the purpose of providing information needed for administrative approval, manufacture, use, import of a patented drug or a patented medical apparatus, and solely for such manufacture, import of a patented drug or a patented medical apparatus.

12.9.2 This provision was added to the Patent Law in the 2009 amendments. Before this, Chinese courts had previously found clinical trials did not constitute patent infringement even though there was no specific exception in the legislation pertaining to clinical trials. In a case decided by the Beijing No. 1 Intermediate Court in December 2006, *Sankyo v. Wansheng*, the court ruled that:

> The Defendant manufactured the drug in question using the patented process in suit for the purpose of clinical trial and its application for a permit for production. The said manufacture was to fulfill the relevant government authority's requirement in relation to drug registration, and to test the safeties and effectiveness of the drug in question. Given that the Defendant's manufacture of the drug in question was not directly for the purpose of sale, such an act does not fall into the prohibited act as provided in the PRC Patent Law, i.e., exploit the patent for production or business purposes. Therefore, this court determines that the Defendant's activities in question do not constitute patent infringement.

12.10 INNOCENCE

1.10.1 After China became a member of the World Trade Organization (WTO), it revised the Patent Law in 2002 to include an innocent infringer defense as to damages.[4] Article 70 of the Patent Law provides

> Any person, who, for business purposes, uses, offers to sell or sells a patented product without knowing that it was made and sold without the authorization of the patentee, shall not be liable for any damages if he can prove that he obtained the product from a legitimate source.

12.10.2 The onus of proof is on the defendant to prove the defense by showing that it did not know the product was unauthorized and it was bought from legitimate channels. Normally, the defendant will need to show that they bought the product under a normal sales contract, at a fair price from an identified seller. The defense is often relied upon and often successful for retailers or wholesalers who have been joined to an action in order to obtain jurisdiction in the city in which the retailer or wholesaler is located.

12.10.3 Defendants will sometimes argue they had no prior knowledge that they were infringing another's patent rights as the patent markings and patent number were not displayed on the plaintiff's products. In the author's

---

4. Patent Law, Article 63.

experience, this defense has not been accepted by the courts, who consider that displaying patent markings and patent number on patented products are rights of the patent rights-holder, rather than a legal duty.

12.10.4 It is important to note that, although the defense excuses the defendant from paying damages, it does not prevent them from being ordered by the court to cease selling the infringing products.

12.11 LIMITATION DEFENSE

12.11.1 Defendants may claim that an action is statute barred because it has been brought outside the limitation period. Limitation periods have been discussed above.

12.11.2 It should be emphasized that a defendant must raise a limitation defense in the first instance trial and not on appeal. If the case is appealed, the defendant must also use this as a ground of appeal.

12.11.3 The case of *Fugui v. Zhang Wenlin, Cao Yanpeng* (*Fugui*)[5] emphasized the importance of asserting the limitation defense as early as possible. The case was an appeal from the Changchun Intermediate People's Court in 2006 that was heard by the Jilin Higher People's Court in 2007. In this case, the plaintiff was shown to have known about the patent infringement in 2000, but had only filed suit in 2005. The chief piece of evidence used to prove this claim was the registration records of the State Administration of Industry and Commerce. However, the Jilin Higher People's Court noted that the appellant had not raised the limitation of action issue, and also had not raised these as grounds for appealing the case. As a result, in its judgment, the Jilin Higher People's Court ruled that the limitation defense would not be considered by the court.

12.12 BREACH OF ANTI-MONOPOLY LAW

12.12.1 Although not a direct defense under the Patent Law, Article 48(2) of the Patent Law provides that where it has been legally determined that the enforcement of the patent right by the patentee is an act of monopoly under the Anti-Monopoly Law (which came into force in 2008), an entity or individual can apply for a compulsory license of the Patent Law.

---

5. Jilin Higher People's Court Final Instance Judgment No. 80. (2007).

12.12.2 Article 55 of the Anti-Monopoly Law provides:

> This Law does not govern the conduct of business operators to exercise their intellectual property rights under laws and relevant administrative regulations on intellectual property rights; however, business operators' conduct to eliminate or restrict market competition by abusing their intellectual property rights shall be governed by this Law.

12.12.3 To date, no compulsory license has been applied for under Article 48(2) of the Patent Law, and no further regulations have been issued to clarify the relationship between the Anti-Monopoly Law and the Patent Law. Presumably, if a defendant to a patent suit took legal action to have the patentee's acts declared to be an act of monopoly, a court trying an infringement case would either stay or slow down an action pending a decision by either an administrative body or the courts as to whether this was an act of monopoly.

12.13 PATENT INCORPORATED INTO STANDARD

12.13.1 If a patent is for a product or process that has been incorporated into a standard, the court may also find non-infringement.

12.13.2 In 2008, in reply to the Liaoning Higher People's Court, the Supreme People's Court Response as to whether Chaoyang Xingnuo Company's Conduct Constitutes Patent Infringement by Exploiting Patent(s) in Designs and Constructions Pursuant to the Industry-Standard Issued by the Ministry of Construction on Design Rules for Composite Medium Ram-Expansion Stakes, stated:

> Since at present the government's standards-setting agencies in China have not set out rules for the use and disclosure of patent information in standards, if a patentee has participated in standard-setting or allowed to let its patent to be incorporated into national, sectorial (industrial) or local standards, it is considered that the patentee permits others to exploit the patent while implementing the standard, and the other parties' exploitation of the patent does not constitute infringement that is stipulated in Article 11 of the Patent Law. The patentee may request that a party who exploits the patent to pay a royalty. However, the amount of payment shall be significantly lower than the normal licensing fees. If the patentee has promised to give up the royalty, the promise shall be honored.

12.13.3 In the first draft of the 2010 Judicial Interpretation, Article 20, a similar provision was included, stating that if a patent was part of a standard, it would be deemed to be licensed. The full text of the draft of Article 20 is set out in Chapter 14, "Remedies," because it principally addresses how the royalty would be calculated.

12.13.4 These provisions are contentious as the question of whether patents included in a standard are licensed is a major issue in patent litigation worldwide. They may not be followed in the case of international standards.

CHAPTER 13

Design Patents

13.1 INTRODUCTION

13.1.1 Design patents are essentially an entirely different right compared to invention patents and utility model patents.

13.1.2 This chapter provides a brief introduction to design patent invalidation and infringement proceedings and identifies the key areas of difference in design actions when compared to invention patent and utility model proceedings.

13.2 STAY OF INFRINGEMENT PROCEEDINGS

13.2.1 The circumstances under which a court will stay infringement proceedings pending a defendant's request for a declaration of invalidity are the same as for utility models. See Chapter 9, Preliminary and Interlocutary Issues. Essentially, provided an application is made for a stay within the period for filing a defense, the court should stay the infringement proceedings unless the design has already been held to be valid in other proceedings.

13.3 GROUNDS FOR INVALIDATING DESIGN PATENT

13.3.1 Article 65 of the Implementing Regulations of the Patent Law (Patent Law Implementing Regulations) provide a design patent may be

Patent Law	Summary of Provision
Article 2(4)	*Design* means a new design proposed for a product's shape, pattern, or the combination thereof, or the combination of its color and shape and/or pattern, that creates an aesthetic feeling and is suitable for industrial application.
Article 23	Design rights shall not belong to an existing design.
Article 25(6)	Two-dimensional designs of images, colors, or combinations of the two that mainly serve as indicators.
Article 27(2)	Design drawing should clearly identify the design.
Article 33	Amendments to the patent application have gone beyond the scope of the initial application.

invalidated on the basis that the design patent does not comply with the following provisions:

Prohibitions in the Patent Law	
Article 5(1)	The subject matter of the patent is contrary to law or social morality or detrimental to the public interest.
Article 9	Patent should be granted to earlier applicant when two or more patents are filed for same invention.

13.3.2 The Guidelines for Patent Examination (Examination Guidelines), Part IV, Chapter 5, set out rules for handling invalidation actions for design rights under Article 23 and Article 9. For other Articles of the law, Part I, Chapter 3, is to be applied.[1]

13.4 DEFINITION OF DESIGN

13.4.1 The Examination Guidelines provide that "Article 2(4) is the general definition of a design which may obtain patent protection. It is not a specific examination standard for determining whether designs are identical or substantively identical." The examiner will determine whether a design is new based on the common sense of normal consumers.[2]

13.4.2 A number of examples are given of items that are not patentable under Section 2(4). These include bridges or buildings that depend on their specific location and cannot be rebuilt elsewhere; any product with no fixed shape, pattern, or color because it contains a substance such as gas, liquid, or powder with no fixed shape; components of parts that cannot be

1. Examination Guidelines, Chapter 5, Part IV, Section 1.
2. Examination Guidelines, Chapter 5, Part IV, Chapter 3, Section 7.3.

sold separately, such as the heel of a sock; works of fine art or penmanship; and a design patent showing if a product is electrified.[3]

13.5 DESIGN RIGHTS SHALL NOT BELONG TO AN EXISTING DESIGN

13.5.1 Identity or Similarity with an existing design is the main ground for seeking to invalidate a design patent.

13.5.2 Article 23 of the Patent Law provides

> Any design for which a patent right may be granted must not belong to an prior design; nor has any entity or individual previously filed before the date of filing with the patent administration department under the State Council an application on an identical design which was published in patent documents after the said date of filing.
> The design for which a patent right may be granted must be substantially different from prior designs or a combination of the features of prior designs.
> Any design for which a patent right may be granted must not be in conflict with any prior legal rights of any other person.
> The prior design referred to in this Law means any design known to the public before the filing date of the patent application in China or abroad.

13.5.3 Part IV, Chapter 5, Sections 2 to 7, of the Examination Guidelines provide comprehensive guidelines for determining whether a design patent breaches Article 23. These are summarized in the following sections.

13.6 IDENTICAL OR NOT SUBSTANTIALLY DIFFERENT DESIGNS

13.6.1 The initial steps to be undertaken to determine whether a design is the same as or not substantially different to a prior design under Article 23(1) and (2) of the Patent Law are:

(a) Identify the prior design. In addition to drawings or photos, any explanation of the object of judgment which, for example, claims protection for color, needs to be considered.[4]

(b) Consider the designs from the standpoint of an ordinary consumer of that product who has some capability of distinguishing differences in shape, patterns, and colors.[5]

---

3. Examination Guidelines, Part I, Chapter 3, Section 7.4.
4. Examination Guidelines, Part IV, Chapter 5, Section 3.
5. Examination Guidelines, Part IV, Chapter 5, Section 4.

Examination in Accordance with Article 23(1)

13.6.2 For examination under Article 23(1) as to whether a design is a prior design, the following rules are applied:

(a) Identity of designs means the patent concerned and the prior design are designs for the same category of products and are identical in shape, pattern, and color.[6]

(b) Substantially identical designs means the designs are in the same or approximate category of products. Approximate categories of products mean products with similar use. For products with multiple uses, one similar use is sufficient.[7]

(c) If to an ordinary consumer, the differences fall into the following categories, they are substantially identical:[8]

(1) Slight changes in fine details that cannot be noticed paying normal attention;

(2) Differences in parts that cannot normally be seen;

(3) The substitution of a well-known design element for the products; for example, changing the shape of a cookie jar with pattern and color from a cube to a cuboid;

(4) Increase or decrease a continuous arrangement; for example, the number of seats in a theater;

(5) Mirror images are a prior design.

13.6.3 When making the judgment above, an examiner should make one-to-one comparisons, by direct observation, targeting only the appearance of the product. They should then make a whole observation and comprehensive judgment.[9]

Examination in Accordance with Article 23(2)

13.6.4 For examination under Article 23(2) as to whether a design is not significantly different from a prior design, under the Examination Guidelines the following rules are applied:[10]

(a) The patent concerned is not significantly different from the prior design of the product in the same or approximate category.

---

6. Examination Guidelines, Part IV, Chapter 5, Section 5.1.
7. Examination Guidelines, Part IV, Chapter 5, Section 5.1, paragraphs 1 and 2.
8. Examination Guidelines, Part IV, Chapter 5, Section 5.1, paragraph 3.
9. Examination Guidelines, Part IV, Chapter 5, Section 5.2.
10. Examination Guidelines, Part IV, Chapter 5, Section 6.

(b) The patent concerned is transformed from the prior design with very slight differences, and the prior design had inspiration for the transformation.

(c) The patent concerned is a combination of prior designs, and the corresponding parts are identical or only have slight differences.

13.6.5 The examination should be done from the viewpoint of a normal consumer[11] and according to the following:

(a) More attention shall be paid to parts that can be seen easily in use.

(b) If some parts of the design are usual parts, more attention shall be paid to changes to other parts.

(c) A special shape exclusively determined by the function of the product generally does not notably influence the overall visual effect.

(d) Minor changes in fine details are not sufficient.

13.7 CONFLICT WITH PRIOR LEGAL RIGHTS

13.7.1 The Examination Guidelines provide that a design patent that conflicts with another person's legal right obtained before the filing or priority date is invalid. Legitimate rights refer to rights recognized by the laws of the People's Republic of China (PRC or China), including trademark rights registered in the PRC, copyright, enterprise names and trade names, image rights, and the right to special packaging. To be in conflict means that to exploit the design would infringe the legitimate right. The petitioner bears the burden of proving their legitimate right.[12]

13.7.2 For well-known trademarks, "the category of product can be properly broadened" in determining whether there is a conflict of rights.[13]

13.8 TWO-DIMENSIONAL DESIGNS THAT MAINLY SERVE AS INDICATORS

13.8.1 Part I, Chapter 3, Section 6.2, of the Examination Guidelines sets out the rules for examining an application for compliance with Article 25(1)(6) of the Patent Law. This section provides that a patent right will not be granted if:

(a) The product for which the design is applied is a two-dimensional pattern for printed goods;

(b) The design is made of patterns, colors, or their combination; and

(c) The design mainly serves as an indicator.

---

11. Examination Guidelines, Part IV, Chapter 5, Section 6.1.
12. Examination Guidelines, Part IV, Chapter 5, Section 7.
13. Examination Guidelines, Part IV, Chapter 5, Section 7.1.

13.8.2 With regard to this latter element, the "serve mainly as an indicator" means "the main purpose of the design is to help the public identify the related product, the origin of the service, etc." That is, it principally serves the function of a trademark.

13.8.3 Article 25(1)(6) was introduced to the patent law in the 2009 amendments. The main purpose of this amendment was to stop applicants applying for trademarks as designs. This was a particular problem for luxury goods in which the trademarks are part of the designs. Applicants would apply for designs incorporating the trademarks and seek to avoid trademark infringement actions by claiming they had a design registration.

13.9 THE DESIGN DRAWING SHOULD CLEARLY IDENTIFY THE DESIGN

1.9.1 The Examination Guidelines in Part I, Chapter 3, Section 4.2, set out the rules for design drawings and photographs. In essence, these provide that drawings or photographs should be clear. Drawings should be of normal projection and width of lines.[14] Shadow lines and dotted lines should not be used. Photos should have clear backgrounds, be taken in conformity with rules of projection, and not have reflections or shadows.[15]

13.10 AMENDMENTS BEYOND THE SCOPE OF THE INITIAL APPLICATION

13.10.1 Amendments to a design application may be made in response to a Notification for Rectification made after preliminary examination by SIPO. The Examination Guidelines simply provide that the amendments should not go beyond the original scope of disclosure in the drawings or photos filed on the date of filing.[16]

13.11 CONTRARY TO LAW OR SOCIAL MORALITY, OR DETRIMENTAL TO THE PUBLIC INTEREST

13.11.1 These grounds have been discussed in relation to the invalidation of invention patents and utility models (See Chapter 6, "Grounds for Invalidating a Patent"). Part I, Chapter 3, Section 6.1, of the Examination

---

14. Examination Guidelines, Part IV, Chapter 5, Part I, Chapter 3, Section 4.2.2.
15. Examination Guidelines, Part IV, Chapter 5, Section 4.2.2.
16. Examination Guidelines, Part IV, Chapter 5, Section 3.4.

Guidelines provides specific guidelines in relation to designs. With relation to social morality, drawings or photographs of violence, murder, and pornography may not be registered.[17] With regard to the public interest, designs for famous buildings, such as the Tiananmen Gate, or designs with the Chinese national emblem or pattern, cannot be registered.[18]

13.12 IDENTICAL INVENTION-CREATION

13.12.1 Article 9 of the Patent Law, which prohibits patents for identical invention-creations, is essentially the same test as that provided for novelty in Article 23. The Examination Guidelines provide in Part IV, Chapter 5, Section 8:

> "Identical Invention-Creation" referred to in Article 9 means for designs, that the claimed designs for the product shall be identical or substantially identical. The comparison shall be based on the comparison of all design elements. . . .
>
> With respect to the judgment of identical or substantially identical designs, Section 5 of this chapter (*i.e.*, that dealing with applications under Article 23) shall apply.

13.13 INFRINGEMENT OF DESIGN PATENTS

Acts of Infringement

13.13.1 Article 11(2) of the Patent Law sets out the exclusive rights of a patentee of a design patent:

> After the grant of the patent right for a design, no entity or individual may, without the authorization of the patentee, exploit the design, namely make, offer to sell, sell, or import the design patented product for production or business purposes.

13.13.2 The words "offer to sell" were added in the 2009 amendments to the Patent Law to address the difficulty patentees had with proving infringement if products were offered on the Internet but not sold at physical locations in China.

---

17. Examination Guidelines, Part IV, Chapter 5, Section 6.1.2.
18. Examination Guidelines, Part IV, Chapter 5, Section 6.1.3.

Scope of Protection

13.13.3 Article 59(2) of the Patent Law provides:

> The scope of protection for a design patent shall be determined by the product's design shown in the drawings or photographs. The brief statement of the patent could be used to interpret the design of the product shown in the drawings or photographs.

Determining Identity or Similarity

13.13.4 Under Article 8 of the Supreme Court Interpretation on Several Issues Regarding Legal Application in the Adjudication of Patent Infringement Cases (2010 Judicial Interpretation), a product that is identical to or similar to a product that is the subject of a design patent is infringing.

13.13.5 The People's Court shall determine whether the type of the products is similar or identical based on the purpose of the product subject to the design patent. To determine the purpose of the product, the People's Court may refer to the brief description of the design, the International Classification for Industrial Designs, the function of the product, and the situations of sale and actual use, etc., of the products.[19]

Ordinary Consumer Test

13.13.6 In determining whether the design is identical or similar, the People's Court shall apply the standard of the level of knowledge and the cognitive ability of the ordinary customers of the product which is subject to the design patent.[20]

Total Visual Effect

13.13.7 Article 11 of the 2010 Judicial Interpretation then provides a comprehensive test for determining whether the designs are similar:

> in determining whether a design is identical or similar, [the court] shall according to the design features of the granted design and the accused infringing design patent, conduct a comprehensive determination based on the total visual effect of the design; however,

---

19. 2010 Judicial Interpretation, Article 9.
20. 2010 Judicial Interpretation, Article 10.

design features that are determined mainly by technical functions as well as features that which do not affect the total visual effect such as materials and internal construction shall not be considered.

The following conditions usually have more influence on the total visual effect of a design:

(a) Parts of the product that in normal use are easily observed directly relative other parts;
(b) Design features of the granted design that differ from existing designs relative to other design features of the granted design.

If the alleged infringing design does not differ from the granted design in terms of total visual effect, the People's Court shall determine the two to be the same; if no substantial difference in total visual effect exists, the two shall be determined to be similar.

13.13.8 In practice, the effect of these rule are that courts will find designs that are similar to a design patent even where there are differences between the alleged infringing product and the design patent. The issue to be determined is the total visual effect to an ordinary consumer.

13.14 DESIGNS INCORPORATED INTO OTHER PRODUCTS

13.14.1 Article 12(2) of the 2010 Judicial Interpretation provides that an infringing use occurs if a product which infringes design patent rights is used as a component to manufacture for sale another product.

13.14.2 Article 12(2) does provide a defense that there will be no infringement if the infringing design patent product only has technical functions in the other product.

13.14.3 This would cover, for example, car parts manufactured for sale. The use of the external car parts would be infringing because they would have other than technical functions. Engine parts, on the other hand, that would most likely only have technical functions, would not be infringing.

13.14.4 Article 12(3) further provides that, if the accused infringers have cooperated and divided the labor in making and using the parts, their acts shall be deemed to be joint infringement.

13.15 DEFENSES

13.15.1 The defenses discussed in Chapter 12, "Defenses," as far as relevant, can also be relied upon in design patent litigation.

13.16 PRIOR ART DEFENSE

13.16.1 Article 62 of the Patent Law provides the prior art defense applies to design patents as well as invention patents and utility models.

13.16.2 Article 14(2) of the 2010 Judicial Interpretation provides that if the accused infringing design is identical to or without substantial differences from a prior design, then the prior art defense may be relied upon.

13.17 DAMAGES

13.17.1 Damages for design infringement will be assessed in the same way as for inventions and utility models. (See Chapter 14, "Remedies")

13.17.2 With regard to design patent for packaging, the 2010 Judicial Interpretation provides:

> If the product infringing a design patent is a packaging, the People's Court shall reasonably determine the amount of damages based on the factors including the value of the packaging itself and its in realizing the profits of the packaged product, etc.[21]

---

21. 2010 Judicial Interpretation, Article 16(3).

CHAPTER 14

Remedies

14.1 REMEDIES AVAILABLE IN CHINA

14.1.1 The principal remedies available for patent infringement in China are provided for in Articles 118 and 134 of the General Principles of Civil Law, which provide for a general right to relief for infringement of intellectual property rights. As it applies to patents, Article 118 of the General Principles of Civil Law provides:

> If a citizen's or legal entity's . . . patent rights. . . . are infringed upon by such means as plagiarism, alteration or imitation, they shall have the right to demand that the infringement be stopped, its ill effects be eliminated and the damages be compensated for.

14.1.2 Article 134 of the Civil Procedure Law provides:

> The main methods of bearing civil liability shall be:
>
> (1) Cessation of infringements;
> (2) Removal of obstacles;
> (3) Elimination of dangers;
> (4) Return of property;
> (5) Restoration of original condition;
> (6) Repair, reworking, or replacement;
> (7) Compensation for losses;
> (8) Payment of breach of contract damages;
> (9) Elimination of ill effects and rehabilitation of reputation; and
> (10) Extension of apology.
>
> The above methods of bearing civil liability may be applied exclusively or concurrently.
>
> When hearing civil cases, a People's Court, in addition to applying the above stipulations, may serve admonitions, order the offender to sign a pledge of repentance,

and confiscate the property used in carrying out illegal activities and the illegal income obtained therefrom. It may also impose fines or detentions as stipulated by law.

14.1.3 The Patent Law also specifically provides for a reasonable fee for pre-grant use of a patent and damages.

14.1.4 Therefore, in patent cases, there are five principal remedies under the General Principles of Civil Law and Patent Law, namely:

(a) Injunctions (stopping of infringement)
(b) Reasonable fee for pre-grant use
(c) Damages
(d) Elimination of ill effects
(e) Order to give an apology

14.1.5 These are discussed in the order below, followed by a discussion on the enforcement of damages awards and injunctions.

14.2 INJUNCTIONS

14.2.1 The Patent Law does not, itself, contain a statutory basis for the granting of permanent injunctions directly by the courts, rather, Article 118 of the General Principles of Civil Law is relied upon.

14.2.2 It should be noted however, that:

(a) Article 60 of the Patent Law specifically provides that the State Intellectual Property Office (SIPO) may issue an order that infringing acts be stopped and that SIPO may apply to the People's Court to enforce such an order.

(b) Article 66 of the Patent Law also makes specific provision for pretrial injunctions to be granted.

14.2.3 As a general practice, injunctions are generally granted in patent cases in China if they are sought by the plaintiff.

14.3 CIRCUMSTANCES IN WHICH AN INJUNCTION WILL NOT BE GRANTED

14.3.1 Although the general rule has been that injunctions would be granted, in the process of the drafting of the 2009 amendments to the Patent Law and Supreme People's Court of the People's Republic of China (Supreme Court or Supreme People's Court) Interpretation on Several Issues Regarding Legal Application in the Adjudication of Patent Infringement

Cases (2010 Judicial Interpretation), provisions that would have limited the right to injunctions were included in the drafts, but not finally enacted.

14.3.2 In the drafting of the Patent Law, a provision introducing the concept of acquiescence was sought to be introduced whereby, if a patentee had not taken action for five years despite knowing of infringement and the defendant was willing to pay reasonable royalties, the court could decide to grant an injunction.[1] A further late amendment was also proposed, which would allow a court to decline to grant an injunction if it was in the public interest to do so.[2]

14.3.3 These provisions were not enacted. However, the 2009 Economic Conditions Opinion includes two provisions that introduce a concept of acquiescence and give courts the ability not to grant injunctions. A decision of the Supreme Court in late 2009 also declined to grant an injunction on public interest grounds.

14.3.4 With regard to acquiescence the 2009 Economic Conditions Opinion provides:[3]

> Where the right holder has for a long period of time acquiesced in infringement and not enforced its rights, at the time it makes a claim for cessation of damage, if ordering cessation of the act would result in a relatively large imbalance between the interests of the parties, you may consider carefully not to order cessation of infringing acts but without affecting giving reasonable compensation in accordance with law.

14.3.5 With regard to whether or not to grant injunction, the 2009 Economic Conditions Opionion provides:[4]

> If stopping the relevant conduct will cause a significant imbalance of interests between the parties, or is contrary to public interest, or in fact can not be performed, you may in accordance with the specific situation of the case proceed to balance the interests and decide not to stop the infringing acts and adopt more substantial compensation or alternative measures such as economic compensation.

14.3.6 In December 2009, the Supreme Court handed down a decision in the case *China Environmental Project Tech Inc. v. Fujikasui Engineering Co., Ltd., Huayang Electric Power Co., Ltd*, in relation to gas flue desulphurization technology that had been installed in a power plant. The first instance court had not granted an injunction against the Huayang Electric on the basis

---

1. Proposed Amendment A13, issued July 31, 2006.
2. This was included in the draft proposed to the State Council Law Administration Office.
3. 2009 Economic Conditions Opinion, Article 15.
4. 2009 Economic Conditions Opinion, Article 15.

that it would have a large social impact. The court did grant an injunction against Fujikasui from further sales. The Supreme Court, in relation to the decision not to grant an injunction against Huayang Electric, held:

> Whereas in relation to the spray desulphurization system that has been installed and is in actual operation in the power plant of Huayang Company, if ordered its cease its activities, this will have a major impact on the local social public interests, therefore the first trial decision after considering fully the rights holders interests and social public interest, did not uphold CEPT's claim to stop infringing activities, but instead ordered Huayang Co during the period the equipment is in use during the life of the patent to pay annually for each unit Renminbi 240,000 Yuan, there is nothing wrong with this.

14.3.7 Patentees should therefore proceed on the basis that injunctions will not necessarily be granted and damages or royalties may instead be ordered.

14.4 REASONABLE FEE FOR PRE-GRANT USE

14.4.1 For invention patents, a patentee, after grant of the patent can make a claim for a reasonable fee if a party has been working the patent between publication and grant.[5] The limitation period is two years from when the patentee knew or ought to have known of the infringing act; or if they know about it before grant, two years from the grant of the patent.[6]

14.4.2 There is no such provision for utility models and design patents, as they are not examined and are granted on publication.

14.5 DAMAGES FOR POST-GRANT INFRINGEMENT

14.5.1 Article 65 of the Patent Law provides damages should be assessed in one of the following ways, in descending order of importance.

(a) Patentee's lost profits due to infringement
(b) Infringer's gains from infringement
(c) Reasonable Royalties
(d) Statutory Damages

14.5.2 Articles 20–22 of the 2001 Patent Trial Guidelines provide some further clarification on how damages are to be assessed. It is important to note the burden of proof remains on the plaintiff to prove damages, even

---

5. Patent Law, Article 13 and Article 68(2).
6. Patent Law, Article 68(2).

though much of the evidence to prove damages is in the hands of the defendant. The 2009 Economic Conditions Opinions encourages courts to guide parties to base their damages claims on lost profits or profits made.[7]

Patentee's Lost Profits Due to Infringement

14.5.3 The lost profits can be determined by multiplying the total decrease in the number of the patentee's products sold, with the profit for each product that patentee can reasonably expect. If the decrease in sales is difficult to determine, the lost profit can be determined by multiplying the total number of items that the infringer sold with the profit for each product that the patentee can reasonably expect.[8]

Infringer's Gains Because of Infringement

14.5.4 Damages can also be determined from infringer's gains. The infringer's gains can be calculated by multiplying the total number of items that the infringer sold with the reasonable profit for each product sold by the infringer.[9]

Reasonable Royalty

14.5.5 If neither the patentee's loss nor the infringer's gain can be ascertained, damages are calculated with reference to the reasonable royalty of a patent license. The damages awarded can be a multiple of between one and three times, of the reasonable royalty.[10] If the plaintiff has licensed its patent, reasonable royalties can be proved by producing its license agreements. If it does not license, the plaintiff can seek to introduce evidence of industry standards. The 2009 Economic Conditions Opinion provides that courts should:[11]

> Pay attention to comparability when referring to licensing fees when calculating compensation, fully consider normal licensing and the way in which infringement actually occurred, and differences between the timing and scale etc, and reflect the spirit that infringement damages should be appropriately higher than normal licensing fees.

---

7. 2009 Economic Conditions Opinion, Article 16.
8. 2001 Patent Trial Guidelines, Article 20(1).
9. 2001 Patent Trial Guidelines, Article 20(3).
10. 2001 Patent Trial Guidelines, Article 21.
11. 2009 Economic Conditions Opinion, Article 16.

Statutory Damages

14.5.6 If it is difficult to determine the losses which the patentee has suffered, the profits which the infringer has earned, or the royalty fee for patent exploitation, the people's court may award damages no less than ten thousand renminbi and no more than one million renminbi depending on the type of patent right, and the nature and gravity of the infringing act.[12] Such damages are often called *statutory damages*. Strictly speaking they are not, as there is no specific statutory amount set out for each infringing act. Courts will often award damages on this basis given the difficulty the plaintiff faces proving losses. The 2009 Economic Conditions Opinion provides that where there is evidence the loss is significantly more than the maximum statutory damages, greater damages may be awarded.[13]

Evidence of Profits or Losses

14.5.7 As noted, in order to prove damages, the burden of proof remains on the plaintiff to prove damages. In proving the plaintiff's loss, i.e., the infringer's profits, or the amount of a reasonable royalty, evidence must be produced that shows the amount of sales made by the defendant of infringing products. It can be very difficult to gather such evidence. The 2009 Economic Conditions Opinion does however encourage the courts to give an interpretation of evidence advantageous to the plaintiff when assessing damages.[14]

14.5.8 Some courts are willing to conduct evidence preservation to obtain the necessary sales and accounting records.[15] However, this is rare. Usually, the plaintiff will need to gather whatever evidence it can to prove damages. This can come from a number of sources such as any public statements or notices by the defendants concerning their sales; or from statements made by the defendant during investigations as to their sales of products.

Apportionment of Damages

14.5.9 Article 16 of the 2010 Judicial Interpretation provides that, when calculating damages based on the infringer's profit, the courts should

---

12. Patent Law, Article 65(2). A similar provision was previously included in Article 21 of the 2001 Patent Trial Guidelines, but is now superseded by Article 65(2).
13. 2009 Economic Conditions Opinion, Article 16.
14. 2009 Economic Conditions Opinion, Article 16.
15. For example, in CHINT v. Schneider, the court conducted evidence preservation twice.

determine the profit that is obtained *due to the infringement of the patent* (instead of all profits made from selling the infringing product). Article 16 provides:

> profits of the infringer that have been generated due to other rights shall be excluded.

14.5.10 The provision further specifies that if only a component of a final product infringes, the court shall determine the amount of damages based on factors such as the value of that component and its contribution to the total profit of the final product. Similarly, if the packaging of a product infringes a design patent, the amount of damages shall be based on factors such as the value of the packaging and its contribution to the profits of the product being packaged.

14.5.11 This rule of apportionment limits a court's power to granting unreasonably large damage awards and is a welcome clarification in the law. In two cases decided in 2007 and 2008, courts in Zhejiang granted very high damages against foreign defendants. In *CHINT v. Schneider Electronics Co.*, in 2007, the Wenzhou Intermediate People's Court order damages of over 350 million renminbi and in *Zhejiang Holley Telecommunication Group Co. Ltd v. Shenzhen Samsung Kejian Mobile Technology Co,. Ltd.* in 2008, the Hangzhou Intermediate People's Court awarded damages of 50 million renminbi. In the CHINT case, the award was reduced by half in a negotiated settlement. In the Holley case, the patent was invalidated on appeal in the Beijing Intermediate People's Court.

14.5.12 In the CHINT case, the Wenzhou court specifically did not apportion damages awarding damages based on the total profit made by the defendant for each infringing product.

Reasonable Expenses

14.5.13 The court may, at the request of the patentee, also award reasonable expenses associated with the investigation and prevention of the infringing acts to be included in the award for damages.[16] Courts will sometimes award some damages as reasonable expense to cover investigation costs. This is usually not substantial.

---

16. Patent Law, Article 65(1); 2001 Patent Trial Guidelines, Article 22.

Royalty for Product Found to Be Part of a Standard

14.5.14 As discussed in the Chapter 12, "Defenses," the Supreme People's Court has held in the Chaoyang Xingnuo case that if an alleged infringing product is part of a national, sectorial, or industry standard (which are standards made by government bodies under the National Standards Law), then there is no infringement, but:

> The patentee may request that a party who exploits the patent to pay a royalty. However, the amount of payment shall be significantly lower than the normal licensing fee.

14.5.15 In the first draft of the 2010 Judicial Interpretation, the following clause was included to provide guidance on how to calculate this license fee. It was, however, not included in the final version, indicating that there remain disagreements as to how to deal with standards.[17]

> If, with the patentee's consent, the patent has been included in a standard published by a national, industry, or local standard-setting organization, and if the standard has not disclosed the patent, the People's Court may deem that the patentee has licensed others to implement its patents when implementing the standard. However, this does not apply to the situation where, according to the law, the implementation must take place in the form of standards. If the patentee requests that a party which has implemented the standard pays licensing fees, the People's Court shall reasonably determine the amount of licensing fees by comprehensively considering the factors including the inventiveness of the patent, its function within the standard, the technical area of the standard, the nature of the standard, and the scope of implementation of the standard, etc. However, this does not apply to the situation where the patentee has undertaken to waive the licensing fees.
>
> If the standard has disclosed the patent and the conditions for licensed implementation, if a third party did not implement the patent in accordance with the disclosed conditions, and if the party contends that the implementation should take place in accordance with the disclosed conditions, the People's Court shall support that position. If the disclosed conditions are obviously unreasonable, based upon a party's request, the People's Court may properly adjust the conditions. If the conditions for licensed implementation have not been disclosed or if the conditions for licensed implementation are uncertain, the parties may resolve the dispute through discussions. If the discussions are not successful, the parties may request that the People's Court determines the conditions.
>
> If the laws or administrative regulations otherwise provide rules regarding implementing patents in standards, they shall be adhered to.

---

17. Draft 2010 Judicial Interpretation, Article 20.

14.6 ELIMINATING ILL EFFECTS

14.6.1 Courts will order the destruction of molds and other items used to make infringing products in order to eliminate the ill effects of infringement. The Supreme Court in the 2009 Economic Situation Opinion made it clear that these orders should be limited to items that can solely be used to make infringing products.[18]

14.7 APOLOGY

14.7.1 Courts do from time to time order a defendant to apologize for infringement. This is usually done by public notice published in a local newspaper.

14.8 THE ENFORCEMENT OF DAMAGES AWARDS

14.8.1 The financial part of any effective judgment of a People's Court may be enforced by that court or any other court in China of equal status at the place where the defendant's assets are located.[19] Applications for enforcement are made to the enforcement chambers of the court.

14.8.2 The most common way in which damages are enforced is by freezing bank accounts and having the money transferred to the court and then on to the successful party.[20] If money has already been frozen under a pretrial asset freezing order, this will be transferred to the court.

14.8.3 Enforcement may also be done by the seizing and auctioning of assets[21] or by garnisheeing income.[22]

14.9 THE ENFORCEMENT OF INJUNCTIONS

14.9.1 The enforcement on injunctions is not a well developed area of law in China. There is no concept of contempt of court, so courts do not have the power to enforce their own orders by contempt.

---

18. 2009 Economic Situation Opinion, Article 15.
19. Civil Procedure Law, Article 201.
20. Civil Procedure Law, Article 218.
21. Civil Procedure Law, Article 223.
22. Civil Procedure Law, Article 219.

14.9.2 Article 102 of the Civil Procedure Law does allow the People's Courts to fine individuals and entities as well as detain individuals who do acts that will affect the administration of justice including breaching court orders or refusing to perform a legally effective judgment or ruling issued by the People's Court. Detention may be ordered against the key personnel of an entity if the entity is in breach of the order.

14.9.3 In case the activities constitute a criminal offense, the person can also be prosecuted for a crime. As patent infringement is not a crime, this latter provision does not assist in patent cases.

14.9.4 Article 104 of the Civil Procedure Law provides that the maximum fine that can be imposed on an individual is 10 thousand renminbi. For an entity, the fine can be between 10 thousand and 300 thousand renminbi. For detention, the courts are required to hand the individuals to the Public Security Bureau. The maximum period of detention is fifteen days. If, during the period of detention, the person admits and corrects their mistake, the People's Court may release them.

14.9.5 Any fine or imprisonment must be approved by the President of the Court.[23]

14.9.6 Despite these provisions, court orders in China are often not obeyed, and indeed flagrantly violated.

---

23. Civil Procedure Law, Article 105.

Concluding Remarks

As can be seen from the preceding chapters, there is a large body of substantive law to be considered in bringing or defending patent litigation in China. The system has become more and more complex since the introduction of the patent law in the 1980s and is certain to become more complex in coming years.

Chinese courts are seeing more and more complex cases brought before them, and a lot of study and discussion is going on within the government, the State Intellectual Property Office (SIPO), and the judiciary as to how to improve the handling of such cases.

We can expect to see in years to come changes to the rules of evidence to make the collection and admission of evidence easier. Courts are far more likely to draw inference from proven facts, and, hopefully, the onerous requirements on foreign parties to notarize and legalize powers of attorneys and evidence will be relaxed.

The greatest change that I have been lobbying for for many years is the establishment of a single patent court of appeal to hear appeals from all first instance cases anywhere in China. This is in line with international practice in the United States, Japan, and the United Kingdom and necessary to ensure consistency of decisions in a complex area of law.

By its very definition, the existence of a uniform court of appeal will lead to the decline of local protectionism, and Chinese patent law jurisprudence will improve dramatically. Future editions of this book and others like it will be able to cite, with confidence, cases that provide guidance as to how future decisions will be made.

There are other improvements that can be made, but the establishment of a court of appeals is a game changer that will bring Chinese patent law up to international standards in a very short period of time.

In the interim, plaintiffs and defendants will need to navigate the system as it is. I hope that this book will be of assistance.

Finally, I would add that from time to time Chinese judges are quoted stating that the courts need to consider the national interest in deciding cases, and in particular, intellectual property cases. In the Article 19 of the 2009 Economic Conditions Opinion it is specifically stated that courts should "always pay attention to safeguard national interests and economic security." Courts have no role to play in determining or safeguarding national interests and economic security. That is the role of the executive and the legislature. The best way that courts can safeguard national interests is to decide cases fairly according to law. The introduction of a concept of national interest into judicial decision making is guaranteed to encourage local protectionism and a weakened judiciary.

Tables

Table 1: PATENT APPLICATIONS

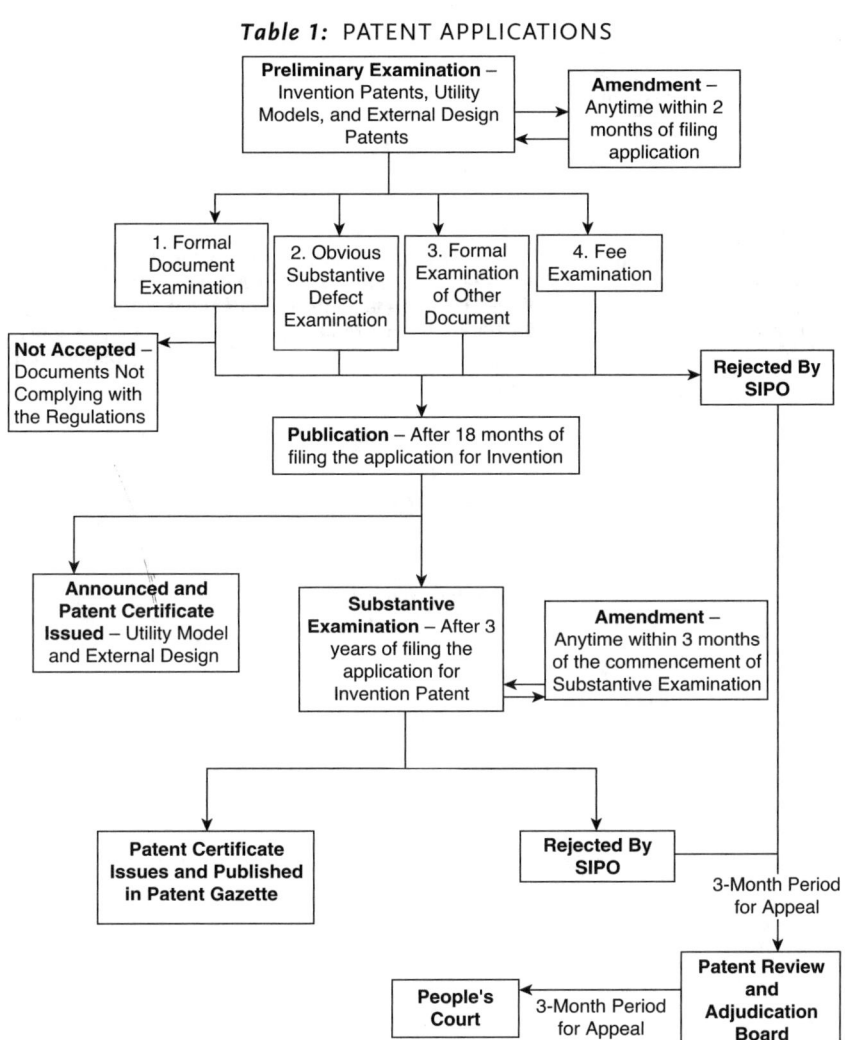

Table 2: PATENT INFRINGEMENT LITIGATION

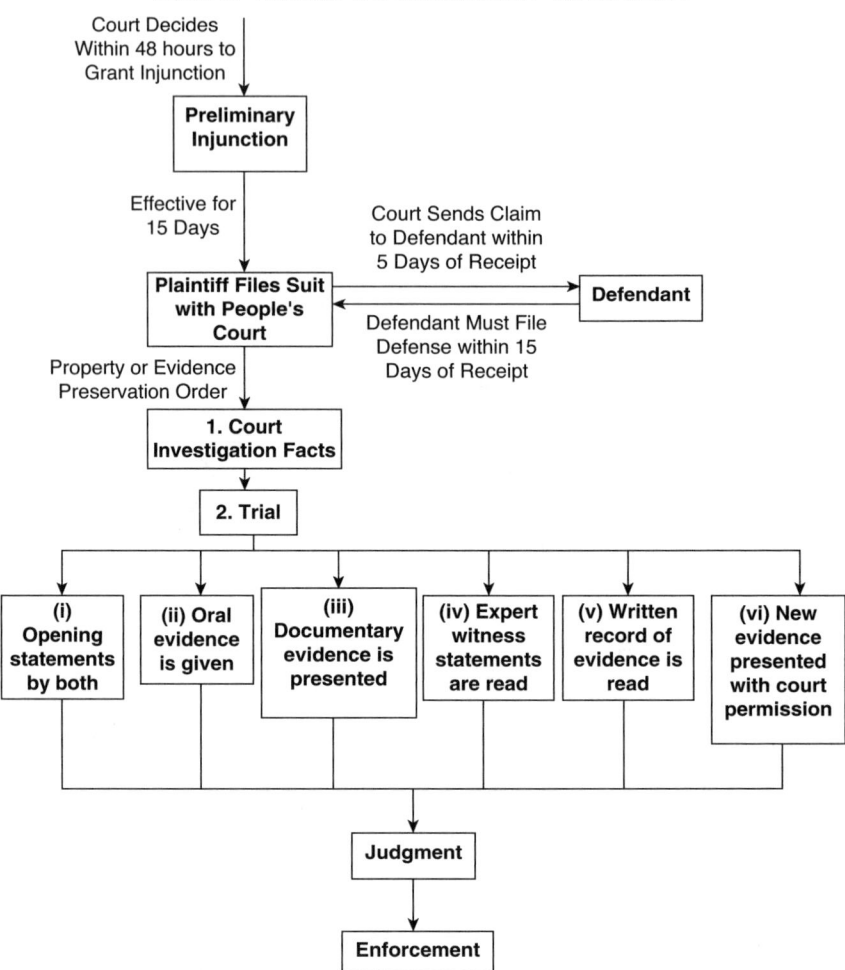

Table 3: PATENT PRELITIGATION, LITIGATION OFFICIAL COURT, AND ENFORCEMENT COST PROJECTIONS

(i) **Patent Prelitigation Official Court Cost Projections**[1]

Value of the Property (Yuan)	Official Amount to Be Paid (Yuan)
1000	Each item 30 Yuan
1000–10,000	1%
100,000	0.5%

Note: The expenses for property preservation measures cannot exceed 5,000 Yuan according to the *Methods for the Payment of Litigation Fees*.

(ii) **Civil Patent Litigation Official Court Cost Projections**[2]

Amount of Damages (Yuan)	Sum or Percentage Payable to the Court (Yuan)
< 10,000	50 Yuan
10,000–100,000	2.5%
100,000–200,000	2%
200,000–500,000	1.5%
500,000–1 million	1%
1 million–2 million	0.9%
2 million–5 million	0.8%
5 million–10 million	0.7%
10 million–20 million	0.6%
> 20 million	0.5%

1. *Methods for the Payment of Litigation Fees*, Article 14(2).
2. *See id.*, Article 13(3)(iii).

(iii) Administrative Litigation Official Court Cost Projections[3]

Amount of Damages (Yuan)	Sum or Percentage Payable to the Court (Yuan)
Any amount	100 Yuan

(iv) Civil Patent Litigation Official Enforcement of Judgment Cost Projections[4]

Value of the Enforcement (Yuan)	Official Enforcement Cost to Be Paid (Yuan)
No Total Amount or Value	50 Yuan–500 Yuan
< 10,000	50 Yuan
> 10,000–500,000	1.5%
500,000–5,000,000	1%
5,000,000–10,000,000	0.1%

---

3. *See id.*, Article 13(5)(i).
4. *See id.*, Article 14(i)–(ii).

Appendices

APPENDIX 1
Patent Law of the People's Republic of China
中华人民共和国专利法

(Third Revision - In Effect October 1, 2009)

第一章 总则	**Chapter I General Provisions**
第一条 为了保护专利权人的合法权益，鼓励发明创造，推动发明创造的应用，提高创新能力，促进科学技术进步和经济社会发展，制定本法。	Article 1 This law is enacted in order to protect the legitimate rights of patentee, encourage invention-creation, promote the application of invention-creation, increase the capacity for innovation, and promote the progress of science and technology, as well as the development of economic society.
第二条 本法所称的发明创造是指发明、实用新型和外观设计。	Article 2 "Invention-creation" referred to in this law means invention, utility model and design.
发明，是指对产品、方法或者其改进所提出的新的技术方案。	"Invention" refers to a new technical solution proposed for a product, method or the improvement thereof.
实用新型，是指对产品的形状、构造或者其结合所提出的适于实用的新的技术方案。	"Utility model" refers to a new technical solution proposed for a product's form, structure, or the combination thereof, that is suitable for utility.
外观设计，是指对产品的形状、图案或者其结合以及色彩与形状、图案的结合所作出的富有美感并适于工业应用的新设计。	"Design" means a new design proposed for a product's shape, pattern or the combination thereof, or the combination of its colour and shape and/or pattern, that creates an aesthetic feeling and is suitable for industrial application.

第三条
国务院专利行政部门负责管理全国的专利工作；统一受理和审查专利申请，依法授予专利权。

省、自治区、直辖市人民政府管理专利工作的部门负责本行政区域内的专利管理工作。

Article 3
The patent administrative department under the State Council is responsible for the nation-wide patent work. It accepts and examines patent applications and grants patent rights in accordance with law.

The administrative departments for patent work under the people's governments of provinces, autonomous regions and municipalities directly under the Central Government are responsible for administering patent work in their respective administrative areas.

第四条
申请专利的发明创造涉及国家安全或者重大利益需要保密的，按照国家有关规定办理。

Article 4
If an invention-creation for which a patent is applied involves national security or other vital interests of the State that require secrecy, the matter is treated in accordance with the relevant provisions of the State.

第五条
对违反国家法律、社会公德或者妨害公共利益的发明创造，不授予专利权。

对违反法律、行政法规的规定获取或者利用遗传资源，并依赖该遗传资源完成的发明创造，不授予专利权。

Article 5
Patent right is not granted for any invention-creation that violates the laws of the State or social morality or that is detrimental to the public interest.

Patent right is not granted for any invention-creation which violates the laws and administrative regulations to acquire or use genetic resources, and relies on the said genetic resources for completion.

第六条
执行本单位的任务或者主要是利用本单位的物质技术条件所完成的发明创造为职务发明创造。职务发明创造申请专利的权利属于该单位；申请被批准后，该单位为专利权人。

非职务发明创造，申请专利的权利属于发明人或者设计人；申请被批准后，该发明人或者设计人为专利权人。

利用本单位的物质技术条件所完成的发明创造，单位与发明人或者设计人订有合同，对申请专利的权利和专利权的归属作出约定的，从其约定。

Article 6
An invention-creation, completed in performing the tasks of the unit to which he belongs, or completed mainly by using the material and technical means of the unit is a service invention-creation. The right to apply for a patent for a service intention-creation belongs to the unit. After the application is approved, the unit shall be the patentee.

For a non-service invention-creation, the right to apply for a patent belongs to the inventor or creator. After the application is approved, the inventor or creator shall be the patentee.

In respect of an invention-creation completed by a person using the material and technical means of a unit to which he belongs, where the unit and the inventor or creator have entered into a contract in which the right to apply for a patent and the ownership of the patent right is agreed upon, such agreement shall control.

第七条
对发明人或者设计人的非职务发明创造专利申请，任何单位或者个人不得压制。

Article 7
Any unit or individual must not suppress applications for a non-service invention-creation patent of an inventor or designer.

Article 8

第八条
两个以上单位或者个人合作完成的发明创造、一个单位或者个人接受其他单位或者个人委托所完成的发明创造，除另有协议的以外，申请专利的权利属于完成或者共同完成的单位或者个人；申请被批准后，申请的单位或者个人为专利权人。

For an invention-creation jointly completed by two or more units or individuals, or completed by a unit or individual entrusted by another unit or individual, the right to apply for a patent, unless otherwise agreed upon, belongs to the unit or individual that completed, or to the units or individuals that jointly completed, the invention-creation. After the application is approved, the unit or individual that makes the application shall be the patentee.

Article 9

第九条
同样的发明创造只能授予一项专利权。但是，同一申请人同日对同样的发明创造既申请实用新型专利又申请发明专利，先获得的实用新型专利权尚未终止，且申请人声明放弃该实用新型专利权的，可以授予发明专利权。

两个以上的申请人分别就同样的发明创造申请专利的，专利权授予最先申请的人。

For the same invention-creation, only one patent right can be granted. However, when the same applicant applied for both a utility model patent and an invention patent on the same day, the invention patent may be granted if the utility model patent right that is obtained first is not yet terminated, and the applicant declares to renounce the said utility model patent right.

If two or more applicants apply separately for a patent on the same invention-creation, the patent right is granted to the person who applies first.

Article 10

第十条
专利申请权和专利权可以转让。

中国单位或者个人向外国人、外国企业或者外国其他组织转让专利申请权或者专利权的，应当依照有关法律、行政法规的规定办理手续。

转让专利申请权或者专利权的，当事人应当订立书面合同，并向国务院专利行政部门登记，由国务院专利行政部门予以公告。专利申请权或者专利权的转让自登记之日起生效。

The right to apply for a patent and the patent right may be assigned.

Any assignment of the right to apply for a patent or of the patent right from a Chinese unit or individual to a foreigner, foreign enterprise or other foreign organizations, shall follow the procedures in accordance of the relevant laws and administrative regulations.

Where the right to apply for a patent or the patent right is assigned, the parties shall conclude a written contract and register it with the patent administrative department under the State Council. The registration is publicly announced by the patent administrative department under the State Council. The assignment of the right to apply for a patent or the patent right takes effect as of the date of registration.

Article 11

第十一条
发明和实用新型专利权被授予后，除本法另有规定的以外，任何单位或者个人未经专利权人许可，都不得实施其专利，即不得为生产经营目的制造、使用、许诺销售、销售、进口其专利产品，或者使用其专利方法以及使用、许诺销售、销售、进口依照该专利方法直接获得的产品。

After the grant of the invention or utility model patent right, except where otherwise provided for in this Law, any unit or individual must not, without the authorization of the patentee, exploit the patent, that is, for production or business purposes, to make, use, offer to sell, sell or import the patented product, or use the patented method, or use, offer to sell, sell or import the product directly obtained through the patented method.

外观设计专利权被授予后，任何单位或者个人未经专利权人许可，都不得实施其专利，即不得为生产经营目的制造、许诺销售、销售、进口其外观设计专利产品。	After the grant of the design patent, any unit or individual must not, without the authorization of the patentee, exploit the patent, that is for production or business purposes, to make, offer to sell, sell, or import the patented design product.
第十二条 任何单位或者个人实施他人专利的，应当与专利权人订立实施许可合同，向专利权人支付专利使用费。被许可人无权允许合同规定以外的任何单位或者个人实施该专利。	Article 12 Any unit or individual exploiting the patent of another shall conclude with the patentee a licensing contract for exploitation and pay the patentee a fee for the exploitation of the patent. The licensee has no right to authorize any unit or individual, other than those specified in the licensing contract, to exploit the patent.
第十三条 发明专利申请公布后，申请人可以要求实施其发明的单位或者个人支付适当的费用。	Article 13 After the publication of the application for an invention patent, the applicant may require the unit or individual exploiting the invention to pay an appropriate fee.
第十四条 国有企业事业单位的发明专利，对国家利益或者公共利益具有重大意义的，国务院有关主管部门和省、自治区、直辖市人民政府报经国务院批准，可以决定在批准的范围内推广应用，允许指定的单位实施，由实施单位按照国家规定向专利权人支付使用费。	Article 14 Where an invention patent, belonging to any State-owned enterprise or institution, is of great significance to the interest of the State or to the public interest, the relevant departments in charge under the State Council and the people's governments of provinces, autonomous regions or municipalities directly under the Central Government may, after reporting to the State Council and getting approval, decide that the invention patent be popularized and applied within the approved limits, and allow designated units to exploit that invention. The exploiting unit, according to the regulations of the State, pay a fee for exploitation to the patentee.
第十五条（新增） 专利申请权或者专利权的共有人对权利的行使有约定的，从其约定。没有约定的，共有人可以单独实施或者以普通许可方式许可他人实施该专利；许可他人实施该专利的，收取的使用费应当在共有人之间分配。 除前款规定的情形外，行使共有的专利申请权或者专利权应当取得全体共有人的同意。	Article 15 If the co-owners of a patent application right or patent right have an agreement on the exercise of those rights, the agreement shall apply. If there is no such agreement, a co-owner may independently exploit or license others to exploit the patent through simple licensing; Royalties received from licensing others to exploit the patent shall be distributed amongst the co-owners. Except for the situation provided in the preceding paragraph, consent shall be obtained from all co-owners to exercise of a jointly-owned patent application right or patent right.

第十六条 被授予专利权的单位应当对职务发明创造的发明人或者设计人给予奖励；发明创造专利实施后，根据其推广应用的范围和取得的经济效益，对发明人或者设计人给予合理的报酬。	Article 16 The unit that is granted a patent right shall reward to the inventor or creator of a service invention--creation; and after exploitation of the patented invention-creation, gives the inventor or designer a reasonable remuneration based on the extent the invention-creation is popularized and applied and the economic benefits it yields.
第十七条（由原15及17条合并） 发明人或者设计人有权在专利文件中写明自己是发明人或者设计人。 专利权人有权在其专利产品或者该产品的包装上标明专利标识。	Article 17 The inventor or designer is entitled to be named as such in the patent document. The patentee is entitled to put patent notice on the patented product or the package thereof.
第十八条 在中国没有经常居所或者营业所的外国人、外国企业或者外国其他组织在中国申请专利的，依照其所属国同中国签订的协议或者共同参加的国际条约，或者依照互惠原则，根据本法办理。	Article 18 Where foreigners, foreign enterprises or other foreign organizations having no regular habitual residence or business office in China files an application for a patent in China, the application is treated pursuant to this Law, and in accordance with the agreement concluded between the country to which the applicant belongs and China, or in accordance with any international treaty which is joined by both parties, or on the basis of the principle of reciprocity.
第十九条 在中国没有经常居所或者营业所的外国人、外国企业或者外国其他组织在中国申请专利和办理其他专利事务的，应当委托依法设立的专利代理机构办理。 中国单位或者个人在国内申请专利和办理其他专利事务的，可以委托依法设立的专利代理机构办理。 专利代理机构应当遵守法律、行政法规，按照被代理人的委托办理专利申请或者其他专利事务；对被代理人发明创造的内容，除专利申请已经公布或者公告的以外，负有保密责任。专利代理机构的具体管理办法由国务院规定。	Article 19 Where foreigners, foreign enterprises or other foreign organizations having no regular habitual residence or business office in China applies for a patent or has other patent matters to handle in China, he or it shall entrust a legally established patent agency to handle. Chinese unit or individual applying for a patent or handling other patent matters may entrust any legally established patent agency to handle. The patent agency shall comply with the laws and administrative regulations, and handle patent applications and other patent matters according to the delegation of the entrusting principal. In respect of the contents of the entrusting principal's inventions-creations, except for those that have been published or announced, the agency shall bear the responsibility of keeping them confidential. The specific measure governing the patent agency shall be formulated by the State Council.
第二十条 任何单位或者个人将在中国完成的发明或者实用新型向外国申请专利的，应当事先	Article 20 Any entity or individual filing a patent application in a foreign country for an invention-creation made in

报经国务院专利行政部门进行保密审查。保密审查的程序、期限等按照国务院的规定执行。	China, shall apply in advance for the confidentiality examination conducted by the patent administrative department under the State Council. The procedures and duration of the confidentiality examination shall be enforced in accordance with the provisions of the State Council.
中国单位或者个人可以根据中华人民共和国参加的有关国际条约提出专利国际申请。申请人提出专利国际申请的，应当遵守前款规定。	Any Chinese unit or individual may file an international application for a patent in accordance with any international treaty concerned to which China is a party. The applicant filing an international application for a patent shall comply with the provisions of the preceding paragraph.
国务院专利行政部门依照中华人民共和国参加的有关国际条约、本法和国务院有关规定处理专利国际申请。	The patent administrative department under the State Council shall handle any international application for patent in accordance with the international treaty concerned to which China is a party, this Law and the relevant provisions of the State Council.
对违反本条第一款规定向外国申请专利的发明或者实用新型，在中国申请专利的，不授予专利权。	Regarding an invention or utility model for which a foreign patent application is filed in violation of the first paragraph of this article, and for which a patent application is filed in China, patent right will not be granted
第二十一条 国务院专利行政部门及其专利复审委员会应当按照客观、公正、准确、及时的要求，依法处理有关专利的申请和请求。	Article 21 The patent administrative department under the State Council and the Patent Reexamination Board under the department shall handle patent-related application and request in accordance with laws and in conformity with the requirements for being objective, fair, correct and timely.
国务院专利行政部门应当完整、准确、及时发布专利信息，定期出版专利公报。	The patent administrative department under the State Council shall completely, correctly and timely publish the patent information, and periodically publish the patent gazette.
在专利申请公布或者公告前，国务院专利行政部门的工作人员及有关人员对其内容负有保密责任。	Until the publication or announcement of the patent, staff members of the patent administrative department under the State Council and relevant personnel bear the responsibility of keeping its contents confidential.
第二章 授予专利权的条件	**Chapter II Conditions for Grant of Patent Right**
第二十二条 授予专利权的发明和实用新型，应当具备新颖性、创造性和实用性。	Article 22 Any invention or utility model for which patent right is granted shall possess the characteristics of novelty, inventiveness and practical applicability.
新颖性，是指该发明或者实用新型不属于现有技术；也没有任何单位或者个人就同样的发明或者实用新型在申请日以前向国	Novelty means that the invention or utility model neither belongs to an existing technology, nor has any entity or individual previously filed before the

务院专利行政部门提出过申请，并记载在申请日以后公布的专利申请文件或者公告的专利文件中。	date of filing with the patent administrative department under the State Council an application on an identical invention or utility model recorded in patent application documents published or patent documents announced after the said date of filing.
创造性，是指与现有技术相比，该发明具有突出的实质性特点和显著的进步，该实用新型具有实质性特点和进步。	Inventiveness means that, as compared with the existing technology, the invention has prominent and substantive features and represents a notable progress, or the utility model possesses substantive features and represents progress.
实用性，是指该发明或者实用新型能够制造或者使用，并且能够产生积极效果。	Practical applicability means that the invention or utility model can be made or used and can produce positive results.
本法所称现有技术，是指申请日以前在国内外为公众所知的技术。	The existing technology referred to in this Law means any technology known to the public before the date of filing in China or abroad.
第二十三条 （修改） 授予专利权的外观设计，应当不属于现有设计；也没有任何单位或者个人就同样的外观设计在申请日以前向国务院专利行政部门提出过申请，并记载在申请日以后公告的专利文件中。	Article 23 Any design for which a patent right is granted shall not belong to an existing design; nor has any unit or individual previously filed before the date of filing with the patent administrative department under the State Council an application on an identical design recorded in patent documents announced after the said date of filing.
授予专利权的外观设计与现有设计或者现有设计特征的组合相比，应当具有明显区别。	The design for which a patent right is granted shall significantly differ as compared to the existing design or combination of the features of the existing design.
授予专利权的外观设计不得与他人在申请日以前已经取得的合法权利相冲突。	Any design for which a patent right is granted must not be in conflict with legitimate rights obtained before the said filing date by other people.
本法所称现有设计，是指申请日以前在国内外为公众所知的设计。	The existing design referred to in this Law means any design known to the public before the date of filing in China or abroad.
第二十四条 申请专利的发明创造在申请日以前六个月内，有下列情形之一的，不丧失新颖性： （一）在中国政府主办或者承认的国际展览会上首次展出的； （二）在规定的学术会议或者技术会议上首次发表的； （三）他人未经申请人同意而泄露其内容的。	Article 24 Any invention-creation for which a patent is applied does not lose its novelty where, within six months before the filing date of the application, one of the following events occurred: (1) where it was exhibited for the first time at an international exhibition sponsored or recognized by the Chinese Government; (2) where it was made public for the first time at a prescribed academic or technical conference; or (3) where the content was disclosed by other person without the consent of the applicant.

第二十五条
对下列各项，不授予专利权：

（一）科学发现；
（二）智力活动的规则和方法；
（三）疾病的诊断和治疗方法；
（四）动物和植物品种；
（五）用原子核变换方法获得的物质；
（六）对平面印刷品的图案、色彩或者二者的结合作出的主要起标识作用的设计。
对前款第（四）项所列产品的生产方法，可以依照本法规定授予专利权。

Article 25
For any of the following, no patent right is granted:

(1) scientific discoveries;
(2) rules and methods for mental activities;
(3) methods for the diagnosis or for the treatment of diseases;
(4) animal and plant varieties;
(5) substances obtained by means of nuclear transformation;
(6) designs that serve mainly as indicators of two-dimensional printing goods' pattern, the colour or the combination of the two.
For processes used in producing products referred to in item (4) of the preceding paragraph, patent right may be granted in accordance with the provisions of this Law.

第三章 专利的申请

Chapter III Application for Patent

第二十六条
申请发明或者实用新型专利的，应当提交请求书、说明书及其摘要和权利要求书等文件。

请求书应当写明发明或者实用新型的名称，发明人的姓名，申请人姓名或者名称、地址，以及其他事项。

说明书应当对发明或者实用新型作出清楚、完整的说明，以所属技术领域的技术人员能够实现为准；必要的时候，应当有附图。摘要应当简要说明发明或者实用新型的技术要点。

权利要求书应当以说明书为依据，清楚、简要地限定要求专利保护的范围。

依赖遗传资源完成的发明创造，申请人应当在专利申请文件中说明该遗传资源的直接来源和原始来源；申请人无法说明原始来源的，应当陈述理由。

Article 26
Where a patent application for invention or utility model is filed, a request, a specification and its abstract, and claims shall be submitted.

The request shall state the title of the invention or utility model, the name of the inventor, the name and address of the applicant and other related matters.

The description shall describe the invention or utility model in a manner sufficiently clear and complete so that a person skilled in the relevant field of technology to carry it out; where necessary, drawings shall be appended. The abstract shall state briefly the technical essentials of the invention or utility model.

The claims shall, on the basis of the description, define the scope of the patent protection sought for in a clear and concise manner.

Where an invention-creation is developed relying on the genetic resources, the applicant shall indicate, in the patent application documents, the direct and original source of such genetic resources; where the applicant is unable to indicate the original source, he or it shall state the reasons thereof.

第二十七条
申请外观设计专利的，应当提交请求书、该外观设计的图片或者照片以及对该外观设计的简要说明等文件。

申请人提交的有关图片或者照片应当清楚地显示要求专利保护的产品的外观设计。

Article 27
When a patent application is filed for a design, a request, drawings or photographs of the design and a brief explanation of the design shall be submitted.

The relevant drawings or photographs submitted by the applicant should clearly indicate the design for which the patent protection is sought.

第二十八条
国务院专利行政部门收到专利申请文件之日为申请日。如果申请文件是邮寄的,以寄出的邮戳日为申请日。

Article 28
The date on which the patent administrative department under the State Council receives the patent application documents shall be the date of filing. If the application documents are sent by mail, the date of mailing indicated by the postmark shall be the date of filing.

第二十九条
申请人自发明或者实用新型在外国第一次提出专利申请之日起十二个月内,或者自外观设计在外国第一次提出专利申请之日起六个月内,又在中国就相同主题提出专利申请的,依照该外国同中国签订的协议或者共同参加的国际条约,或者依照相互承认优先权的原则,可以享有优先权。

Article 29
Where, within twelve months from the date on which an applicant first filed in a foreign country an application for a patent for invention or utility model, or within six months from the date on which any applicant first filed in a foreign country an application for a patent for design, he or it files in China an application for a patent for the same subject matter, he or it may, in accordance with any agreement concluded between the said foreign country and China, or in accordance with any international treaty to which both countries are party, or on the basis of the principle of mutual recognition of the right of priority, enjoy a right of priority.

申请人自发明或者实用新型在中国第一次提出专利申请之日起十二个月内,又向国务院专利行政部门就相同主题提出专利申请的,可以享有优先权。

Where, within twelve months from the date on which an applicant first filed in China an application for a patent for invention or utility model, he or it files with the patent administrative department under the State Council an application for a patent for the same subject matter, he or it may enjoy a right of priority.

第三十条
申请人要求优先权的,应当在申请的时候提出书面声明,并且在三个月内提交第一次提出的专利申请文件的副本;未提出书面声明或者逾期未提交专利申请文件副本的,视为未要求优先权。

Article 30
An applicant who claims the right of priority shall make a written declaration when the application is filed, and submit, within three months, a copy of the patent application documents that was first filed; if the applicant fails to make the written declaration or fails to submit a copy of the patent application documents within the time limit, the claim to the right of priority shall be deemed not to have been made.

第三十一条
一件发明或者实用新型专利申请应当限于一项发明或者实用新型。属于一个总的发明构思的两项以上的发明或者实用新型,可以作为一件申请提出。

Article 31
A patent application for invention or utility model shall be limited to one invention or utility model. Two or more inventions or utility models belonging to a single general inventive concept may be filed as one application.

一件外观设计专利申请应当限于一项外观设计。同一产品两项以上的相似外观设计,或者用于同一类别并且成套出售或者使用的产品的两项以上外观设计,可以作为一件申请提出。

A patent application for design shall be limited to one design. Two or more similar designs for the same product, or two or more designs which are incorporated in products belonging to the same class and sold or used in sets may be filed as one application.

Article 32

An applicant may withdraw the patent application at any time before the patent right is granted.

Article 33

An applicant may amend his or its application documents for a patent, but the amendment to the application documents for a patent for invention or utility model must not go beyond the scope of the disclosure contained in the original specification and the claims, and the amendment to the application documents for a patent for design must not go beyond the scope of the disclosure as shown in the original drawings or photographs.

Chapter IV Examination and Approval of Patent Application

Article 34

Where, after receiving an application for a patent for invention, the patent administrative department under the State Council, upon preliminary examination, finds the application to be in conformity with the requirements of this Law, it shall publish the application promptly after the expiration of eighteen months from the date of filing. Upon the request of the applicant, the patent administrative department under the State Council may publish the application earlier.

Article 35

Upon the applicant's request for a patent for invention, made at any time within three years from the filing date of an application, the patent administrative department under the State Council may carry out substantive examination of that application. If, without any justified reason, the applicant fails to meet the time limit for requesting such substantive examination, the application shall be deemed to have been withdrawn.

The patent administrative department under the State Council may, on its own initiative, carry out substantive examination of an application for a patent for invention when it deems it necessary.

Article 36

When the applicant for a patent for invention requests substantive examination, the applicant shall furnish reference materials concerning the invention that were available prior to the filing date of the application.

发明专利已经在外国提出过申请的，国务院专利行政部门可以要求申请人在指定期限内提交该国为审查其申请进行检索的资料或者审查结果的资料；无正当理由逾期不提交的，该申请即被视为撤回。

For an application for a patent for invention that has been already filed in a foreign country, the patent administrative department under the State Council may ask the applicant to furnish within a specified time limit documents concerning any search made for the purpose of examining that application, or concerning the results of any examination made, in that country. If, at the expiration of the specified time limit, without any justified reason, the said documents are not furnished, the application shall be deemed to have been withdrawn.

第三十七条
国务院专利行政部门对发明专利申请进行实质审查后，认为不符合本法规定的，应当通知申请人，要求其在指定的期限内陈述意见，或者对其申请进行修改；无正当理由逾期不答复的，该申请即被视为撤回。

Article 37
Where the patent administrative department under the State Council, after it has made the substantive examination of the application for a patent for invention, finds that the application is not in conformity with the provisions of this Law, it shall notify the applicant and request him or it to submit, within a specified time limit, his or its observations or to amend the application. If, without any justified reason, the time limit for making response is not met, the application shall be deemed to have been withdrawn.

第三十八条
发明专利申请经申请人陈述意见或者进行修改后，国务院专利行政部门仍然认为不符合本法规定的，应当予以驳回。

Article 38
Where after the applicant has made the observations or amendments, the patent administrative department under the State Council finds that the application for a patent for invention is still not in conformity with the provisions of this Law, the application shall be rejected.

第三十九条
发明专利申请经实质审查没有发现驳回理由的，由国务院专利行政部门作出授予发明专利权的决定，发给发明专利证书，同时予以登记和公告。发明专利权自公告之日起生效。

Article 39
Where it is found after substantive examination that there is no cause for rejection of the application for a patent for invention, the patent administrative department under the State Council makes a decision to grant the patent right for invention, issues the certificate of patent for invention, and registers and announces it. The patent right for invention takes effect as of the date of the announcement.

第四十条
实用新型和外观设计专利申请经初步审查没有发现驳回理由的，由国务院专利行政部门作出授予实用新型专利权或者外观设计专利权的决定，发给相应的专利证书，同时予以登记和公告。实用新型专利权和外观设计专利权自公告之日起生效。

Article 40
Where it is found after preliminary examination that there is no cause for rejection of the application for a patent for utility model or design, the patent administrative department under the State Council makes a decision to grant the patent right for utility model or the patent right for design, issues the relevant patent certificate, and registers and announces it. The patent right for utility model or design takes effect as of the date of the announcement.

第四十一条
国务院专利行政部门设立专利复审委员会。专利申请人对国务院专利行政部门驳回申请的决定不服的，可以自收到通知之日起三个月内，向专利复审委员会请求复审。专利复审委员会复审后，作出决定，并通知专利申请人。

专利申请人对专利复审委员会的复审决定不服的，可以自收到通知之日起三个月内向人民法院起诉。

Article 41
The patent administrative department under the State Council sets up a Patent Reexamination Board. Where an applicant for patent is not satisfied with the decision of rejecting his or its application for patent issued by the patent administrative department under the State Council, such applicant may, within three months from the date of receipt of the notification, make a request for a reexamination to the Patent Reexamination Board. The Patent Reexamination Board, after reexamination, makes a decision and notifies the applicant for patent.

Where the applicant for patent is not satisfied with the decision of the Patent Reexamination Board, the applicant may, within three months from the date of receipt of the notification, institute legal proceedings in the people's court.

第五章 专利权的期限、终止和无效

Chapter V Duration, Cessation and Invalidation of Patent Right

第四十二条
发明专利权的期限为二十年，实用新型专利权和外观设计专利权的期限为十年，均自申请日起计算。

Article 42
The duration of patent right for invention is twenty years, and the duration of the patent right for utility model and patent right for design is ten years, counted from the date of filing.

第四十三条
专利权人应当自被授予专利权的当年开始缴纳年费。

Article 43
The patentee shall pay an annual fee beginning with the year in which the patent right is granted.

第四十四条
有下列情形之一的，专利权在期限届满前终止：
（一）没有按照规定缴纳年费的；
（二）专利权人以书面声明放弃其专利权的。
专利权在期限届满前终止的，由国务院专利行政部门登记和公告。

Article 44
In any of the following situations, the patent right ceases before the expiration of its duration:

(1) if the annual fee is not paid as prescribed; or
(2) if the patentee renounces his or its patent right by a written declaration.

Where the patent right ceases before the expiration of its duration, the patent administrative department under the State Council registers and announces it.

第四十五条
自国务院专利行政部门公告授予专利权之日起，任何单位或者个人认为该专利权的授予不符合本法有关规定的，可以请求专利复审委员会宣告该专利权无效。

Article 45
Where, starting from the date of the announcement of the grant of the patent right by the patent administrative department under the State Council, any unit or individual considers that the grant of the said patent right is not in conformity with the relevant provisions of this Law, it or he may request the Patent Reexamination Board to declare the patent right invalid.

第四十六条
专利复审委员会对宣告专利权无效的请求应当及时审查和作出决定，并通知请求人和专利权人。宣告专利权无效的决定，由国务院专利行政部门登记和公告。

对专利复审委员会宣告专利权无效或者维持专利权的决定不服的，可以自收到通知之日起三个月内向人民法院起诉。人民法院应当通知无效宣告请求程序的对方当事人作为第三人参加诉讼。

Article 46

The Patent Reexamination Board shall examine the request for invalidation of the patent right promptly, make a decision on it, and notify the person who made the request and the patentee. The decision declaring the patent right invalid is registered and announced by the patent administrative department under the State Council.

Where the patentee or the person who makes the request for invalidation is not satisfied with the decision of the Patent Reexamination Board declaring the patent right invalid or upholding the patent right, such party may, within three months from receipt of the notification, institute legal proceedings in the people's court. The people's court shall notify the person that is the opponent party of that party in the invalidation procedure to appear as a third party in the legal proceedings.

第四十七条
宣告无效的专利权视为自始即不存在。

宣告专利权无效的决定，对在宣告专利权无效前人民法院作出并已执行的专利侵权的判决、调解书，已经履行或者强制执行的专利侵权纠纷处理决定，以及已经履行的专利实施许可合同和专利权转让合同，不具有追溯力。但是因专利权人的恶意给他人造成的损失，应当给予赔偿。

依照前款规定不返还专利侵权赔偿金、专利使用费、专利权转让费，明显违反公平原则的，应当全部或者部分返还。

Article 47

The patent right which has been declared invalid shall be deemed to be non-existent from the beginning.

The decision declaring the patent right invalid has no retroactive effect on the judgment, mediation decision of patent infringement which has been issued and enforced by the people's court, as well as on the decision concerning the handling of disputes over patent infringement which has been complied with or compulsorily executed, or on any contract of patent license or of assignment of patent right which has been performed prior to the declaration of the patent right invalid; however, the damage caused to other persons in bad faith on the part of the patentee shall be compensated.

Where, pursuant to the provisions of the preceding paragraph, the monetary damages for patent infringement, the fees for exploitation of the patent or fees for the assignment of the patent right is not returned, but such non-return is obviously contrary to the principle of equity, the whole or part of above-mentioned fees should be returned.

第六章 专利实施的强制许可

Chapter VI Compulsory Licence for Patent Exploitation

第四十八条 （修改）
有下列情形之一的，国务院专利行政部门根据具备实施条件的单位或者个人的申请，可以给予实施发明专利或者实用新型专利的强制许可：

Article 48
In any of the following situations, the patent administrative department under the State Council may, upon the application of a unit or individual which is qualified to exploit the invention or utility

（一）专利权人自专利权被授予之日起满三年，且自提出专利申请之日起满四年，无正当理由未实施或者未充分实施其专利的； （二）专利权人行使专利权的行为被依法认定为垄断行为，为消除或者减少该行为对竞争产生的不利影响的。	model, grant a compulsory license to exploit the patent for the invention or utility model. (1) where the patentee after the expiration of three years from the date of granting the patent right, and the expiration of four years from the date of filing, has not exploited the patent or has not sufficiently exploited the patent without any justified reasons; (2) where the exercising of the patent right by the patentee is legally determined as an act of monopoly, for the purpose of eliminating or reducing the adverse effects of said act on the competition.
第四十九条 在国家出现紧急状态或者非常情况时，或者为了公共利益的目的，国务院专利行政部门可以给予实施发明专利或者实用新型专利的强制许可。	Article 49 Where a national emergency or an extraordinary state of affairs occurs, or for the purpose of the public interest, the patent administrative department under the State Council may grant a compulsory license to exploit the patent for invention or utility model.
第五十条（新增） 为了公共健康目的，对取得专利权的药品，国务院专利行政部门可以给予制造并将其出口到符合中华人民共和国参加的有关国际条约规定的国家或者地区的强制许可。	Article 50 (newly added) For the purpose of public health, with regard to a pharmaceutical product which has been granted patent right, the patent administrative department under the State Council may grant a compulsory license to manufacture it and to export it to the countries or regions specified in the relevant international treaties to which China is a party.
第五十一条 一项取得专利权的发明或者实用新型比前已经取得专利权的发明或者实用新型具有显著经济意义的重大技术进步，其实施又有赖于前一发明或者实用新型的实施的，国务院专利行政部门根据后一专利权人的申请，可以给予实施前一发明或者实用新型的强制许可。	Article 51 Where the invention or utility model for which the patent right has been granted has important technical advance of considerable economic significance compared with another invention or utility model for which a patent right has been granted earlier and the exploitation of the later invention or utility model depends on the exploitation of the earlier invention or utility model, the patent administrative department under the State Council may, upon the request of the later patentee, grant a compulsory license to exploit the earlier invention or utility model.
在依照前款规定给予实施强制许可的情形下，国务院专利行政部门根据前一专利权人的申请，也可以给予实施后一发明或者实用新型的强制许可。	Where, according to the preceding paragraph, a compulsory license is granted, the patent administrative department under the State Council may, upon the request of the earlier patentee, also grant a compulsory license to exploit the later invention or utility model.

第五十二条（新增） 强制许可涉及的发明创造为半导体技术的，其实施限于公共利益的目的和本法第四十八条第（二）项规定的情形。	Article 52 Where the invention-creation involved in the compulsory license is semi-conductor technology, the exploitation thereof is limited for the purpose of public interest or under the conditions as provided in Article 48(2) of this Law.
第五十三条（新增） 除依照本法第四十八条第（二）项、第五十条规定给予的强制许可外，强制许可的实施应当主要为了供应国内市场。	Article 53 Except for compulsory licenses granted in accordance with the provisions of Article 48(2) or 50 of this Law, the exploitation of compulsory licenses shall be executed mainly for the supply of the domestic market.
第五十四条（原第51条修改） 依照本法第四十八条第（一）项、第五十一条规定申请强制许可的单位或者个人应当提供证据，证明其以合理的条件请求专利权人许可其实施专利，但未能在合理的时间内获得许可。	Article 54 In accordance with the provisions of Article 48(1) or Article 51 of this Law, the unit or individual applying for a compulsory license shall furnish proof to show that it or he has made requests for authorization from the patentee to exploit the patent on reasonable terms and conditions but was not authorized within a reasonable period of time.
第五十五条 国务院专利行政部门作出的给予实施强制许可的决定，应当及时通知专利权人，并予以登记和公告。	Article 55 The decision made by the patent administrative department under the State Council granting a compulsory license for exploitation shall be notified promptly to the patentee concerned, and shall be registered and announced.
给予实施强制许可的决定，应当根据强制许可的理由规定实施的范围和时间。强制许可的理由消除并不再发生时，国务院专利行政部门应当根据专利权人的请求，经审查后作出终止实施强制许可的决定。	In the decision granting the compulsory license for exploitation, the scope and duration of the exploitation shall be specified on the basis of the reasons justifying the grant. When the reason justifying compulsory license cease to exist and does not recur, the patent administrative department under the State Council may, upon the request of the patentee, terminate the compulsory license after examination.
第五十六条 取得实施强制许可的单位或者个人不享有独占的实施权，并且无权允许他人实施。	Article 56 The unit or individual that is granted a compulsory licence for exploitation does not have an exclusive right to exploit, and does not have the right to authorize others to exploit.
第五十七条 （原第54条修改） 取得实施强制许可的单位或者个人应当付给专利权人合理的使用费，或者依照中华人民共和国参加的有关国际条约的规定处理使用费问题。付给使用费的，其数额由双方协商；双方不能达成协议的，由国务院专利行政部门裁决。	Article 57 The unit or individual that is granted a compulsory licence shall pay the patentee a reasonable exploitation fee or deal with the issue of exploitation fee according to relevant provisions of international treaties to which China is a party. Where the exploitation fee is paid, the amount of the

	exploitation fee is negotiated by both parties. Where the parties fail to reach an agreement, the patent administrative department under the State Council adjudicate.
第五十八条 专利权人对国务院专利行政部门关于实施强制许可的决定不服的，专利权人和取得实施强制许可的单位或者个人对国务院专利行政部门关于实施强制许可的使用费的裁决不服的，可以自收到通知之日起三个月内向人民法院起诉。	Article 58 Where the patentee is not satisfied with the decision of the patent administrative department under the State Council regarding granting a compulsory license for exploitation, or where the patentee or the unit or individual that is granted the compulsory license for exploitation is not satisfied with the ruling made by the patent administrative department under the State Council regarding the fee for exploitation, he or it may, within three months from the date of receipt of the notification, institute legal proceedings in the people's court.
第七章 专利权的保护	**Chapter VII Protection of Patent Right**
第五十九条（修改原第56条修改） 发明或者实用新型专利权的保护范围以其权利要求的内容为准，说明书及附图可以用于解释权利要求的内容。 外观设计专利权的保护范围以表示在图片或者照片中的该产品的外观设计为准，简要说明可以用于解释图片或者照片所表示的该产品的外观设计。	Article 59 The scope of protection of patent right for invention or utility model is determined by the terms of the claims. The specification and attached drawings may be used to interpret the terms of the claims. The scope of protection of patent right for design is determined by the product's design as shown in the drawings or photographs. The brief statement of the patent may be used to interpret the design as shown in the drawings or photographs.
第六十条 未经专利权人许可，实施其专利，即侵犯其专利权，引起纠纷的，由当事人协商解决；不愿协商或者协商不成的，专利权人或者利害关系人可以向人民法院起诉，也可以请求管理专利工作的部门处理。管理专利工作的部门处理时，认定侵权行为成立的，可以责令侵权人立即停止侵权行为，当事人不服的，可以自收到处理通知之日起十五日内依照《中华人民共和国行政诉讼法》向人民法院起诉；侵权人期满不起诉又不停止侵权行为的，管理专利工作的部门可以申请人民法院强制执行。进行处理的管理专利工作的部门应当事人的请求，可以就侵犯专利权的赔偿数额进行调解；调解不成的，当事人可以依照《中华人民共和国民事诉讼法》向人民法院起诉。	Article 60 Where a dispute arises as a result of the exploitation of a patent without the authorization of the patentee, that is, the infringement of the patent right of the patentee, it shall be settled through consultation by the parties. Where the parties are not willing to consult with each other or where the consultation fails, the patentee or the interested party may institute legal proceedings in the people's court, or request the administrative authority for patent affairs to handle the matter. When the administrative authority for patent affairs handling the matter considers that the infringement is established, it may order the infringer to stop the infringing act immediately. If the party is not satisfied with the order, he may, within 15 days from the date of receipt of the notification of the order, institutes legal proceedings in the people's court in accordance with the Administrative Procedure Law of the People's Republic of China. If, within the said time limit, the infringer does not institute the legal proceedings and does not stop the infringing act, the administrative

authority for patent affairs may approach the people's court for compulsory execution. The authority handling the patent matter may, upon the request of the parties, mediate in the amount of compensation for the infringement of the patent right. If the mediation fails, the parties may institute legal proceedings in the people's court in accordance with the Civil Procedure Law of the People's Republic of China.

第六十一条（原第57条修改）
专利侵权纠纷涉及新产品制造方法的发明专利的，制造同样产品的单位或者个人应当提供其产品制造方法不同于专利方法的证明。

Article 61
Where a infringement dispute relates to a patent for invention for a process for the manufacture of a new product, the unit or individual manufacturing the identical product shall furnish proof to show that the process used in the manufacture of its or his product is different from the patented process.

专利侵权纠纷涉及实用新型专利或者外观设计专利的，人民法院或者管理专利工作的部门可以要求专利权人或者利害关系人出具由国务院专利行政部门对相关实用新型或者外观设计进行检索、分析和评价后作出的专利权评价报告，作为审理、处理专利侵权纠纷的证据。

Where the patent infringement dispute relates to a patent for utility model or design, the people's court or the administrative authority for patent affairs may require the patentee or the interested party to furnish an evaluation report of patent issued by the patent administrative department under the State Council after having conducted search, analysis and evaluation of the relevant utility model or design, and use it as evidence for hearing or handling the patent infringement dispute.

第六十二条（新增）
在专利侵权纠纷中，被控侵权人有证据证明其实施的技术或者设计属于现有技术或者现有设计的，不构成侵犯专利权。

Article 62
In a patent infringement dispute, where the alleged infringer has evidence to prove the technology or design exploited by it or him belongs to the existing technology or existing design, such exploitation does not constitute infringement of patent right.

第六十三条（原第58，59条修改）
假冒专利的，除依法承担民事责任外，由管理专利工作的部门责令改正并予公告，没收违法所得，可以并处违法所得四倍以下的罚款；没有违法所得的，可以处二十万元以下的罚款；构成犯罪的，依法追究刑事责任。

Article 63
Where any person passes off a patent, he shall, in addition to bearing the civil liability according to law, be ordered by the administrative authority for patent affairs to correct his act, and the order shall be announced. The illegal earnings shall be confiscated and a fine of not more than four times of the illegal earnings may be imposed; if there is no illegal earnings, a fine of not more than RMB 200,000 Yuan can be imposed; where the infringement constitutes a crime, the infringer shall be prosecuted for his criminal liability.

第六十四条 （新增）
管理专利工作的部门根据已经取得的证据，对涉嫌假冒专利行为进行查处时，可以询问有关当事人，调查与涉嫌违法行为

Article 64
When the administrative authority for patent affairs, based on the evidence obtained, investigates and prosecutes the suspected act of passing off a patent,

有关的情况；对当事人涉嫌违法行为的场所实施现场检查；查阅、复制与涉嫌违法行为有关的合同、发票、账簿以及其他有关资料；检查与涉嫌违法行为有关的产品，对有证据证明是假冒专利的产品，可以查封或者扣押。

it may query the parties concerned and investigate the relevant circumstances of the suspected illegal act; carry out an on-the-spot inspection of the where the party's suspected illegal acts took place; review and reproduce the contracts, invoices, account books and other relevant materials related to the suspected illegal act; examine the products related to suspected illegal act, and may seal up or withhold the products proved to pass off the patented product.

管理专利工作的部门依法行使前款规定的职权时，当事人应当予以协助、配合，不得拒绝、阻挠。

When the administrative authority for patent affairs performs its functions and duties specified in the preceding paragraph in accordance with the law, the parties concerned shall assist and cooperate, shall not refuse or interfere with the performance.

第六十五条（原第60条修改）
侵犯专利权的赔偿数额按照权利人因被侵权所受到的实际损失确定；实际损失难以确定的，可以按照侵权人因侵权所获得的利益确定。权利人的损失或者侵权人获得的利益难以确定的，参照该专利许可使用费的倍数合理确定。赔偿数额还应当包括权利人为制止侵权行为所支付的合理开支。

Article 65
The amount of compensation for the damage caused by the infringement of the patent right shall be assessed on the basis of the actual loss suffered by the right holder because of the infringement; where it is difficult to determine the actual loss, the amount may be assessed on the basis of the profits the infringer has earned because of the infringement. Where it is difficult to determine the losses the right holder has suffered or the profits the infringer has earned, the amount may be assessed by reference to the appropriate multiple of the amount of the exploitation fee. The amount of compensation for damage shall also include the reasonable expenses of the right holder incurred for stopping the infringing act.

权利人的损失、侵权人获得的利益和专利许可使用费均难以确定的，人民法院可以根据专利权的类型、侵权行为的性质和情节等因素，确定给予一万元以上一百万元以下的赔偿。

Where it is difficult to determine the losses suffered by the right holder, the profits the infringer has earned, or the exploitation fee of the patent under a licence, the people's court may award damage of not less than RMB 10,000 Yuan and not more than RMB 1,000,000 Yuan, in light of such factors, as the type of patent right, the nature and the circumstances of the infringing act.

第六十六条（原第61条修改）
专利权人或者利害关系人有证据证明他人正在实施或者即将实施侵犯专利权的行为，如不及时制止将会使其合法权益受到难以弥补的损害的，可以在起诉前向人民法院申请采取责令停止有关行为的措施。

Article 66
Where any patentee or interested party has evidence to prove that another person is infringing or will soon infringe its or his patent right and that if such infringing act is not stopped from occurring in time, it is likely to cause irreparable harm to it or him, it or he may, before legal proceedings are instituted, petition the people's court to adopt measures to stop the relevant acts.

申请人提出申请时，应当提供担保；不提供担保的，驳回申请。

When a petition is filed, the petitioner shall provide a guaranty; if the petitioner fails to do so, the petition is rejected.

人民法院应当自接受申请之时起四十八小时内作出裁定；有特殊情况需要延长的，可以延长四十八小时。裁定责令停止有关行为的，应当立即执行。当事人对裁定不服的，可以申请复议一次；复议期间不停止裁定的执行。

The people's court shall make a ruling within 48 hours after receiving the petition; Where there are special circumstances that require a delayed ruling, the court may make the ruling in another 48 hours. If the ruling is made to stop the related acts, this ruling shall be enforced immediately. If any interested party is not satisfied with the ruling, it or he may apply for reconsideration once; the enforcement of the ruling is not suspended during the reconsideration.

申请人自人民法院采取责令停止有关行为的措施之日起十五日内不起诉的，人民法院应当解除该措施。

Where the petitioner fails to institute legal proceedings within 15 days after the people's court issued the ruling to stop the relevant act, the people's court shall lift the measures.

申请有错误的，申请人应当赔偿被申请人因停止有关行为所遭受的损失。

If the petition is made in error, the petitioner shall compensate respondent for the losses caused by stopping the relevant acts.

第六十七条（新增）
为了制止专利侵权行为，在证据可能灭失或者以后难以取得的情况下，专利权人或者利害关系人可以在起诉前向人民法院申请保全证据。

Article 67
In order to stop patent infringement, under the circumstances where the evidence might be destroyed or where it would be difficult to obtain in the future, the patentee or the interested party may petition the people's court for evidence preservation before instituting legal proceedings.

人民法院采取保全措施，可以责令申请人提供担保；申请人不提供担保的，驳回申请。

When adopting preservation measures, the people's court may order the applicant to provide a guaranty for the petition; if the petitioner fails to provide the guaranty, the petition shall be rejected.

人民法院应当自接受申请之时起四十八小时内作出裁定；裁定采取保全措施的，应当立即执行。

The people's court shall make a ruling within 48 hours after receiving the petition; If the court rules to adopt preservation measures, the ruling shall be enforced immediately.

申请人自人民法院采取保全措施之日起十五日内不起诉的，人民法院应当解除该措施。

Where the petitioner fails to institute legal proceedings within 15 days after the people's court adopted the preservation measures, the people's court shall lift the measures.

第六十八条
侵犯专利权的诉讼时效为二年，自专利权人或者利害关系人得知或者应当得知侵权行为之日起计算。

Article 68
Prescription for instituting legal proceedings concerning the infringement of patent right is two years, counted from the date on which the patentee or the interested party acquires knowledge or should have acquired knowledge of the infringing act.

发明专利申请公布后至专利权授予前使用该发明未支付适当使用费的，专利权人要求支付使用费的诉讼时效为二年，自专利权人得知或者应当得知他人使用其发明之日起计算，但是，专利权人于专利权授予之日前即已得知或者应当得知的，自专利权授予之日起计算。

During the period from the publication of the application for patent for invention to the grant of patent right to the said invention, where no appropriate fee for exploitation of the invention is paid, prescription for instituting legal proceedings by the patentee to demand the said fee is two years, counted from the date on which the patentee acquires or should have obtained knowledge of the exploitation of his invention by another person.

However, where the patentee has already acquired or should have acquired knowledge before the date of the grant of the patent right, the prescription shall be counted from the date of the grant.

第六十九条（原第63条修改）
有下列情形之一的，不视为侵犯专利权：

（一）专利产品或者依照专利方法直接获得的产品，由专利权人或者经其许可的单位、个人售出后，使用、许诺销售、销售、进口该产品的；
（二）在专利申请日前已经制造相同产品、使用相同方法或者已经作好制造、使用的必要准备，并且仅在原有范围内继续制造、使用的；
（三）临时通过中国领陆、领水、领空的外国运输工具，依照其所属国同中国签订的协议或者共同参加的国际条约，或者依照互惠原则，为运输工具自身需要而在其装置和设备中使用有关专利的；
（四）专为科学研究和实验而使用有关专利的；
（五）为提供行政审批所需要的信息，制造、使用、进口专利药品或者专利医疗器械的，以及专门为其制造、进口专利药品或者专利医疗器械的。

Article 69
None of the following shall be deemed an infringement of the patent right:

(1) Where, after the sale of a patented product or products directly obtained using the patented process, by the patentee or a unit or individual authorized by the patentee, any other person uses, offers to sell, sells or imports that product;
(2) Where before the date of filing the application for patent, any person who has already made the identical product, used the identical process, or made necessary preparations for its making or using, continues to make or use it within the original scope only;
(3) Where any foreign means of transport which temporarily passes through the territory, territorial waters or territorial airspace of China uses the patent concerned, in accordance with any agreement concluded between the country to which the foreign means of transport belongs and China, or in accordance with any international treaty to which both countries are party, or on the basis of the principle of reciprocity, for its own needs, in its devices and installations;
(4) Where any person uses the patent concerned solely for the purposes of scientific research and experiments;
(5) For the purpose of providing information needed for administrative examination and approval, any person makes, uses, imports a patented medicine or a patented medical apparatus, and where any person makes, imports the patented medicine or the patented medical apparatus exclusively for such person.

第七十条（原第63条修改）
为生产经营目的使用、许诺销售或者销售不知道是未经专利权人许可而制造并售出的专利侵权产品，能证明该产品合法来源的，不承担赔偿责任。

Article 70
Any person, who, for production and business purposes, uses, offers to sell or sells a patented product without knowing that it was made and sold without the authorization of the patentee, is not liable to compensate for the damage if he can prove the legitimate source of the product.

第七十一条
违反本法第二十条规定向外国申请专利，泄露国家秘密的，由所在单位或者上级主管机关给予行政处分；构成犯罪的，依法追究刑事责任。

Article 71
Where any person, in violation of the provisions of Article 20 of this Law, files in a foreign country an application for patent that divulges State secrets, he is subject to administrative sanction by the unit to

which he belongs or by the competent authority at a higher level. Where the case constitutes a crime, he is prosecuted for the criminal liability in accordance with law.

第七十二条
侵夺发明人或者设计人的非职务发明创造专利申请权和本法规定的其他权益的，由所在单位或者上级主管机关给予行政处分。

Article 72
Where any person usurps the right of an inventor or designer to apply for a patent for a non-service invention-creation or usurps the other rights or interests of an inventor or designer prescribed in this Law, he is subjected to administrative sanction by the unit to which be belongs or by the competent department at a higher level.

第七十三条
管理专利工作的部门不得参与向社会推荐专利产品等经营活动。

管理专利工作的部门违反前款规定的，由其上级机关或者监察机关责令改正，消除影响，有违法收入的予以没收；情节严重的，对直接负责的主管人员和其他直接责任人员依法给予行政处分。

Article 73
The administrative authority for patent affairs must not take part in recommending any patented product for sale to the public or any such commercial activities.

Where the administrative authority for patent affairs violates the provisions of the preceding paragraph, it shall be ordered by the authority at the next higher level or the supervisory authority to correct its mistakes and eliminate the effects. The illegal earnings, if any, shall be confiscated. Where the circumstances are serious, the persons who are directly in charge and the other persons who are directly responsible shall be given administrative sanction in accordance with law.

第七十四条
从事专利管理工作的国家机关工作人员以及其他有关国家机关工作人员玩忽职守、滥用职权、徇私舞弊，构成犯罪的，依法追究刑事责任；尚不构成犯罪的，依法给予行政处分。

Article 74
Where any State functionary working for patent administration or any other State functionary working for patent administration or any other State functionary concerned neglects his duty, abuses his power, or engages in malpractice for personal gain, which constitutes a crime, shall be prosecuted for his criminal liability in accordance with law. If the case is not serious enough to constitute a crime, he shall be given administrative sanction in accordance with law.

第八章 附则

Chapter VIII Supplementary Provisions

第七十五条
向国务院专利行政部门申请专利和办理其他手续，应当按照规定缴纳费用。

Article 75
Any application for a patent and any proceedings before, the Patent Administration Department under the State Council shall pay a fee as prescribed.

第七十六条
本法自1985年4月1日起施行。

Article 76
This Law enters into effect on April 1, 1985.

APPENDIX 2
Implementing Regulations of the Patent Law of the People's Republic of China
中华人民共和国专利法实施细则

(In effect 1 February 2010)

目录	TABLE OF CONTENTS
第一章 总则	CHAPTER 1 GENERAL PROVISIONS
第二章 专利的申请	CHAPTER 2 APPLICATION FOR PATENT
第三章 专利申请的审查和批准	CHAPTER 3 EXAMINATION AND APPROVAL OF APPLICATION FOR PATENT
第四章 专利申请的复审与专利权的无效宣告	CHAPTER 4 REEXAMINATION OF PATENT APPLICATIONS AND INVALIDATION OF PATENT RIGHTS
第五章 专利实施的强制许可	CHAPTER 5 COMPULSORY LICENSES FOR EXPLOITATION OF PATENT
第六章 对职务发明创造的发明人或者设计人的奖励和报酬	CHAPTER 6 REWARD AND REMUNERATION FOR INVENTORS OR CREATORS OF SERVICE INVENTION CREATION INVENTOR OR DESIGNER
第七章 专利权的保护	CHAPTER 7 PROTECTION OF PATENT RIGHTS

第八章 专利登记和专利公报	CHAPTER 8 PATENT REGISTRATION AND PATENT GAZETTE
第九章 费用	CHAPTER 9 FEES
第十章 关于国际申请的特别规定	CHAPTER 10 SPECIAL PROVISIONS CONCERNING INTERNATIONAL APPLICATION
第十一章 附则	CHAPTER 11 SUPPLEMENTARY PROVISIONS

Implementing Regulations (Chinese) | **Implementing Regulations (English translation)**

第一章 总则	**Chapter 1 GENERAL PROVISIONS**
第一条 根据《中华人民共和国专利法》（以下简称专利法），制定本细则。	Article 1 These Implementing Regulations are enacted in accordance with the *Patent Law of the People's Republic of China* (hereinafter referred to as the *Patent Law*).
第二条 专利法和本细则规定的各种手续，应当以书面形式或者国务院专利行政部门规定的其他形式办理。	Article 2 Any formalities prescribed by the Patent Law and these Implementing Regulations shall be complied with in a written form or in any other form prescribed by the patent administration department under the State Council.
第三条 依照专利法和本细则规定提交的各种文件应当使用中文；国家有统一规定的科技语的，应当采用规范词；外国人名、地名和科技术语没有统一中文译文的，应当注明原文。	Article 3 Any document submitted in accordance with the provisions of the patent law and these Implementing Regulations shall be in Chinese; the standard scientific and technical terms shall be used if there is a prescribed one set forth by the State; where no generally accepted translation in Chinese can be found for a foreign name or scientific or technical term, the one in the original language shall be also indicated.
依照专利法和本细则规定提交的各种证件和证明文件是外文的，国务院专利行政部门认为必要时，可以要求当事人在指定期限内附送中文译文；期满未附送的，视为未提交该证件和证明文件。	Where any certificate or certifying document submitted in accordance with the provisions of the Patent Law and these Implementing Regulations is in a foreign language, the patent administration department under the State Council may, when it deems necessary, request a Chinese translation of the certificate or the certifying document be submitted within a specified time limit; where the translation is not submitted within the specified time limit, the certificate or certifying document shall be deemed not to have been submitted.

Implementing Regulations (Chinese)	Implementing Regulations (English translation)
第四条 向国务院专利行政部门邮寄的各种文件，以寄出的邮戳日为递交日；邮戳日不清晰的，除当事人能够提出证明外，以国务院专利行政部门收到日为递交日。	Article 4 Where any document is sent by mail to the patent administration department under the state council, the date of mailing indicated by the postmark on the envelope shall be deemed to be the date of filing; where the date of mailing indicated by the postmark on the envelope is illegible, the date on which the patent administration department under the State Council receives the document shall be the date of filing, except where the date of mailing is proved by the party concerned.
国务院专利行政部门的各种文件，可以通过邮寄、直接送交或者其他方式送达当事人。当事人委托专利代理机构的，文件送交专利代理机构；未委托专利代理机构的，文件送交请求书中指明的联系人。	Any document of the patent administration department under the State Council may be served by mail, by personal delivery or by other forms. Where any party concerned appoints a patent agency, the document shall be sent to the patent agency; where no patent agency is appointed, the document shall be sent to the contacting person named in the request.
国务院专利行政部门邮寄的各种文件，自文件发出之日起满15日，推定为当事人收到文件之日。	Where any document is sent by mail by the patent administration department under the State Council, the 16th day from the date of mailing shall be presumed to be the date on which the party concerned receives the document.
根据国务院专利行政部门规定应当直接送交的文件，以交付日为送达日。	Where any document is delivered personally in accordance with the provisions of the patent administration department under the State Council, the date of delivery is the date on which the party concerned receives the document.
文件送交地址不清，无法邮寄的，可以通过公告的方式送达当事人。自公告之日起满1个月，该文件视为已经送达。	Where the address of any document is not clear and it cannot be sent by mail, the document may be served by making an announcement. At the expiration of one month from the date of the announcement, the document shall be deemed to have been served.
第五条 专利法和本细则规定的各种期限的第一日不计算在期限内。期限以年或者月计算的，以其最后一月的相应日为期限届满日；该月无相应日的，以该月最后一日为期限届满日；期限届满日是法定休假日的，以休假日后的第一个工作日为期限届满日。	Article 5 The first day of any time limit prescribed in the Patent Law and these Implementing Regulations shall not be counted in the time limit. Where the lime limit is counted by year or by month, it shall expire on the corresponding day of the last month; if there is no corresponding day in that month, the lime limit shall expire on the last day of that month; if a time limit expires on an official holiday, it shall expire on the first working day following that official holiday.

Implementing Regulations (Chinese)	Implementing Regulations (English translation)
第六条 当事人因不可抗拒的事由而延误专利法或者本细则规定的期限或者国务院专利行政部门指定的期限，导致其权利丧失的，自障碍消除之日起2个月内，最迟自期限届满之日起2年内，可以向国务院专利行政部门请求恢复权利。	Article 6 Where a time limit prescribed in the Patent Law or these Implementing Regulations or specified by the patent administration department under the State Council is not observed by a party concerned because of *force majeure*, resulting in loss of his or its rights, he or it may, within two months from the date on which the impediment is removed, at the latest within two years immediately following the expiration of that lime limit request the patent administration department under the State Council to restore his or its rights. Except for circumstances prescribed in preceding paragraph, where a lime limit prescribed in the Patent Law or these Implementing Regulations or specified by the patent administration department under the State Council is not observed by a party concerned because of any other justified reason, resulting in loss of his or its rights, he or it may, within two months from the date of receipt of a notification from the patent administration department under the State Council, request the patent administration department under the State Council to restore his or its rights.
当事人依照本条第一款或者第二款的规定请求恢复权利的，应当提交恢复权利请求书，说明理由，必要时附具有关证明文件，并办理权利丧失前应当办理的相应手续；依照本条第二款的规定请求恢复权利的，还应当缴纳恢复权利请求费。	Where any party concerned requests to restore his or its right according to paragraph one or paragraph two of this Article, he or it shall submit a request for restoration of his or its right, stating the reasons, attaching, if necessary, the relevant certifying documents, and go through the relevant formalities which should have been complied with before the loss of his or its right. Where the party concerned requests for restoration of his or its right according to paragraph two of this Article, he or it shall pay the fee for request for restoration of right.
当事人请求延长国务院专利行政部门指定的期限的，应当在期限届满前，向国务院专利行政部门说明理由并办理有关手续。	Where the party concerned makes a request for an extension of a time limit specified by the patent administration department under the State Council, he or it shall, before the time limit expires, state the reasons to the patent administration department under the State Council and go through the relevant formalities.
本条第一款和第二款的规定不适用专利法第二十四条、第二十九条、第四十二条、第六十八条规定的期限。	The provisions of paragraphs one and two of this Article shall not be applicable to the time limit referred to in Articles 24, 29, 42 and 68 of the Patent Law.

Implementing Regulations (Chinese)	Implementing Regulations (English translation)
第七条 专利申请涉及国防利益需要保密的，由国防专利机构受理并进行审查；国务院专利行政部门受理的专利申请涉及国防利益需要保密的，应当及时移交国防专利机构进行审查。经国防专利机构审查没有发现驳回理由的，由国务院专利行政部门作出授予国防专利权的决定。	Article 7 Where an application for a patent relates to the interests of national defense and is required to be kept secret, the application for patent shall be filed with and examined by the patent department of national defense. Where an application for patent received by the patent administration department under the State Council relates to the interests of national defense and is required to be kept secret, the application shall be promptly forwarded to the patent department of national defense to carry out the examination. Where it is found after examination by the patent department of national defense there is no cause for rejection of the application, the patent administration department under the State Council shall make a decision to grant the patent right concerning national defense.
国务院专利行政部门认为其受理的发明或者实用新型专利申请涉及国防利益以外的国家安全或者重大利益需要保密的，应当及时作出按照保密专利申请处理的决定，并通知申请人。保密专利申请的审查、复审以及保密专利权无效宣告的特殊程序，由国务院专利行政部门规定。	Where the patent administration department under the State Council finds that an application for patent for invention or patent for utility model filed with it relates to national security or other vital interests other than interests concerning national defense and is required to be kept secret, it shall promptly make a decision on handling it as an application for secret patent and notify the applicant accordingly. The special procedures for the examination and reexamination of application for secret patent as well as the invalidation of secret patent shall be provided for by the patent administration department under the State Council.
第八条 专利法第二十条所称在中国完成的发明或者实用新型，是指技术方案的实质性内容在中国境内完成的发明或者实用新型。	Article 8 The invention or utility model developed in China as mentioned in Article 20 of the Patent Law refers to an invention or utility model of which the substantive contents of the technical solution were made within the territory of China.
任何单位或者个人将在中国完成的发明或者实用新型向外国申请专利的，应当按照下列方式之一请求国务院专利行政部门进行保密审查：	Where any unit or individual intends to file an application for patent abroad for the invention or utility model developed in China, it or he shall request, by one of the following manner, the patent administration department under the State Council to conduct confidentiality examination:
（一）直接向外国申请专利或者向有关国外机构提交专利国际申请的，应当事先向国务院专利行政部门提出请求，并详细说明其技术方案；	(1) where any unit or individual intends to file an application for patent directly in a foreign country or an international patent application with a relevant foreign organization, it or he shall file a request for confidentiality examination in advance with the patent administration department under the State Council and describe the related technical solution in detail;

Implementing Regulations (Chinese)	Implementing Regulations (English translation)
（二）向国务院专利行政部门申请专利后拟向外国申请专利或者向有关外国机构提交专利国际申请的，应当在向外国申请专利或者向有关国外机构提交专利国际申请前向国务院专利行政部门提出请求。	(2) where after having filed an application for patent with the patent administration department under the State Council, the applicant intends to file an application for patent in a foreign country or an international patent application with a relevant foreign organization, it or he shall file the request for confidentiality examination with the patent administration department under the State Council before filing of the application for patent in a foreign country or the international patent application with the relevant foreign organization.
向国务院专利行政部门提交专利国际申请的，视为同时提出了保密审查请求。	Where the applicant files an international patent application with the patent administration department under the State Council, it or he shall be deemed to have simultaneously filed the request for confidentiality examination.
第九条 国务院专利行政部门收到依照本细则第八条规定递交的请求后，经过审查认为该发明或者实用新型可能涉及国家安全或者重大利益需要保密的，应当及时向申请人发出保密审查通知；申请人未在其请求递交日起4个月内收到保密审查通知的，可以就该发明或者实用新型向外国申请专利或者向有关国外机构提交专利国际申请。	Article 9 Where the patent administration department under the State Council receives a request filed under Article 8 of these Implementing Regulations and finds, upon examination, that the invention or utility model may relate to the security or vital interest of the State and is required to be kept secret, it shall promptly issue a notification of confidentiality examination to the applicant. If the applicant fails to receive the notification of confidentiality examination within four months from the date of filing its or his request, it or he may file, in respect of the invention or utility model, an application for patent in a foreign country or an international patent application with the relevant foreign organization.
国务院专利行政部门依照前款规定通知进行保密审查的，应当及时作出是否需要保密的决定，并通知申请人。申请人未在其请求递交日起6个月内收到需要保密的决定的，可以就该发明或者实用新型向外国申请专利或者向有关国外机构提交专利国际申请。	Where the patent administration department under the State Council carries out a confidentiality examination in accordance with the notification prescribed in the preceding paragraph, it shall promptly make a decision on whether the invention or utility mode is required to be kept secret and notify the applicant accordingly. If the applicant fails to receive such a decision within six months from the date of filing its or his request, it or he may file, in respect of the invention or utility model, an application for patent in a foreign country or an international patent application with the relevant foreign organization.
第十条 专利法第五条所称违反法律的发明创造，不包括仅其实施为法律所禁止的发明创造。	Article 10 Any invention-creation that is contrary to the laws referred to in Article 5 of the Patent Law shall not include the invention-creation merely because the exploitation of which is prohibited by the laws.

Implementing Regulations (Chinese)	Implementing Regulations (English translation)
第十一条 除专利法第二十八条和第四十二条规定的情形外，专利法所称申请日，有优先权的，指优先权日。 本细则所称申请日，除另有规定的外，是指专利法第二十八条规定的申请日。	Article 11 The date of filing referred to in the Patent Law, except for those referred to in Articles 28 and 42, means the priority date where priority is claimed. The date of filing referred to in these Implementing Regulations, except as otherwise prescribed, means the date of filing prescribed in Article 28 of the Patent Law.
第十二条 专利法第六条所称执行本单位的任务所完成的职务发明创造，是指： （一）在本职工作中作出的发明创造； （二）履行本单位交付的本职工作之外的任务所作出的发明创造； （三）退休、调离原单位后或者劳动、人事关系终止后1年内作出的，与其在原单位承担的本职工作或者原单位分配的任务有关的发明创造。 专利法第六条所称本单位，包括临时工作单位；专利法第六条所称本单位的物质技术条件，是指本单位的资金、设备、零部件、原材料或者不对外公开的技术资料等。	Article 12 "A service invention-creation completed in performing the tasks of the unit to which he belongs" referred to in Article 6 of the Patent Law means any invention-creation made: (1) in the course of performing his own duty; (2) in execution of any task, other than his own duty, which was entrusted to him by the unit to which he belongs; (3) within one year from his retirement, resignation or from termination of his employment or personnel relationship with the unit to which he previously belonged, where the invention-creation relates to his own duty or the other task entrusted to him by the unit to which he previously belonged. "The unit to which he belongs" referred to in Article 6 of the Patent Law includes the unit in which the person concerned is a temporary staff member. "Material and technical means of the unit" referred to in Article 6 of the Patent Law mean the unit's money, equipment, spare parts, raw materials or technical materials which are not disclosed to the public, etc.
第十三条 专利法所称发明人或者设计人，是指对发明创造的实质性特点作出创造性贡献的人。在完成发明创造过程中，只负责组织工作的人、为物质技术条件的利用提供方便的人或者从事其他辅助工作的人，不是发明人或者设计人。	Article 13 "Inventor" or "creator" referred to in the Patent Law means any person who makes creative contributions to the substantive features of an invention-creation. Any person who, during the course of accomplishing the invention-creation, is responsible only for organizational work, or who only offers facilities for making use of material and technical means, or who only takes part in other auxiliary functions, is not the inventor or creator.
第十四条 除依照专利法第十条规定转让专利权外，专利权因其他事由发生转移的，当事人应当凭有关证明文件或者法律文书向国务院专利行政部门办理专利权转移手续。	Article 14 Except for the assignment of the patent right in accordance with Article 10 of the Patent Law, where the patent right is transferred because of any other reason, the person or persons concerned shall,

Implementing Regulations (Chinese)	Implementing Regulations (English translation)
	accompanied by relevant certified documents or legal papers, request the patent administration department under the State Council to register the change in the owner of the patent right.
专利权人与他人订立的专利实施许可合同，应当自合同生效之日起3个月内向国务院专利行政部门备案。	Any license contract for exploitation of a patent which has been concluded by the patentee with others shall, within three months from the date of entry into force of the contract, be submitted to the patent administration department under the State Council for the record.
以专利权出质的，由出质人和质权人共同向国务院专利行政部门办理出质登记。	Where any patent right is pledged, both the pledger and the pledgee shall jointly register the contract of pledge with the patent administration department under the State Council.
第二章 专利的申请	**Chapter 2 Application for Patent**
第十五条 以书面形式申请专利的，应当向国务院专利行政部门提交申请文件一式两份。	Article 15 Anyone who applies for a patent in written form shall file with the patent administration department under the State Council application documents in two copies.
以国务院专利行政部门规定的其他形式申请专利的，应当符合规定的要求。	Anyone who applies for a patent in other forms as provided by the patent administration department under the State Council shall comply with the relevant provisions.
申请人委托专利代理机构向国务院专利行政部门申请专利和办理其他专利事务的，应当同时提交委托书，写明委托权限。	Any applicant who appoints a patent agency for applying for a patent, or for having other patent matters to attend to before the patent administration department under the State Council, shall submit at the same time a power of attorney indicating the scope of the power entrusted.
申请人有2人以上且未委托专利代理机构的，除请求书中另有声明的外，以请求书中指明的第一申请人为代表人。	Where there are two or more applicants and no patent agency is appointed, unless otherwise stated in the request, the applicant named first in the request shall be the representative.
第十六条 发明、实用新型或者外观设计专利申请的请求书应当写明下列事项： （一）发明、实用新型或者外观设计的名称； （二）申请人是中国单位或者个人的，其名称或者姓名、地址、邮政编码、组织机构代码或者居民身份证件号码；申请人是外国人、外国企业或者外国其他组织的，其姓名或者名称、国籍或者注册的国家或者地区；	Article 16 The request of application for patent for invention, utility model or design, shall state the following: (1) the title of the invention, utility model or design; (2) where the applicant is a Chinese unit or individual, its or his title or name, address, postal code, the code of the organization or the citizen identification card number; where the applicant is a foreigner, a foreign enterprise or other foreign organization, his or its name or title, the nationality or the country or region in which the applicant is registered;

Implementing Regulations (Chinese)	Implementing Regulations (English translation)
（三）发明人或者设计人的姓名； （四）申请人委托专利代理机构的，受托机构的名称、机构代码以及该机构指定的专利代理人的姓名、执业证号码、联系电话； （五）要求优先权的，申请人第一次提出专利申请（以下简称在先申请）的申请日、申请号以及原受理机构的名称； （六）申请人或者专利代理机构的签字或者盖章； （七）申请文件清单； （八）附加文件清单； （九）其他需要写明的有关事项。	(3) the name of the inventor or creator; (4) where the applicant has appointed a patent agency, the name of the appointed agency, the agency's organizational code and the name, the professional certificate number and the telephone number of the patent agent assigned by the agency; (5) where the right of priority is claimed, the filing date on which the applicant filed the application the first time (hereinafter referred to as the earlier application), the filing number of the application and the title of the authority with which the application was first filed; (6) the signature or seal of the applicant or the patent agency; (7) a list of the documents constituting the application; (8) a list of the documents appending the application; and (9) any other related matters which needs to be indicated.
第十七条 发明或者实用新型专利申请的说明书应当写明发明或者实用新型的名称，该名称应当与请求书中的名称一致。说明书应当包括下列内容： （一）技术领域：写明要求保护的技术方案所属的技术领域； （二）背景技术：写明对发明或者实用新型的理解、检索、审查有用的背景技术；有可能的，并引证反映这些背景技术的文件； （三）发明内容：写明发明或者实用新型所要解决的技术问题以及解决其技术问题采用的技术方案，并对照现有技术写明发明或者实用新型的有益效果； （四）附图说明：说明书有附图的，对各幅附图作简略说明； （五）具体实施方式：详细写明申请人认为实现发明或者实用新型的优选方式；必要时，举例说明；有附图的，对照附图。	Article 17 The description of an application for a patent for invention or a patent for utility model shall state the title of the invention or utility model, which shall be the same as it appears in the request. The description shall include the following: (1) technical field: specifying the technical field to which the technical solution for which protection is sought pertains; (2) background art: indicating the background art which can be regarded as useful for the understanding, searching and examination of the invention or utility model, and when possible, citing the documents reflecting such art; (3) contents of the invention: disclosing the technical problem the invention or utility model aims to settle and the technical solution adopted to resolve the problem; and stating, with reference to the prior art, the advantageous effects of the invention or utility model; (4) description of figures: briefly describing each figure in the drawings, if any; (5) embodiment of carrying out the invention or utility model: describing in detail the optimally selected mode contemplated by the applicant for carrying out the invention or utility model; where necessary, examples can be listed for explanation, and with reference to the drawings, if any;

Implementing Regulations (Chinese)	Implementing Regulations (English translation)
发明或者实用新型专利申请人应当按照前款规定的方式和顺序撰写说明书，并在说明书每一部分前面写明标题，除非其发明或者实用新型的性质用其他方式或者顺序撰写能节约说明书的篇幅和使他人能够准确理解其发明或者实用新型。	The manner and order referred to in the preceding paragraph shall be followed by the applicant for a patent for invention or a patent for utility model, and each of the parts shall be preceded by a heading, unless, because of the nature of the invention or utility model, a different manner or order would result in a better understanding and a more economical presentation.
发明或者实用新型说明书应当用词规范、语句清楚，并不得使用"如权利要求……所述的……"一类的引用语，也不得使用商业性宣传用语。	The description of the invention or utility model shall use standard terms and be in clear wording, and shall not contain such references to the claims as: "as described in claim . . ." nor shall it contain commercial advertising.
发明专利申请包含一个或者多个核苷酸或者氨基酸序列的，说明书应当包括符合国务院专利行政部门规定的序列表。申请人应当将该序列表作为说明书的一个单独部分提交，并按照国务院专利行政部门的规定提交该序列表的计算机可读形式的副本。	Where an application for a patent for invention contains disclosure of one or more nucleotide and/or amino acid sequences, the description shall contain a sequence listing in compliance with the standard prescribed by the patent administration department under the State Council. The sequence listing shall be submitted as a separate part of the description, and a copy of the said sequence listing in machine-readable form shall also be submitted in accordance with the provisions of the patent administration department under the State Council.
实用新型专利申请说明书应当有表示要求保护的产品的形状、构造或者其结合的附图。	The description of an application for patent for utility model shall include the drawings showing the shape, structure or their combination of the product for which protection is sought
第十八条 发明或者实用新型的几幅附图应当按照"图1，图2，……"顺序编号排列。	Article 18 The figures of drawings of the invention or utility model shall be numbered and arranged in numerical order consecutively as "Figure 1, Figure 2…"
发明或者实用新型说明书文字部分中未提及的附图标记不得在附图中出现，附图中未出现的附图标记不得在说明书文字部分中提及。申请文件中表示同一组成部分的附图标记应当一致。	Reference signs not mentioned in the text of the description of the invention or utility model shall not appear in the drawings. Reference signs not mentioned in the drawings shall not appear in the text of the description. Reference signs for the same composite part shall be used consistently throughout the application document.
附图中除必需的词语外，不应当含有其他注释。	The drawings shall not contain any other explanatory notes, except words which are indispensable.
第十九条 权利要求书应当记载发明或者实用新型的技术特征。	Article 19 The claims shall specify the technical features of the invention or utility model.
权利要求书有几项权利要求的，应当用阿拉伯数字顺序编号。	If there are several claims, they shall be numbered consecutively in Arabic numerals.

Implementing Regulations (Chinese)	Implementing Regulations (English translation)
权利要求书中使用的科技术语应当与说明书中使用的科技术语一致，可以有化学式或者数学式，但是不得有插图。除绝对必要的外，不得使用"如说明书……部分所述"或者"如图……所示"的用语。	The scientific and technical terms used in the claims shall be consistent with that used in the description. The claims may contain chemical or mathematical formulae but no drawings. They shall not, except where absolutely necessary, contain such references to the description or drawings as: "as described in part... of the description", or "as illustrated in Figure... of the drawings".
权利要求中的技术特征可以引用说明书附图中相应的标记，该标记应当放在相应的技术特征后并置于括号内，便于理解权利要求。附图标记不得解释为对权利要求的限制。	The technical features mentioned in the claims may, in order to facilitate the understanding of the claim, make reference to the corresponding reference signs in the drawings. Such reference signs shall follow the corresponding technical features and be placed in parentheses. The reference signs shall not be construed as limiting the claims.
第二十条 权利要求书应当有独立权利要求，也可以有从属权利要求。	Article 20 The claims shall have an independent claim, and may also contain dependent claims.
独立权利要求应当从整体上反映发明或者实用新型的技术方案，记载解决技术问题的必要技术特征。	The independent claim shall outline the technical solution of an invention or utility model and state the essential technical features necessary for the solution of its technical problem.
从属权利要求应当用附加的技术特征，对引用的权利要求作进一步限定。	The dependent claim shall, by additional technical features, further define the claim which it refers to.
第二十一条 发明或者实用新型的独立权利要求应当包括前序部分和特征部分，按照下列规定撰写：	Article 21 An independent claim of an invention or utility model shall contain a preamble portion and a characterizing portion, and be presented in the following form:
（一）前序部分：写明要求保护的发明或者实用新型技术方案的主题名称和发明或者实用新型主题与最接近的现有技术共有的必要技术特征； （二）特征部分：使用"其特征是……"或者类似的用语，写明发明或者实用新型区别于最接近的现有技术的技术特征。这些特征和前序部分写明的特征合在一起，限定发明或者实用新型要求保护的范围。	(1) a preamble portion: indicating the title of the claimed subject matter of the technical solution of the invention or utility model, and those technical features which are necessary for the definition of the claimed subject matter but which, in combination, are part of the most related prior art; (2) a characterizing portion: stating, in such words as "its characterization is" or in similar expressions, the technical features of the invention or utility model, which distinguish it from the most related prior art. Those features, in combination with the features stated in the preamble portion, serve to define the extent of protection of the invention or utility model.

Implementing Regulations (Chinese)	Implementing Regulations (English translation)
发明或者实用新型的性质不适于用前款方式表达的，独立权利要求可以用其他方式撰写。	Where the manner specified in the preceding paragraphs is not appropriate to be followed because of the nature of the invention or utility model, an independent claim may be presented in a different manner.
一项发明或者实用新型应当只有一个独立权利要求，并写在同一发明或者实用新型的从属权利要求之前。	An invention or utility model shall have only one independent claim, which shall precede all the dependent claims relating to the same invention or utility model.
第二十二条 发明或者实用新型的从属权利要求应当包括引用部分和限定部分，按照下列规定撰写： （一）引用部分：写明引用的权利要求的编号及其主题名称； （二）限定部分：写明发明或者实用新型附加的技术特征。	Article 22 Any dependent claim of an invention or utility model shall contain a reference portion and a characterizing portion, and be presented in the following manner: (1) a reference portion: indicating the serial number(s) of the claim(s) referred to, and the title of the subject matter; (2) a characterizing portion: stating the additional technical features of the invention or utility model.
从属权利要求只能引用在前的权利要求。引用两项以上权利要求的多项从属权利要求，只能以择一方式引用在前的权利要求，并不得作为另一项多项从属权利要求的基础。	Any dependent claim shall only refer to the preceding claim or claims. Any multiple dependent claims, which refers to two or more claims, shall refer to the preceding claims in the alternative only, and shall not serve as a basis for any other multiple dependent claims.
第二十三条 说明书摘要应当写明发明或者实用新型专利申请所公开内容的概要，即写明发明或者实用新型的名称和所属技术领域，并清楚地反映所要解决的技术问题、解决该问题的技术方案的要点以及主要用途。	Article 23 The abstract shall consist of a summary of the disclosure as contained in the application for patent for invention or utility model. The summary shall indicate the title of the invention or utility model, and the technical field to which the invention or utility model pertains, and shall be drafted in a way which allows the clear understanding of the technical problem, the gist of the technical solution to that problem, and the principal use or uses of the invention or utility model.
说明书摘要可以包含最能说明发明的化学式；有附图的专利申请，还应当提供一幅最能说明该发明或者实用新型技术特征的附图。附图的大小及清晰度应当保证在该图缩小到4厘米×6厘米时，仍能清晰地分辨出图中的各个细节。摘要文字部分不得超过300个字。摘要中不得使用商业性宣传用语。	The abstract may contain the chemical formula which best characterizes the invention. In an application for a patent which contains drawings, the applicant shall provide a figure which best characterizes the technical features of the invention or utility model. The scale and the distinctness of the figure shall be as such that a reproduction with a linear reduction in size to 4cm x 6cm would still enable all details to be clearly distinguished. The whole text of the abstract shall contain not more than 300 words. There shall be no commercial advertising in the abstract.

Implementing Regulations (Chinese)	Implementing Regulations (English translation)
第二十四条 申请专利的发明涉及新的生物材料，该生物材料公众不能得到，并且对该生物材料的说明不足以使所属领域的技术人员实施其发明的，除应当符合专利法和本细则的有关规定外，申请人还应当办理下列手续：	Article 24 Where an invention for which a patent is applied for concerns a new biological material which is not available to the public and which cannot be described in the application in such a manner as to enable the invention to be carried out by a person skilled in the art, the applicant shall, in addition to the other requirements provided for in the Patent Law and these Implementing Regulations, go through the following formalities:
（一）在申请日前或者最迟在申请日（有优先权的，指优先权日），将该生物材料的样品提交国务院专利行政部门认可的保藏单位保藏，并在申请时或者最迟自申请日起4个月内提交保藏单位出具的保藏证明和存活证明；期满未提交证明的，该样品视为未提交保藏； （二）在申请文件中，提供有关该生物材料特征的资料； （三）涉及生物材料样品保藏的专利申请应当在请求书和说明书中写明该生物材料的分类命名（注明拉丁文名称）、保藏该生物材料样品的单位名称、地址、保藏日期和保藏编号；申请时未写明的，应当自申请日起4个月内补正；期满未补正的，视为未提交保藏。	(1) depositing a sample of the biological material with a depositary institution designated by the patent administration department under the State Council before, or at the latest, on the date of filing (or the priority date where priority is claimed), and submit at the time of filing or at the latest, within four months from the date of filing, a receipt of deposit and the viability proof from the depositary institution; where they are not submitted within the specified time limit, the sample of the biological material shall be deemed not to have been deposited; (2) giving in the application document relevant information of the characteristics of the biological material; (3) indicating, where the application relates to the deposit of a sample of the biological material, in the request and the description the scientific name (with its Latin name) and the title and address of the depositary institution, the date on which the sample of the biological material was deposited and the accession number of the deposit; where, at the time of filing, they are not indicated, they shall be supplied within four months from the date of filing; where after the expiration of the time limit they are not supplied, the sample of the biological material shall be deemed not to have been deposited.
第二十五条 发明专利申请人依照本细则第二十四条的规定保藏生物材料样品的，在发明专利申请公布后，任何单位或者个人需要将该专利申请所涉及的生物材料作为实验目的使用的，应当向国务院专利行政部门提出请求，并写明下列事项：	Article 25 Where the applicant for a patent for invention has deposited a sample of the biological material in accordance with the provisions of Article 24 of these Implementing Regulations, and after the application for patent for invention is published, any unit or individual that intends to make use of the biological material to which the application relates, for the purpose of experiment, shall make a request to the patent administration department under the State Council, containing the following items:
（一）请求人的姓名或者名称和地址；	(1) the title or name and address of the requesting person;

Implementing Regulations (Chinese)	Implementing Regulations (English translation)
（二）不向其他任何人提供该生物材料的保证； （三）在授予专利权前，只作为实验目的使用的保证。	(2) an undertaking not to make the biological material available to any other person; (3) an undertaking to use the biological material for experimental purpose only before the grant of the patent right.
第二十六条 专利法所称遗传资源，是指取自人体、动物、植物或者微生物等含有遗传功能单位并具有实际或者潜在价值的材料；专利法所称依赖遗传资源完成的发明创造，是指利用了遗传资源的遗传功能完成的发明创造。 就依赖遗传资源完成的发明创造申请专利的，申请人应当在请求书中予以说明，并填写国务院专利行政部门制定的表格。	Article 26 The genetic resources referred to in the Patent Law mean the material obtained from such as human body, animal, plant, or microorganism which contains functional units of heredity and is of actual or potential value. The invention-creation is developed relying on the genetic resources referred to in the Patent Law means that the invention-creation is developed relying on the use of the heredity function of the genetic resources. Where an application for patent is filed for an invention-creation the development of which relies on the use of genetic resources, the applicant shall state that fact in the request, and fill in the forms provided by the patent administration department under the State Council.
第二十七条 申请人请求保护色彩的，应当提交彩色图片或者照片。 申请人应当就每件外观设计产品所需要保护的内容提交有关图片或者照片。	Article 27 Where an application for a patent for design seeking protection of colours is filed, drawings or photographs in colour shall be submitted. The applicant shall, in respect of the subject matter of the product incorporating the design which is in need of protection, submit the relevant drawings or photographs.
第二十八条 外观设计的简要说明应当写明外观设计产品的名称、用途，外观设计的设计要点，并指定一幅最能表明设计要点的图片或者照片。省略视图或者请求保护色彩的，应当在简要说明中写明。 对同一产品的多项相似外观设计提出一件外观设计专利申请的，应当在简要说明中指定其中一项作为基本设计。 简要说明不得使用商业性宣传用语，也不能用来说明产品的性能。	Article 28 The brief explanation of application for patent for design shall indicate the title and the use of the product incorporating the design, the essential feature of the design, and designate a drawing or photograph capable of best showing the essential feature of the design. Where a view of the product incorporating the design is omitted or where concurrent protection for colour is claimed, it shall be indicated in the brief explanation. Where an application for patent for design is filed for two or more similar designs incorporated in the same product, one of these designs shall be indicated as the main design in the brief explanation. The brief explanation shall not contain any commercial advertising and shall not be used to indicate the function of the product.

Implementing Regulations (Chinese)	Implementing Regulations (English translation)
第二十九条 国务院专利行政部门认为必要时，可以要求外观设计专利申请人提交使用外观设计的产品样品或者模型。样品或者模型的体积不得超过30厘米×30厘米×30厘米，重量不得超过15公斤。易腐、易损或者危险品不得作为样品或者模型提交。	Article 29 Where the patent administration department under the State Council deems necessary, it may require the applicant for a patent for design to submit a sample or model of the product incorporating the design. The volume of the sample or model submitted shall not exceed 30cm x 30cm x 30cm, and its weight shall not surpass 15 kilograms. Articles that are easy to get rotten or broken or articles that are dangerous shall not be submitted as sample or model.
第三十条 专利法第二十四条第（一）项所称中国政府承认的国际展览会，是指国际展览会公约规定的在国际展览局注册或者由其认可的国际展览会。	Article 30 The international exhibition recognized by the Chinese Government referred to in Article 24, subparagraph (1) of the Patent Law means the international exhibition that is registered with or recognized by the International Exhibitions Bureau as stipulated by the International Exhibitions Convention.
专利法第二十四条第（二）项所称学术会议或者技术会议，是指国务院有关主管部门或者全国性学术团体组织召开的学术会议或者技术会议。	The academic or technological conference referred to in Article 24, subparagraph (2) of the Patent Law means any academic or technological meeting organized by a competent department concerned of the State Council or by a national academic or technological association.
申请专利的发明创造有专利法第二十四条第（一）项或者第（二）项所列情形的，申请人应当在提出专利申请时声明，并自申请日起2个月内提交有关国际展览会或者学术会议、技术会议的组织单位出具的有关发明创造已经展出或者发表，以及展出或者发表日期的证明文件。	Where any invention-creation for which a patent is applied falls under the provisions of Article 24, subparagraph (I) or (2) of the Patent Law, the applicant shall, when filing the application, make a declaration and, within a time limit of two months from the date of filing, submit certifying documents issued by the unit which organized the international exhibition or academic or technological meeting, stating the fact that the invention-creation was exhibited or published and with the date of its exhibition or publication.
申请专利的发明创造有专利法第二十四条第（三）项所列情形的，国务院专利行政部门认为必要时，可以要求申请人在指定期限内提交证明文件。	Where any invention-creation for which a patent is applied falls under the provisions of Article 24, subparagraph (3) of the Patent Law, the patent administration department under the State Council may, when it deems necessary, require the applicant to submit the relevant certifying documents within the specified time limit.
申请人未依照本条第三款的规定提出声明和提交证明文件的，或者未依照本条第四款的规定在指定期限内提交证明文件的，其申请不适用专利法第二十四条的规定。	Where the applicant fails to make a declaration and submit certifying documents as required in paragraph three of this Article, or fails to submit certifying documents within the specified time limit as required in paragraph four of this Article, the provisions of Article 24 of the Patent Law shall not apply to the application.

Implementing Regulations (Chinese)	Implementing Regulations (English translation)
第三十一条 申请人依照专利法第三十条的规定要求外国优先权的，申请人提交的在先申请文件副本应当经原受理机构证明。依照国务院专利行政部门与该受理机构签订的协议，国务院专利行政部门通过电子交换等途径获得在先申请文件副本的，视为申请人提交了经该受理机构证明的在先申请文件副本。要求本国优先权，申请人在请求书中写明在先申请的申请日和申请号的，视为提交了在先申请文件副本。	Article 31 Where an applicant claims the right of foreign priority in accordance with the provisions of Article 30 of the Patent Law, the copy of the earlier application documents submitted by the applicant shall be certified by the authority with which the earlier application was filed. Where, in accordance with the agreement between the patent administration department under the State Council and the said authority, the patent administration department under the State Council obtains a copy of the earlier application documents through electronic transmission or in any other manner, the copy of the earlier application documents certified by the authority shall be deemed to have been submitted by the applicant. Where the right of domestic priority is claimed, if the date of filing and the filing number of the earlier application are indicated in the request by the applicant, the copy of the earlier application documents shall be deemed to have been submitted.
要求优先权，但请求书中漏写或者错写在先申请的申请日、申请号和原受理机构名称中的一项或者两项内容的，国务院专利行政部门应当通知申请人在指定期限内补正；期满未补正的，视为未要求优先权。	Where such one or two items as the date of filing, the filing number of the earlier application or the title of the authority with which the earlier application was filed are missing or incorrect in the request when claiming for right of priority, the patent administration department under the State Council shall notify the applicant to make rectification within the specified time limit. Where the applicant fails to make the rectification within the time limit, the right of priority shall be deemed not to have been claimed.
要求优先权的申请人的姓名或者名称与在先申请文件副本中记载的申请人姓名或者名称不一致的，应当提交优先权转让证明材料，未提交该证明材料的，视为未要求优先权。	Where the name or title of the applicant who claims the right of priority is not the same as the one recorded in the copy of the earlier application, the applicant shall submit document certifying the assignment of right of priority. If no such document is submitted, the right of priority shall be deemed not to have been claimed.
外观设计专利申请的申请人要求外国优先权，其在先申请未包括对外观设计的简要说明，申请人按照本细则第二十八条规定提交的简要说明未超出在先申请文件的图片或者照片表示的范围的，不影响其享有优先权。	Where any applicant claims a right of foreign priority for patent application for design, and no brief explanation of the design was contained in the earlier application, he or it will not be adversely affected as for enjoying the right of priority if the brief explanation submitted by the applicant in accordance with the provisions of Article 28 of these Regulations does not go beyond the scope as shown in the drawings or photographs of the earlier application.

Implementing Regulations (Chinese)	Implementing Regulations (English translation)
第三十二条 申请人在一件专利申请中，可以要求一项或者多项优先权；要求多项优先权的，该申请的优先权期限从最早的优先权日起计算。 申请人要求本国优先权，在先申请是发明专利申请的，可以就相同主题提出发明或者实用新型专利申请；在先申请是实用新型专利申请的，可以就相同主题提出实用新型或者发明专利申请。但是，提出后一申请时，在先申请的主题有下列情形之一的，不得作为要求本国优先权的基础： （一）已经要求外国优先权或者本国优先权的； （二）已经被授予专利权的； （三）属于按照规定提出的分案申请的。 申请人要求本国优先权的，其在先申请自后一申请提出之日起即视为撤回。	Article 32 An applicant may claim one or more priorities for an application for a patent; where multiple priorities are claimed, the priority period for the application shall be calculated from the earliest priority date. Where an applicant claims the right of domestic priority, if the earlier application is one for a patent for invention, he or it may file an application for a patent for invention or utility model for the same subject matter; if the earlier application is one for a patent for utility model, he or it may file an application for a patent for utility model or invention for the same subject matter. However, when the later application is filed, if the subject matter of the earlier application falls under any of the following, it may not be taken as the basis for claiming domestic priority: (1) where the applicant has claimed foreign or domestic priority; (2) where it has been granted a patent right; (3) where it is the subject matter of a divisional application filed as prescribed. Where the domestic priority is claimed, the earlier application shall be deemed to be withdrawn from the date on which the later application is filed.
第三十三条 在中国没有经常居所或者营业所的申请人，申请专利或者要求外国优先权的，国务院专利行政部门认为必要时，可以要求其提供下列文件： （一）申请人是个人的，其国籍证明； （二）申请人是企业或者其他组织的，其注册的国家或者地区的证明文件； （三）申请人的所属国，承认中国单位和个人可以按照该国国民的同等条件，在该国享有专利权、优先权和其他与专利有关的权利的证明文件。	Article 33 Where an application for a patent is filed or the right of foreign priority is claimed by an applicant having no habitual residence or business office in China, the patent administration department under the State Council may, when it deems necessary, require the applicant to submit the following documents: (1) if the applicant is an individual, a certificate concerning his nationality; (2) if the applicant is an enterprise or other organization, a document certifying the country or region in which it is registered; (3) a document certifying that the country, to which the foreigner, foreign enterprise or other foreign organization belongs, recognizes that Chinese units and individuals are, under the same conditions as those applied to its nationals, entitled to the patent right, the right of priority and other related rights in that country.
第三十四条 依照专利法第三十一条第一款规定，可以作为一件专利申请提出的属于一个总的发明构思的两项以上的发明或者实用新型，	Article 34 Two or more inventions or utility models belonging to a single general inventive concept which may be filed as one application in accordance with the

Implementing Regulations (Chinese)	Implementing Regulations (English translation)
应当在技术上相互关联，包含一个或者多个相同或者相应的特定技术特征，其中特定技术特征是指每一项发明或者实用新型作为整体，对现有技术作出贡献的技术特征。	provisions of Article 31, paragraph one of the Patent Law shall be technically interrelated and contain one or more of the same or corresponding special technical features. The expression "special technical features" shall mean those technical features that define a contribution which each of those inventions or utility models, considered as a whole, makes over the prior art.
第三十五条 依照专利法第三十一条第二款规定，将同一产品的多项相似外观设计作为一件申请提出的，对该产品的其他设计应当与简要说明中指定的基本设计相似。一件外观设计专利申请中的相似外观设计不得超过10项。	Article 35 Where two or more similar designs of the same product are filed in one application in accordance with the provisions of Article 31, paragraph two of the Patent Law, the other designs of the product shall be similar to the main design indicated in the brief explanation. The number of similar designs contained in an application for patent for design shall not exceed 10.
专利法第三十一条第二款所称同一类别并且成套出售或者使用的产品的两项以上外观设计，是指各产品属于分类表中同一大类，习惯上同时出售或者同时使用，而且各产品的外观设计具有相同的设计构思。	The two or more designs belonging to the same class and sold or used in sets as referred to in Article 31, paragraph two of the Patent Law mean that, each product incorporating the design belongs to the same class in the classification of products and is customarily sold or used at the same time, and the designs incorporated in each product have the same concept of design.
将两项以上外观设计作为一件申请提出的，应当将各项外观设计的顺序编号标注在每件外观设计产品各幅图片或者照片的名称之前。	Where two or more designs are filed as one application, they shall be numbered consecutively and the numbers shall precede the titles of the drawings or photographs of the product incorporating the design.
第三十六条 申请人撤回专利申请的，应当向国务院专利行政部门提出声明，写明发明创造的名称、申请号和申请日。	Article 36 When withdrawing an application for a patent, the applicant shall submit to the patent administration department under the State Council a declaration to that effect stating the title of the invention-creation, the filing number and the date of filing.
撤回专利申请的声明在国务院专利行政部门作好公布专利申请文件的印刷准备工作后提出的，申请文件仍予公布；但是，撤回专利申请的声明应当在以后出版的专利公报上予以公告。	Where a declaration to withdraw an application for a patent is submitted after the preparations for the publication of the application document has been completed by the patent administration department under the State Council, the application document shall be published as scheduled. However, the declaration withdrawing the application for patent shall be published in the next issue of the Patent Gazette.

Implementing Regulations (Chinese)	Implementing Regulations (English translation)
第三章 专利申请的审查和批准	**Chapter 3 Examination and Approval of Application for Patent**
第三十七条 在初步审查、实质审查、复审和无效宣告程序中，实施审查和审理的人员有下列情形之一的，应当自行回避，当事人或者其他利害关系人可以要求其回避： （一）是当事人或者其代理人的近亲属的； （二）与专利申请或者专利权有利害关系的； （三）与当事人或者其代理人有其他关系，可能影响公正审查和审理的； （四）专利复审委员会成员曾参与原申请的审查的。	Article 37 Where any of the following events occurs, a person who makes examination or hears a case in the procedures of preliminary examination, examination as to substance, reexamination or invalidation shall, on his own initiative or upon the request of the parties concerned or any other interested person, be excluded from exercising his function: (1) where he is a close relative of the party concerned or the agent of the party concerned; (2) where he has an interest in the application for patent or the patent right; (3) where he has any other kinds of relations with the party concerned or with the agent of the party concerned that may influence impartial examination and hearing; (4) where a member of the Patent Reexamination Board who has taken part in the examination of the same application.
第三十八条 国务院专利行政部门收到发明或者实用新型专利申请的请求书、说明书（实用新型必须包括附图）和权利要求书，或者外观设计专利申请的请求书、外观设计的图片或者照片和简要说明后，应当明确申请日、给予申请号，并通知申请人。	Article 38 Upon the receipt of an application for a patent for invention or utility model consisting of a request, a description (drawings must be included in an application for utility model) and one or more claims, or an application for a patent for design consisting of a request, one or more drawings or photographs showing the design and a brief explanation, the patent administration department under the State Council shall accord the date of filing, issue a filing number, and notify the applicant.
第三十九条 专利申请文件有下列情形之一的，国务院专利行政部门不予受理，并通知申请人： （一）发明或者实用新型专利申请缺少请求书、说明书（实用新型无附图）或者权利要求书的，或者外观设计专利申请缺少请求书、图片或者照片、简要说明的； （二）未使用中文的；	Article 39 In any of the following circumstances, the patent administration department under the State Council shall refuse to accept the application and notify the applicant accordingly: (1) where the application for a patent for invention or utility model does not contain a request, a description (the description of utility model does not contain drawings) or claims, or the application for a patent for design does not contain a request, drawings or photographs, or a brief explanation; (2) where the application is not written in Chinese;

Implementing Regulations (Chinese)	Implementing Regulations (English translation)
（三）不符合本细则第一百二十一条第一款规定的； （四）请求书中缺少申请人姓名或者名称，或者缺少地址的； （五）明显不符合专利法第十八条或者第十九条第一款的规定的； （六）专利申请类别（发明、实用新型或者外观设计）不明确或者难以确定的。	(3) where the application is not in conformity with the provisions of Article 121, paragraph one of these Implementing Regulations; (4) where the request does not contain the name or title, or address of the applicant; (5) where the application is obviously not in conformity with the provisions of Article 18, or of Article 19, paragraph one of the Patent Law; (6) where the kind of protection (patent for invention, utility model or design) of the application for a patent is not clear and definite or cannot be ascertained.
第四十条 说明书中写有对附图的说明但无附图或者缺少部分附图的，申请人应当在国务院专利行政部门指定的期限内补交附图或者声明取消对附图的说明。申请人补交附图的，以向国务院专利行政部门提交或者邮寄附图之日为申请日；取消对附图的说明的，保留原申请日。	Article 40 Where the description states that it contains explanatory notes to the drawings but the drawings or part of them are missing, the applicant shall, within the time limit specified by the patent administration department under the State Council, either furnish the drawings or make a declaration for the deletion of the explanatory notes to the drawings. If the drawings are submitted later, the date of their delivery at, or mailing to, the patent administration department under the State Council shall be the date of filing of the application; if the explanatory notes to the drawings are to be deleted, the initial date of filing shall be retained.
第四十一条 两个以上的申请人同日（指申请日；有优先权的，指优先权日）分别就同样的发明创造申请专利的，应当在收到国务院专利行政部门的通知后自行协商确定申请人。 同一申请人在同日（指申请日）对同样的发明创造既申请实用新型专利又申请发明专利的，应当在申请时分别说明对同样的发明创造已申请了另一专利；未作说明的，依照专利法第九条第一款关于同样的发明创造只能授予一项专利权的规定处理。	Article 41 Two or more applicants who respectively file, on the same day (means the date of filing or the priority date where priority is claimed), applications for patent for the identical invention-creation, shall, after receipt of a notification from the patent administration department under the State Council, hold consultations among themselves to decide the person or persons who shall be entitled to file the application. Where an applicant files on the same day (means the date of filing) applications for both a patent for utility model and a patent for invention for the identical invention-creation, he or it shall state respectively upon filing the application that another patent application for the identical invention-creation has been filed by him or it. If the applicant fails to do so, the issue shall be handled according to the provisions of Article 9, paragraph one of the Patent Law, only one patent right shall be granted for any identical invention-creation.

国务院专利行政部门公告授予实用新型专利权，应当公告申请人已依照本条第二款的规定同时申请了发明专利的说明。

Where the patent administration department under the State Council makes an announcement of the grant of patent for utility model, the statement of the applicant in accordance with the provision of paragraph two of this Article that he has simultaneously filed an application for a patent for invention shall be announced.

发明专利申请经审查没有发现驳回理由，国务院专利行政部门应当通知申请人在规定期限内声明放弃实用新型专利权。申请人声明放弃的，国务院专利行政部门应当作出授予发明专利权的决定，并在公告授予发明专利权时一并公告申请人放弃实用新型专利权声明。申请人不同意放弃的，国务院专利行政部门应当驳回该发明专利申请；申请人期满未答复的，视为撤回该发明专利申请。

Where it is found after examination that there is no cause for rejection of the application for patent for invention, the patent administration department under the State Council shall notify the applicant to declare, within the specified time limit, the abandonment of his or its patent for utility model. If the applicant so declares, the patent administration department under the State Council shall make the decision to grant a patent for invention, and announce at the same time both the grant of the patent for invention and the declaration of the applicant to abandon his or its patent for utility model. If the applicant refuses to abandon his or its patent for utility model, the patent administration department under the State Council shall reject the application for patent for invention. If the applicant fails to respond within the time limit, the application for patent for invention shall be deemed to have been withdrawn.

实用新型专利权自公告授予发明专利权之日起终止。

The patent right for utility model ceases from the date of the announcement of grant of the patent for invention.

第四十二条
一件专利申请包括两项以上发明、实用新型或者外观设计的，申请人可以在本细则第五十四条第一款规定的期限届满前，向国务院专利行政部门提出分案申请；但是，专利申请已经被驳回、撤回或者视为撤回的，不能提出分案申请。

Article 42
Where an application for a patent contains two or more inventions, utility models or designs, the applicant may, before the expiration of the time limit provided for in Article 54, paragraph one of these Implementing Regulations, submit to the patent administration department under the State Council a divisional application. However, where an application for patent has been rejected, withdrawn or is deemed to have been withdrawn, no divisional application can be filed.

国务院专利行政部门认为一件专利申请不符合专利法第三十一条和本细则第三十四条或者第三十五条的规定的，应当通知申请人在指定期限内对其申请进行修改；申请人期满未答复的，该申请视为撤回。

If the patent administration department under the State Council finds that an application for a patent is not in conformity with the provisions of Article 31 of the Patent Law or of Article 34 or 35 of these Implementing Regulations, it shall invite the applicant to amend the application within a specified time limit; if the applicant fails to make any response after the expiration of the specified time limit, the application shall be deemed to have been withdrawn.

Implementing Regulations (Chinese)	Implementing Regulations (English translation)
分案的申请不得改变原申请的类别。	The divisional application must not change the kind of protection of the initial application.
第四十三条 依照本细则第四十二条规定提出的分案申请，可以保留原申请日，享有优先权的，可以保留优先权日，但是不得超出原申请记载的范围。	Article 43 A divisional application filed in accordance with the provisions of Article 42 of these Implementing Regulations shall be entitled to the filing date and, if priority is claimed, the priority date of the initial application, provided that the divisional application does not go beyond the scope of disclosure contained in the initial application.
分案申请应当依照专利法及本细则的规定办理有关手续。	The divisional application shall go through all the formalities in accordance with the provisions of the Patent Law and these Implementing Regulations.
分案申请的请求书中应当写明原申请的申请号和申请日。提交分案申请时，申请人应当提交原申请文件副本；原申请享有优先权的，并应当提交原申请的优先权文件副本。	The filing number and the date of filing of the initial application shall be indicated in the request of the divisional application. When the divisional application is filed, it shall be accompanied by a copy of the initial application; if priority is claimed for the initial application, a copy of the priority document of the initial application shall also be submitted.
第四十四条 专利法第三十四条和第四十条所称初步审查，是指审查专利申请是否具备专利法第二十六条或者第二十七条规定的文件和其他必要的文件，这些文件是否符合规定的格式，并审查下列各项：	Article 44 "Preliminary examination" referred to in Articles 34 and 40 of the Patent Law means the check of an application for a patent to see whether or not it contains the documents as provided for in Article 26 or 27 of the Patent Law and other necessary documents, and whether or not those documents are in the prescribed form; such check shall also include the following:
（一）发明专利申请是否明显属于专利法第五条、第二十五条规定的情形，是否不符合专利法第十八条、第十九条第一款、第二十条第一款或者本细则第十六条、第二十六条第二款的规定，是否明显不符合专利法第二条第二款、第二十六条第五款、第三十一条第一款、第三十三条或者本细则第十七条至第二十一条的规定； （二）实用新型专利申请是否明显属于专利法第五条、第二十五条规定的情形，是否不符合专利法第十八条、第十九条第一款、第二十条第一款或者本细则第十六条至第十九条、第二十一条至第二十三条的规定，是否明显不符合专利法第二条第三款、第二十二条第二款、第四款、第二十六条第三款、第四款、第三十一条第一	(1) whether or not any application for a patent for invention obviously falls under Article 5 or 25 of the Patent Law, or is not in conformity with the provisions of Article 18, Article 19, paragraph one or Article 20, paragraph one of the Patent Law or Article 16 or Article 26, paragraph two of these Implementing Regulations, or is obviously not in conformity with the provisions of Article 2, paragraph two, Article 26, paragraph five, Article 31, paragraph one, or Article 33 of the Patent Law, or of Article 17 to 21 of these Implementing Regulations; (2) whether or not any application for a patent for utility model obviously falls under Article 5 or 25 of the Patent Law, or is not in conformity with the provisions of Article 18, Article 19, paragraph one or Article 20, paragraph one of the Patent Law or Articles 16 to 19 or Articles 21 to 23 of these Implementing Regulations, or is obviously not in

Implementing Regulations (Chinese)	Implementing Regulations (English translation)
款、第三十三条或者本细则第二十条、第四十三条第一款的规定，是否依照专利法第九条规定不能取得专利权； （三）外观设计专利申请是否明显属于专利法第五条、第二十五条第一款第（六）项规定的情形，是否不符合专利法第十八条、第十九条第一款或者本细则第十六条、第二十七条、第二十八条的规定，是否明显不符合专利法第二条第四款、第二十三条第一款、第二十七条第二款、第三十一条第二款、第三十三条或者本细则第四十三条第一款的规定，是否依照专利法第九条规定不能取得专利权； （四）申请文件是否符合本细则第二条、第三条第一款的规定。	conformity with the provisions of Article 2, paragraph three, Article 22, paragraph two or four, Article 26, paragraph three or four, or of Article 31, paragraph one, or of Article 33 of the Patent Law, or of Article 20 or Article 43, paragraph one of these Implementing Regulations, or is not entitled to a patent right in accordance with the provisions of Article 9 of the Patent Law; (3) whether or not any application for a patent for design obviously falls under Article 5 or Article 25, paragraph one (6) of the Patent Law, or is not in conformity with the provisions of Article 18, Article 19, paragraph one of the Patent Law, or of Article 16, Article 27 or Article 28 of these Implementing Regulations, or is obviously not in conformity with the provisions of Article 2, paragraph four, Article 23, paragraph one, Article 27, paragraph two, Article 31, paragraph two, or of Article 33 of the Patent Law, or of Article 43, paragraph one of these Implementing Regulations, or is not entitled to a patent right in accordance with the provisions of Article 9 of the Patent Law; (4) whether or not any application document is in conformity with the provisions of Article 2 or Article 3, paragraph one of these Implementing Regulations.
国务院专利行政部门应当将审查意见通知申请人，要求其在指定期限内陈述意见或者补正；申请人期满未答复的，其申请视为撤回。申请人陈述意见或者补正后，国务院专利行政部门仍然认为不符合前款所列各项规定的，应当予以驳回。	The patent administration department under the State Council shall notify the applicant of its opinions after checking his or its application and invite him or it to state his or its observations or to rectify his or its application within the specified time limit. If the applicant fails to make any response within the specified time limit, the application shall be deemed to have been withdrawn. Where, after the applicant has made his or its observations or the corrections, the patent administration department under the State Council still finds that the application is not in conformity with the provisions of the Articles cited in the preceding subparagraphs, the application shall be rejected.
第四十五条 除专利申请文件外，申请人向国务院专利行政部门提交的与专利申请有关的其他文件有下列情形之一的，视为未提交： （一）未使用规定的格式或者填写不符合规定的；	Article 45 Apart from the application for patent, any document relating to the patent application which is submitted to the patent administration department under the State Council, shall, in any of the following circumstances, be deemed not to have been submitted: (1) where the document is not presented in the prescribed form or the indications therein are not in conformity with the prescriptions;

Implementing Regulations (Chinese)	Implementing Regulations (English translation)
（二）未按照规定提交证明材料的。 国务院专利行政部门应当将视为未提交的审查意见通知申请人。	(2) where no certifying document is submitted as prescribed. The patent administration department under the State Council shall notify the applicant of its opinion after checking that the document is deemed not to have been submitted.
第四十六条 申请人请求早日公布其发明专利申请的，应当向国务院专利行政部门声明。国务院专利行政部门对该申请进行初步审查后，除予以驳回的外，应当立即将申请予以公布。	Article 46 Where the applicant requests an earlier publication of his or its application for a patent for invention, a statement shall be made to the patent administration department under the State Council. The patent administration department under the State Council shall, after preliminary examination of the application, publish it immediately, unless it is to be rejected.
第四十七条 申请人写明使用外观设计的产品及其所属类别的，应当使用国务院专利行政部门公布的外观设计产品分类表。未写明使用外观设计的产品所属类别或者所写的类别不确切的，国务院专利行政部门可以予以补充或者修改。	Article 47 The applicant shall, when indicating the product incorporating the design and the class to which that product belongs, refer to the classification of products for designs published by the patent administration department under the State Council. Where no indication, or an incorrect indication, of the class to which the product incorporating the design belongs is made, the patent administration department under the State Council shall supply the indication or correct it.
第四十八条 自发明专利申请公布之日起至公告授予专利权之日止，任何人均可以对不符合专利法规定的专利申请向国务院专利行政部门提出意见，并说明理由。	Article 48 Any person may, from the date of publication of an application of a patent for invention till the date of announcing the grant of the patent right, submit to the patent administration department under the State Council his observations, with reasons, on the application which is not in conformity with the provisions of the Patent Law.
第四十九条 发明专利申请人因有正当理由无法提交专利法第三十六条规定的检索资料或者审查结果资料的，应当向国务院专利行政部门声明，并在得到有关资料后补交。	Article 49 Where the applicant for a patent for invention cannot furnish, for justified reasons, the documents concerning any search or results of any examination specified in Article 36 of the Patent Law, he or it shall make a statement to the patent administration department under the State Council and submit them when the said documents are available.

Implementing Regulations (Chinese)	Implementing Regulations (English translation)
第五十条 国务院专利行政部门依照专利法第三十五条第二款的规定对专利申请自行进行审查时，应当通知申请人。	Article 50 The patent administration department under the State Council shall, when proceeding on its own initiative to examine an application for a patent in accordance with the provisions of Article 35, paragraph two of the Patent Law, notify the applicant accordingly.
第五十一条 发明专利申请人在提出实质审查请求时以及在收到国务院专利行政部门发出的发明专利申请进入实质审查阶段通知书之日起的3个月内，可以对发明专利申请主动提出修改。	Article 51 At the time when a request for examination as to substance is made, and when, within the time limit of three months after the receipt of the notification of the patent administration department under the State Council on the entry into examination as to substance of the application, the applicant for a patent for invention may amend the application for a patent for invention on his or its own initiative.
实用新型或者外观设计专利申请人自申请日起2个月内，可以对实用新型或者外观设计专利申请主动提出修改。	Within two months from the date of filing, the applicant for a patent for utility model or design may amend the application for a patent for utility model or design on its or his own initiative.
申请人在收到国务院专利行政部门发出的审查意见通知书后对专利申请文件进行修改的，应当针对通知书指出的缺陷进行修改。	Where the applicant amends the application after receiving the notification of opinions of the examination as to substance of the patent administration department under the State Council, he or it shall make the amendment directed to the defects pointed out by the notification.
国务院专利行政部门可以自行修改专利申请文件中文字和符号的明显错误。国务院专利行政部门自行修改的，应当通知申请人。	The patent administration department under the State Council may, on its own initiative, correct the obvious clerical mistakes and symbol mistakes in the documents of application for a patent. Where the patent administration department under the State Council corrects mistakes on its own initiative, it shall notify the applicant.
第五十二条 发明或者实用新型专利申请的说明书或者权利要求书的修改部分，除个别文字修改或者增删外，应当按照规定格式提交替换页。外观设计专利申请的图片或者照片的修改，应当按照规定提交替换页。	Article 52 When an amendment to the description or the claims in an application for a patent for invention or utility model is made, a replacement sheet in prescribed form shall be submitted, unless the amendment concerns only the alteration, insertion or deletion of a few words. Where an amendment to the drawings or photographs of an application for a patent for design is made, a replacement sheet shall be submitted as prescribed.

Implementing Regulations (Chinese)	Implementing Regulations (English translation)
第五十三条 依照专利法第三十八条的规定，发明专利申请经实质审查应当予以驳回的情形是指： （一）申请属于专利法第五条、第二十五条规定的情形，或者依照专利法第九条规定不能取得专利权的； （二）申请不符合专利法第二条第二款、第二十条第一款、第二十二条、第二十六条第三款、第四款、第五款、第三十一条第一款或者本细则第二十条第二款规定的； （三）申请的修改不符合专利法第三十三条规定，或者分案的申请不符合本细则第四十三条第一款的规定的。	Article 53 In accordance with the provisions of Article 38 of the Patent Law, the circumstances where an application for a patent for invention shall be rejected by the patent administration department under the State Council after examination as to substance are as follows: (1) where the application falls under Article 5 or 25 of the Patent Law, or the applicant is not entitled to a patent right in accordance with the provisions of Article 9 of the Patent Law; (2) where the application does not comply with the provisions of Article 2, paragraph two, Article 20, paragraph one, Article 22, Article 26, paragraph three, four or five, or Article 31, paragraph one of the Patent Law, or of Article 20, paragraph two of these Implementing Regulations. (3) where the amendment to the application does not comply with the provisions of Article 33 of the Patent Law, or the divisional application does not comply with the provisions of Article 43, paragraph one of these Implementing Regulations.
第五十四条 国务院专利行政部门发出授予专利权的通知后，申请人应当自收到通知之日起2个月内办理登记手续。申请人按期办理登记手续的，国务院专利行政部门应当授予专利权，颁发专利证书，并予以公告。 期满未办理登记手续的，视为放弃取得专利权的权利。	Article 54 After the patent administration department under the State Council issues the notification to grant the patent right, the applicant shall go through the formalities of registration within two months from the date of receipt of the notification. If the applicant completes the formalities of registration within the said time limit, the patent administration department under the State Council shall grant the patent right, issue the patent certificate and announce it. If the applicant does not go through the formalities of registration within the time limit, he or it shall be deemed to have abandoned his or its right to obtain the patent right.
第五十五条 保密专利申请经审查没有发现驳回理由的，国务院专利行政部门应当作出授予保密专利权的决定，颁发保密专利证书，登记保密专利权的有关事项。	Article 55 Where it is found after examination that there is no cause for rejection of the application for a secret patent, the patent administration department under the State Council shall make a decision to grant a secret patent, issue the certificate of the secret patent, and register the matters relating to the secret patent.

Implementing Regulations (Chinese)	Implementing Regulations (English translation)
第五十六条 授予实用新型或者外观设计专利权的决定公告后，专利法第六十条规定的专利权人或者利害关系人可以请求国务院专利行政部门作出专利权评价报告。 请求作出专利权评价报告的，应当提交专利权评价报告请求书，写明专利号。每项请求应当限于一项专利权。 专利权评价报告请求书不符合规定的，国务院专利行政部门应当通知请求人在指定期限内补正；请求人期满未补正的，视为未提出请求。	Article 56 After the announcement of the decision to grant a patent for utility model or a patent for design, the patentee or the interested party prescribed in Article 60 of the Patent Law may request the patent administration department under the State Council to make an evaluation report of patent. Where such person requests for an evaluation report of patent, he shall submit a request for the evaluation report of patent, indicating the patent number. Each request shall be limited for one patent. Where the request for the evaluation report of patent does not comply with the requirements as prescribed, the patent administration department under the State Council shall notify the requesting party to rectify the request within a specified time limit. If the requesting party fails to do so within the time limit, the request shall be deemed not to have been submitted.
第五十七条 国务院专利行政部门应当自收到专利权评价报告请求书后2个月内作出专利权评价报告。对同一项实用新型或者外观设计专利权，有多个请求人请求作出专利权评价报告的，国务院专利行政部门仅作出一份专利权评价报告。任何单位或者个人可以查阅或者复制该专利权评价报告。	Article 57 The patent administration department under the State Council shall make the evaluation report of patent within two months from receiving of the request for the evaluation report of patent. Where two or more persons request for the evaluation report of patent in respect of a same patent for utility model or patent for design, the patent administration department under the State Council shall make one evaluation report only. Any unit or individual may view or copy the evaluation report of patent.
第五十八条 国务院专利行政部门对专利公告、专利单行本中出现的错误，一经发现，应当及时更正，并对所作更正予以公告。	Article 58 The patent administration department under the State Council shall correct promptly the mistakes in the patent announcements and patent pamphlets issued by it once they are discovered, and the corrections shall be announced.
第四章　专利申请的复审与专利权的无效宣告	**Chapter 4　Reexamination of Patent Application and Invalidation of Patent Right**
第五十九条 专利复审委员会由国务院专利行政部门指定的技术专家和法律专家组成，主任委员由国务院专利行政部门负责人兼任。	Article 59 The Patent Reexamination Board shall consist of technical and legal experts appointed by the patent administration department under the State Council. The person responsible for the patent administration department under the State Council shall be the Director of the Board.

Implementing Regulations (Chinese)	Implementing Regulations (English translation)
第六十条 依照专利法第四十一条的规定向专利复审委员会请求复审的，应当提交复审请求书，说明理由，必要时还应当附具有关证据。	Article 60 Where the applicant requests the Patent Reexamination Board to make a reexamination in accordance with the provisions of Article 41 of the Patent Law, it or he shall file a request for reexamination, state the reasons and, when necessary, attach the relevant supporting documents.
复审请求不符合专利法第十九条第一款或者第四十一条第一款规定的，专利复审委员会不予受理，书面通知复审请求人并说明理由。	Where the request for reexamination does not comply with the provisions of Article 19, paragraph one or Article 41, Paragraph one of the Patent Law, the Patent Reexamination Board shall refuse to accept it, notify the applicant in written form and state the reasons thereof.
复审请求书不符合规定格式的，复审请求人应当在专利复审委员会指定的期限内补正；期满未补正的，该复审请求视为未提出。	Where the request for reexamination does not comply with the prescribed form, the person making the request shall rectify it within the time limit specified by the Patent Reexamination Board. If the requesting person fails to do so, the request for reexamination shall be deemed not to have been filed.
第六十一条 请求人在提出复审请求或者在对专利复审委员会的复审通知书作出答复时，可以修改专利申请文件；但是，修改应当仅限于消除驳回决定或者复审通知书指出的缺陷。	Article 61 The person making the request may amend its or his patent application at the time when it or he requests reexamination or makes responses to the notification of reexamination of the Patent Reexamination Board. However, the amendments shall be limited only to remove the defects pointed out in the decision of rejection of the application or in the notification of reexamination.
修改的专利申请文件应当提交一式两份。	The amendments to the application for patent shall be in two copies.
第六十二条 专利复审委员会应当将受理的复审请求书转交国务院专利行政部门原审查部门进行审查。原审查部门根据复审请求人的请求，同意撤销原决定的，专利复审委员会应当据此作出复审决定，并通知复审请求人。	Article 62 The Patent Reexamination Board shall remit the request for reexamination which the Board has received to the examination department of the patent administration department under the State Council which has made the examination of the application concerned to make an examination. Where that examination department agrees to revoke its former decision upon the request of the person requesting reexamination, the Patent Reexamination Board shall make a decision accordingly and notify the requesting person.

Implementing Regulations (Chinese)	Implementing Regulations (English translation)
第六十三条 专利复审委员会进行复审后，认为复审请求不符合专利法和本细则有关规定的，应当通知复审请求人，要求其在指定期限内陈述意见。期满未答复的，该复审请求视为撤回；经陈述意见或者进行修改后，专利复审委员会认为仍不符合专利法和本细则有关规定的，应当作出维持原驳回决定的复审决定。	Article 63 Where, after reexamination, the Patent Reexamination Board finds that the request does not comply with relevant provisions of the Patent Law and these Implementing Regulations, it shall invite the person requesting reexamination to submit its or his observations within a specified time limit. If the time limit for making response is not met, the request for reexamination shall be deemed to have been withdrawn. Where, after the requesting person has made its or his observations or amendments, the Patent Reexamination Board still finds that the request does not comply with relevant provisions of the Patent Law and these Implementing Regulations, it shall make a decision of reexamination to maintain the earlier decision rejecting the application.
专利复审委员会进行复审后，认为原驳回决定不符合专利法和本细则有关规定的，或者认为经过修改的专利申请文件消除了原驳回决定指出的缺陷的，应当撤销原驳回决定，由原审查部门继续进行审查程序。	Where, after reexamination, the Patent Reexamination Board finds that the decision rejecting the application does not comply with relevant provisions of the Patent Law and these Implementing Regulations, or that the amended application has removed the defects as pointed out by the decision rejecting the application, it shall make a decision to revoke the decision rejecting the application, and ask the examination department which has made the examination to continue the examination procedure.
第六十四条 复审请求人在专利复审委员会作出决定前，可以撤回其复审请求。	Article 64 At any time before the Patent Reexamination Board makes its decision on the request for reexamination, the requesting person may withdraw its or his request for reexamination.
复审请求人在专利复审委员会作出决定前撤回其复审请求的，复审程序终止。	Where the requesting person withdraws its or his request for reexamination before the Patent Reexamination Board makes its decision, the procedure of reexamination is terminated.
第六十五条 依照专利法第四十五条的规定，请求宣告专利权无效或者部分无效的，应当向专利复审委员会提交专利权无效宣告请求书和必要的证据一式两份。无效宣告请求书应当结合提交的所有证据，具体说明无效宣告请求的理由，并指明每项理由所依据的证据。	Article 65 Anyone requesting invalidation or part invalidation of a patent right in accordance with the provisions of Article 45 of the Patent Law shall submit a request and the necessary evidence in two copies. The request for invalidation shall state in detail the grounds for filing the request, making reference to all the evidence as submitted, and indicate the pieces of evidence to support each ground.

Implementing Regulations (Chinese)	Implementing Regulations (English translation)
前款所称无效宣告请求的理由，是指被授予专利的发明创造不符合专利法第二条、第二十条第一款、第二十二条、第二十三条、第二十六条第三款、第四款、第二十七条第二款、第三十三条或者本细则第二十条第二款、第四十三条第一款的规定，或者属于专利法第五条、第二十五条的规定，或者依照专利法第九条规定不能取得专利权。	The grounds on which the request for invalidation is based, referred to in the preceding paragraph, mean that the invention-creation for which the patent right is granted does not comply with the provisions of Article 2, Article 20, paragraph one, Article 22, Article 23, Article 26, paragraph three or four, Article 27, paragraph two, or Article 33 of the Patent Law, or of Article 20, paragraph two or Article 43, paragraph one of these Implementing Regulations; or the invention-creation falls under the provisions of Article 5 or 25 of the Patent Law; or the applicant is not entitled to be granted the patent right in accordance with the provisions of Article 9 of the Patent Law which each ground is based.
第六十六条 专利权无效宣告请求不符合专利法第十九条第一款或者本细则第六十五条规定的，专利复审委员会不予受理。 在专利复审委员会就无效宣告请求作出决定之后，又以同样的理由和证据请求无效宣告的，专利复审委员会不予受理。 以不符合专利法第二十三条第三款的规定为理由请求宣告外观设计专利权无效，但是未提交证明权利冲突的证据的，专利复审委员会不予受理。 专利权无效宣告请求书不符合规定格式的，无效宣告请求人应当在专利复审委员会指定的期限内补正；期满未补正的，该无效宣告请求视为未提出。	Article 66 Where the request for invalidation does not comply with the provisions of Article 19, paragraph one of the Patent Law, or of Article 65 of these Implementing Regulations, the Patent Reexamination Board shall refuse to accept it. Where, after a decision on any request for invalidation of the patent right is made, invalidation based on the same reasons and evidence is requested once again, the Patent Reexamination Board shall refuse to accept it. Where a request for invalidation of a patent for design is filed on the ground that the patent for design does not comply with the provision of Article 23, paragraph three of the Patent Law, but no evidence is submitted to prove such conflict of rights, the Patent Reexamination Board shall refuse to accept it. Where the request for invalidation of the patent right does not comply with the prescribed form, the person making the request shall rectify it within the time limit specified by the Patent Reexamination Board. If the rectification fails to be made within the time limit, the request for invalidation shall be deemed not to have been made.
第六十七条 在专利复审委员会受理无效宣告请求后，请求人可以在提出无效宣告请求之日起1个月内增加理由或者补充证据。逾期增加理由或者补充证据的，专利复审委员会可以不予考虑。	Article 67 After a request for invalidation is accepted by the Patent Reexamination Board, the person making the request may add reasons or supplement evidence within one month from the date when the request for invalidation is filed. Additional reasons or evidence which are submitted after the specified time limit may be disregarded by the Patent Reexamination Board.

Implementing Regulations (Chinese)	Implementing Regulations (English translation)
第六十八条 专利复审委员会应当将专利权无效宣告请求书和有关文件的副本送交专利权人，要求其在指定的期限内陈述意见。 专利权人和无效宣告请求人应当在指定期限内答复专利复审委员会发出的转送文件通知书或者无效宣告请求审查通知书；期满未答复的，不影响专利复审委员会审理。	Article 68 The Patent Reexamination Board shall send a copy of the request for invalidation of the patent right and copies of the relevant documents to the patentee and invite it or him to present its or his observations within a specified time limit. The patentee and the person making the request for invalidation shall, within the specified time limit, make responses to the notification concerning transmitted documents or the notification concerning the examination of the request for invalidation sent by the Patent Reexamination Board. Where no response is made within the specified time limit, the examination of the Patent Reexamination Board will not be affected.
第六十九条 在无效宣告请求的审查过程中，发明或者实用新型专利的专利权人可以修改其权利要求书，但是不得扩大原专利的保护范围。 发明或者实用新型专利的专利权人不得修改专利说明书和附图，外观设计专利的专利权人不得修改图片、照片和简要说明。	Article 69 In the course of the examination of the request for invalidation, the patentee for the patent for invention or utility model concerned may amend its or his claims, but may not broaden the scope of patent protection. The patentee for the patent for invention or utility model concerned may not amend its or his description or drawings. The patentee for the patent for design concerned may not amend its or his drawings, photographs or the brief explanation of the design.
第七十条 专利复审委员会根据当事人的请求或者案情需要，可以决定对无效宣告请求进行口头审理。 专利复审委员会决定对无效宣告请求进行口头审理的，应当向当事人发出口头审理通知书，告知举行口头审理的日期和地点。当事人应当在通知书指定的期限内作出答复。 无效宣告请求人对专利复审委员会发出的口头审理通知书在指定的期限内未作答复，并且不参加口头审理的，其无效宣告请求视为撤回；专利权人不参加口头审理的，可以缺席审理。	Article 70 The Patent Reexamination Board may, at the request of the parties concerned or in accordance with the needs of the case, decide to hold an oral hearing in respect of a request for invalidation. Where the Patent Reexamination Board decides to hold an oral examination in respect of a request for invalidation, it shall send notifications to the parties concerned, indicating the date and place of the oral procedure to be held. The parties concerned shall make response to the notification within the time limit specified in the notification. Where the person requesting invalidation fails to make response to the notification of the oral examination sent by the Patent Reexamination Board within the specified time limit, and fails to take part in the oral procedure, the request for invalidation shall be deemed to have been withdrawn. Where the patentee fails to take part in the oral examination, the Patent Reexamination Board may proceed to examine by default.

Implementing Regulations (Chinese)	Implementing Regulations (English translation)
第七十一条 在无效宣告请求审查程序中，专利复审委员会指定的期限不得延长。	Article 71 In the course of the examination of a request for invalidation, the time limit specified by the Patent Reexamination Board shall not be extended.
第七十二条 专利复审委员会对无效宣告的请求作出决定前，无效宣告请求人可以撤回其请求。 专利复审委员会作出决定之前，无效宣告请求人撤回其请求或者其无效宣告请求被视为撤回的，无效宣告请求审查程序终止。但是，专利复审委员会认为根据已进行的审查工作能够作出宣告专利权无效或者部分无效的决定的，不终止审查程序。	Article 72 The person requesting invalidation may withdraw his request before the Patent Reexamination Board makes a decision on it. Where the person requesting invalidation withdraws his request or where his request for invalidation is deemed to have been withdrawn before the Patent Reexamination Board makes a decision on it, the examination of the request for invalidation is terminated. Where, based on the examination work it has done, the Patent Reexamination Board finds that it is able to make a decision of invalidation or invalidation in part of the patent right, the examination procedure shall not be terminated.
第五章　专利实施的强制许可	**Chapter 5　Compulsory License for Exploitation of Patent**
第七十三条 专利法第四十八条第（一）项所称未充分实施其专利，是指专利权人及其被许可人实施其专利的方式或者规模不能满足国内对专利产品或者专利方法的需求。 专利法第五十条所称取得专利权的药品，是指解决公共健康问题所需的医药领域中的任何专利产品或者依照专利方法直接获得的产品，包括取得专利权的制造该产品所需的活性成分以及使用该产品所需的诊断用品。	Article 73 The insufficient exploitation of its or his patent mentioned in Article 48, subparagraph (1) of the Patent Law means the manner or scale of the exploitation of patent by the patentee and/or the licensee authorized by it or him cannot meet the demands of the domestic market for the patented product or patented process. The pharmaceutical product to which patent right has been granted as mentioned in Article 50 of the Patent Law means any patented product, or product directly obtained by a patented process, of pharmaceutical sector needed to address public health problems, including the patented active ingredients necessary for the manufacture of the product and the diagnostic kits needed for its use.
第七十四条 请求给予强制许可的，应当向国务院专利行政部门提交强制许可请求书，说明理由并附具有关证明文件。 国务院专利行政部门应当将强制许可请求书的副本送交专利权人，专利权人应当在国务院专利行政部门指定的期限内陈述	Article 74 Any unit or individual requesting a compulsory license shall submit to the patent administration department under the State Council a request for compulsory license, state the reasons thereof, and attach relevant certifying documents. The patent administration department under the State Council shall send a copy of the request for compulsory license to the patentee, who shall make

Implementing Regulations (Chinese)	Implementing Regulations (English translation)
意见；期满未答复的，不影响国务院专利行政部门作出决定。	his or its observations within the time limit specified by the patent administration department under the State Council. Where no response is made within the time limit, the patent administration department under the State Council will not be affected in making its decision.
国务院专利行政部门在作出驳回强制许可请求的决定或者给予强制许可的决定前，应当通知请求人和专利权人拟作出的决定及其理由。	Before making a decision to reject a request for compulsory license or to grant a compulsory license, the patent administration department under the State Council shall, notify the requesting person and the patentee the decision that is to be made on the request and the reasons thereof.
国务院专利行政部门依照专利法第五十条的规定作出给予强制许可的决定，应当同时符合中国缔结或者参加的有关国际条约关于为了解决公共健康问题而给予强制许可的规定，但中国作出保留的除外。	The decision of the patent administration department under the State Council on granting a compulsory license in accordance with Article 50 of the Patent Law, shall be also in conformity with the provisions of the relevant international treaties on granting compulsory license for the purposes of addressing public health issue, to which China is party, except for provisions on which China has made reservation.
第七十五条 依照专利法第五十七条的规定，请求国务院专利行政部门裁决使用费数额的，当事人应当提出裁决请求书，并附具双方不能达成协议的证明文件。国务院专利行政部门应当自收到请求书之日起3个月内作出裁决，并通知当事人。	Article 75 Where any unit or individual requests, in accordance with the provisions of Article 57 of the Patent Law, the patent administration department under the State Council to adjudicate the fees for exploitation, it or he shall submit a request for adjudication and furnish documents showing that the parties concerned have not been able to conclude an agreement in respect of the amount of the exploitation fee. The patent administration department under the State Council shall make adjudication within three months from the date of receipt of the request and notify the parties concerned accordingly.
第六章　对职务发明创造的发明人或者设计人的奖励和报酬	Chapter 6　Reward and Remuneration for Inventors or Creators of Service Inventions-Creations
第七十六条 被授予专利权的单位可以与发明人、设计人约定或者在其依法制定的规章制度中规定专利法第十六条规定的奖励、报酬的方式和数额。	Article 76 The unit to which a patent right is granted may, on the manner and amount of the reward and remuneration as prescribed in Article 16 of the Patent Law, enter into a contract with the inventor or creator, or provide it in its rules and regulations formulated in accordance with the laws.

Implementing Regulations (Chinese)	Implementing Regulations (English translation)
企业、事业单位给予发明人或者设计人的奖励、报酬，按照国家有关财务、会计制度的规定进行处理。	The reward and remuneration awarded to the inventor or creator by any enterprise or institution shall be handled in accordance with the relevant provisions of the State on financial and accounting systems.
第七十七条 被授予专利权的单位未与发明人、设计人约定也未在其依法制定的规章制度中规定专利法第十六条规定的奖励的方式和数额的，应当自专利权公告之日起3个月内发给发明人或者设计人奖金。一项发明专利的奖金最低不少于3000元；一项实用新型专利或者外观设计专利的奖金最低不少于1000元。 由于发明人或者设计人的建议被其所属单位采纳而完成的发明创造，被授予专利权的单位应当从优发给奖金。	Article 77 Where the unit to which a patent right is granted has not entered into a contract with the inventor or creator on the manner and amount of the reward as prescribed in Article 16 of the Patent Law, nor has the unit provided it in its rules and regulations formulated in accordance with the laws, it shall, within three months from the date of the announcement of the grant of the patent right, award to the inventor or creator of a service invention-creation a sum of money as prize. The sum of money prize for a patent for invention shall not be less than RMB 3, 000 Yuan; the sum of money prize for a patent for utility model or design shall not be less than RMB 1, 000 Yuan. Where an invention-creation is made on the basis of an inventor's or creator's proposal adopted by the unit to which he belongs, the unit to which a patent right is granted shall award to him a money prize on favourable terms.
第七十八条 被授予专利权的单位未与发明人、设计人约定也未在其依法制定的规章制度中规定专利法第十六条规定的报酬的方式和数额的，在专利权有效期限内，实施发明创造专利后，每年应当从实施该项发明或者实用新型专利的营业利润中提取不低于2%或者从实施该项外观设计专利的营业利润中提取不低于0.2%，作为报酬给予发明人或者设计人，或者参照上述比例，给予发明人或者设计人一次性报酬；被授予专利权的单位许可其他单位或者个人实施其专利的，应当从收取的使用费中提取不低于10%，作为报酬给予发明人或者设计人。	Article 78 Where the unit to which a patent right is granted has not entered into a contract with the inventor or creator on the manner and amount of the remuneration as prescribed in Article 16 of the Patent law, nor has the unit provided it in its rules and regulations in accordance with the laws, it shall, after exploiting the patent for invention-creation within the duration of the patent right, draw each year from the profits from exploitation of the invention or utility model a percentage of not less than 2%, or from the profits from exploitation of the design a percentage of not less than 0. 2%, and award it to the inventor or creator as remuneration. The unit may, as an alternative, by making reference to the said percentage, award a lump sum of money to the inventor or creator as remuneration once and for all. Where any unit to which a patent right is granted authorizes any other unit or individual to exploit its patent, it shall draw from the exploitation fee it receives a percentage of not less than 10% and award it to the inventor or creator as remuneration.

Implementing Regulations (Chinese)	Implementing Regulations (English translation)
第七章 专利权的保护	**Chapter 7 Protection of Patent Right**
第七十九条 专利法和本细则所称管理专利工作的部门，是指由省、自治区、直辖市人民政府以及专利管理工作量大又有实际处理能力的设区的市人民政府设立的管理专利工作的部门。	Article 79 The administrative authority for patent affairs referred to in the Patent Law and these Implementing Regulations means the department responsible for the administrative work concerning patent affairs set up by the people's government of any province, autonomous region, or municipality directly under the Central Government, or by the people's government of any city which consists of districts, has a large amount of patent administration work to attend to and has the ability to deal with the matter.
第八十条 国务院专利行政部门应当对管理专利工作的部门处理专利侵权纠纷、查处假冒专利行为、调解专利纠纷进行业务指导。	Article 80 The patent administration department under the State Council shall provide professional guidance to the administrative authorities for patent affairs in handling patent infringement disputes, investigating and prosecuting acts of passing off a patent and mediating patent disputes.
第八十一条 当事人请求处理专利侵权纠纷或者调解专利纠纷的，由被请求人所在地或者侵权行为地的管理专利工作的部门管辖。 两个以上管理专利工作的部门都有管辖权的专利纠纷，当事人可以向其中一个管理专利工作的部门提出请求；当事人向两个以上有管辖权的管理专利工作的部门提出请求的，由最先受理的管理专利工作的部门管辖。 管理专利工作的部门对管辖权发生争议的，由其共同的上级人民政府管理专利工作的部门指定管辖；无共同上级人民政府管理专利工作的部门的，由国务院专利行政部门指定管辖。	Article 81 Where any party concerned requests handling of a patent infringement dispute or mediation of a patent dispute, it shall fall under the jurisdiction of the administrative authority for patent affairs where the alleged infringer has his location or where the act of infringement has taken place. Where two or more administrative authorities for patent affairs all have jurisdiction over a patent dispute, any party concerned may file his or its request with one of them to handle or mediate the matter. Where requests are filed with two or more administrative authorities for patent affairs with proper jurisdiction, the administrative authority for patent affairs that first accepts the request shall have jurisdiction. Where administrative authorities for patent affairs have a dispute over their jurisdiction, the administrative authority for patent affairs of their common higher level people's government shall designate the administrative authority for patent affairs to exercise the jurisdiction; if there is no such administrative authority for patent affairs of their common higher level people's government, the patent administration department under the State Council shall designate the administrative authority for patent affairs to exercise the jurisdiction.

Implementing Regulations (Chinese)	Implementing Regulations (English translation)
第八十二条 在处理专利侵权纠纷过程中，被请求人提出无效宣告请求并被专利复审委员会受理的，可以请求管理专利工作的部门中止处理。 管理专利工作的部门认为被请求人提出的中止理由明显不能成立的，可以不中止处理。	Article 82 Where, in the course of handling a patent infringement dispute, the alleged infringer requests invalidation of the patent right and his request is accepted by the Patent Reexamination Board, he may request the administrative authority for patent affairs concerned to suspend the handling of the matter. If the administrative authority for patent affairs considers that the reasons set forth by the alleged infringer for the suspension are obviously untenable, it may not suspend the handling of the matter.
第八十三条 专利权人依照专利法第十七条的规定，在其专利产品或者该产品的包装上标明专利标识的，应当按照国务院专利行政部门规定的方式予以标明。 专利标识不符合前款规定的，由管理专利工作的部门责令改正。	Article 83 Where any patentee affixes a patent indication on the patented product or on the package of that product in accordance with the provisions of Article 17 of the Patent Law, he or it shall make the affixation in the manner as prescribed by the patent administration department under the State Council. Where any patent indication is not in conformity with the provision of the preceding paragraph, the administrative authority for patent affairs shall order to correct it.
第八十四条 下列行为属于专利法第六十三条规定的假冒专利的行为： （一）在未被授予专利权的产品或者其包装上标注专利标识，专利权被宣告无效后或者终止后继续在产品或者其包装上标注专利标识，或者未经许可在产品或者产品包装上标注他人的专利号；（二）销售第（一）项所述产品； （三）在产品说明书等材料中将未被授予专利权的技术或者设计称为专利技术或者专利设计，将专利申请称为专利，或者未经许可使用他人的专利号，使公众将所涉及的技术或者设计误认为是专利技术或者专利设计； （四）伪造或者变造专利证书、专利文件或者专利申请文件； （五）其他使公众混淆，将未被授予专利权的技术或者设计误认为是专利技术或者专利设计的行为。	Article 84 Any of the following is an act of passing off a patent as prescribed in Article 63 of the Patent Law: (1) affixing patent indication on a product or on the package of a product which has not been granted a patent, continuing to affix patent indication on a product or on the package of a product, after the related patent right has been declared invalid or is terminated, or affixing the patent number of another person on a product or on the package of a product without authorization. (2) sale of the product as prescribed in subparagraph (1); (3) indicating a technology or design to which no patent right has been granted as patented technology or patented design, indicating a patent application as patent or using the patent number of another person without authorization, in such materials as specification of product etc. which could mislead the public to regard the related technology or design as patented technology or patented design; (4) counterfeiting or transforming any patent certificate, patent document or patent application document;

Implementing Regulations (Chinese)	Implementing Regulations (English translation)
	(5) any other act which might cause confusion on the part of the public, misleading them to regard a technology or design to which no patent right has been granted as patented technology or patented design.
专利权终止前依法在专利产品、依照专利方法直接获得的产品或者其包装上标注专利标识，在专利权终止后许诺销售、销售该产品的，不属于假冒专利行为。	Affixing patent indication legally on a patented product, or on a product directly obtained by a patented process, or on the package of such products before the termination of the patent right, offering for sale or sale of such products after the termination of the patent right is not an act of passing off a patent.
销售不知道是假冒专利的产品，并且能够证明该产品合法来源的，由管理专利工作的部门责令停止销售，但免除罚款的处罚。	Where any person sells a product passing off a patent without knowing it, and can prove that it or he obtains the product from a legitimate channel, it or he shall be ordered to stop selling the product by the administrative authority for patent affairs, but be exempted from being imposed a fine.
第八十五条 除专利法第六十条规定的外，管理专利工作的部门应当事人请求，可以对下列专利纠纷进行调解： （一）专利申请权和专利权归属纠纷； （二）发明人、设计人资格纠纷； （三）职务发明创造的发明人、设计人的奖励和报酬纠纷； （四）在发明专利申请公布后专利权授予前使用发明而未支付适当费用的纠纷； （五）其他专利纠纷。	Article 85 In addition to the provisions of Article 60 of the Patent Law, the administration authority for patent affairs may also mediate in the following patent disputes at the request of the parties concerned: (1) any dispute over the ownership of the right to apply for patent and the patent right; (2) any dispute over the qualification of the inventor or creator; (3) any dispute over the award and remuneration of the inventor or creator of a sewice invention-creation; (4) any dispute over the appropriate fee to be paid for the exploitation of an invention after the publication of the application for patent but before the grant of patent right; (5) any other patent dispute.
对于前款第（四）项所列的纠纷，当事人请求管理专利工作的部门调解的，应当在专利权被授予之后提出。	In respect of the dispute referred to in subparagraph (4), where the party concerned requests the administrative authority for patent affairs to mediate, the request shall be made after the grant of the patent right.
第八十六条 当事人因专利申请权或者专利权的归属发生纠纷，已请求管理专利工作的部门调解或者向人民法院起诉的，可以请求国务院专利行政部门中止有关程序。	Article 86 Any party involving in a dispute over the ownership of the right of patent application or patent right, who has already applied for mediation with the administrative authority for patent affairs or instituted legal proceedings before the people's court, may request the patent administration department under the State Council to suspend the relevant procedures.

Implementing Regulations (Chinese)	Implementing Regulations (English translation)
依照前款规定请求中止有关程序的，应当向国务院专利行政部门提交请求书，并附具管理专利工作的部门或者人民法院的写明申请号或者专利号的有关受理文件副本。	Any party requesting the suspension of the relevant procedures in accordance with the preceding paragraph, shall submit a request to the patent administration department under the State Council, accompanied by a copy of the document acknowledging that the administrative authority for patent affairs or the people's court has accepted the case, in which the filing number or the patent number concerned has been indicated.
管理专利工作的部门作出的调解书或者人民法院作出的判决生效后，当事人应当向国务院专利行政部门办理恢复有关程序的手续。自请求中止之日起1年内，有关专利申请权或者专利权归属的纠纷未能结案，需要继续中止有关程序的，请求人应当在该期限内请求延长中止。期满未请求延长的，国务院专利行政部门自行恢复有关程序。	After entering into force of the mediation made by the administrative authority for patent affairs or the judgment rendered by the people's court, the parties concerned shall request the patent administration department under the State Council to resume the suspended procedure. If, within one year from the date when the request for suspension is filed, no decision is made on the dispute relating to the ownership of the right to apply for a patent or the patent right, and it is necessary to continue the suspension, the party who made the request shall, within the said time limit, request to extend the suspension. If, at the expiration of the said time limit, no such request for extension is filed, the patent administration department under the State Council shall resume the procedure on its own initiative.
第八十七条 人民法院在审理民事案件中裁定对专利申请权或者专利权采取保全措施的，国务院专利行政部门应当在收到写明申请号或者专利号的裁定书和协助执行通知书之日中止被保全的专利申请权或者专利权的有关程序。保全期限届满，人民法院没有裁定继续采取保全措施的，国务院专利行政部门自行恢复有关程序。	Article 87 Where, in hearing civil cases, the people's court has ordered the adoption of preservation measures on the right of patent application or patent right, the patent administration department under the State Council shall suspend the relevant procedure concerning the patent application or patent under preservation on the date of receiving the judgment order and the notification on assisting the execution of the order indicated with the filing number or the patent number. At the expiration of the time limit for preservation, if there is no order of the people's court to continue the preservation, the patent administration department under the State Council shall resume the relevant procedure on its own initiative.
第八十八条 国务院专利行政部门根据本细则第八十六条和第八十七条规定中止有关程序，是指暂停专利申请的初步审查、实质审查、复审程序，授予专利权程序和专利权无效宣	Article 88 The suspension of relevant procedures carried out by the patent administration department under the State Council in accordance with Article 86 and Article 87 of these Implementing Regulations, refers

Implementing Regulations (Chinese)	Implementing Regulations (English translation)
告程序；暂停办理放弃、变更、转移专利权或者专利申请权手续，专利权质押手续以及专利权期限届满前的终止手续等。	to the suspension of such procedures as preliminary examination, examination as to substance, reexamination of a patent application, granting of patent right and the announcement of invalidation of patent; the suspension of the procedures on handling the abandonment of patent right, changing or transferring patent right or right of patent application, pledge of patent right and the cessation of patent right before the expiration of its duration.
第八章　专利登记和专利公报	**Chapter 8　Patent Registration and Patent Gazette**
第八十九条 国务院专利行政部门设置专利登记簿，登记下列与专利申请和专利权有关的事项： （一）专利权的授予； （二）专利申请权、专利权的转移； （三）专利权的质押、保全及其解除； （四）专利实施许可合同的备案； （五）专利权的无效宣告； （六）专利权的终止； （七）专利权的恢复； （八）专利实施的强制许可； （九）专利权人的姓名或者名称、国籍和地址的变更。	Article 89 The patent administration department under the State Council shall keep a Patent Register in which the registration of the following matters relating to patent application or patent right shall be made: (1) any grant of the patent right; (2) any transfer of the right of patent application or the patent right; (3) any pledge and preservation of the patent right and their discharge; (4) any patent license contract for exploitation submitted for the record; (5) any invalidation of the patent right; (6) any cessation of the patent right; (7) any restoration of the patent right; (8) any compulsory license for exploitation of the patent; (9) any change in the name or title, nationality and address of the patentee.
第九十条 国务院专利行政部门定期出版专利公报，公布或者公告下列内容： （一）发明专利申请的著录事项和说明书摘要； （二）发明专利申请的实质审查请求和国务院专利行政部门对发明专利申请自行进行实质审查的决定； （三）发明专利申请公布后的驳回、撤回、视为撤回、视为放弃、恢复和转移；	Article 90 The patent administration department under the State Council shall publish the Patent Gazette at regular intervals, publishing or announcing the following: (1) the bibliographic data and the abstract of the description of an application for a patent for invention; (2) any request for examination as to substance of an application for a patent for invention and any decision made by the patent administration department under the State Council to proceed on its own initiative to examine as to substance an application for a patent for invention; (3) any rejection, withdrawal, deemed withdrawal, deemed abandonment, restoration and transfer of an application for a patent for invention after its publication;

Implementing Regulations (Chinese)	Implementing Regulations (English translation)
（四）专利权的授予以及专利权的著录事项； （五）发明或者实用新型专利的说明书摘要，外观设计专利的一幅图片或者照片； （六）国防专利、保密专利的解密； （七）专利权的无效宣告； （八）专利权的终止、恢复； （九）专利权的转移； （十）专利实施许可合同的备案； （十一）专利权的质押、保全及其解除； （十二）专利实施的强制许可的给予； （十三）专利权人的姓名或者名称、地址的变更； （十四）文件的公告送达； （十五）国务院专利行政部门作出的更正； （十六）其他有关事项。	(4) any grant of patent right and the bibliographic data of the patent right; (5) the abstract of the description of a patent for invention or a patent for utility model, one drawing or photograph of a patent for design; (6) any declassification of national defense patent or secret patent; (7) any invalidation of the patent right; (8) any cessation or restoration of the patent right; (9) any transfer of the patent right; (10) any patent license contract for exploitation submitted for record; (11) any pledge or preservation of the patent right and their discharge; (12) any grant of compulsory license for exploitation of the patent; (13) any change in the name or title and address of the patentee; (14) any service of documents by way of making an announcement; (15) any correction made by the patent administration department under the State Council; and (16) any other related matters.
第九十一条 国务院专利行政部门应当提供专利公报、发明专利申请单行本以及发明专利、实用新型专利、外观设计专利单行本，供公众免费查阅。	Article 91 The patent administration department under the State Council shall make the patent gazettes, the pamphlets of the application for patent for invention and the pamphlets of patent for invention, patent for utility model and patent for design available to the public for consultation with free of charge.
第九十二条 国务院专利行政部门负责按照互惠原则与其他国家、地区的专利机关或者区域性专利组织交换专利文献。	Article 92 The patent administration department under the State Council is responsible for exchanging, in accordance with the principle of reciprocity, patent documents with the patent authorities of other countries or regions or with the patent authorities of regional patent organizations.
第九章　费用	Chapter 9　Fees
第九十三条 向国务院专利行政部门申请专利和办理其他手续时，应当缴纳下列费用： （一）申请费、申请附加费、公布印刷费、优先权要求费；	Article 93 When any person files an application for a patent with, or has other formalities to go through at, the patent administration department under the State Council, he or it shall pay the following fees: (1) filing fee, additional fee for filing an application, printing fee for publishing the application, and fee for claiming priority;

Implementing Regulations (Chinese)	Implementing Regulations (English translation)
（二）发明专利申请实质审查费、复审费； （三）专利登记费、公告印刷费、年费； （四）恢复权利请求费、延长期限请求费； （五）著录事项变更费、专利权评价报告请求费、无效宣告请求费。 前款所列各种费用的缴纳标准，由国务院价格管理部门、财政部门会同国务院专利行政部门规定。	(2) fee for examination as to substance for an application for patent for invention, and reexamination fee; (3) registration fee for the grant of patent right, printing fee for the announcement of grant of patent right, and annual fee; (4) fee for requesting restoration of right, and fee for requesting extension of time limit; (5) fee for making a change in the bibliographic data, fee for requesting for evaluation report of patent, and fee for requesting for announcement of invalidation of patent. The amount of the fees referred to in the preceding paragraphs shall be prescribed by the price administration department and the finance administration department under the State Council in conjunction with the patent administration department under the State Council.
第九十四条 专利法和本细则规定的各种费用，可以直接向国务院专利行政部门缴纳，也可以通过邮局或者银行汇付，或者以国务院专利行政部门规定的其他方式缴纳。 通过邮局或者银行汇付的，应当在送交国务院专利行政部门的汇单上写明正确的申请号或者专利号以及缴纳的费用名称。不符合本款规定的，视为未办理缴费手续。 直接向国务院专利行政部门缴纳费用的，以缴纳当日为缴费日；以邮局汇付方式缴纳费用的，以邮局汇出的邮戳日为缴费日；以银行汇付方式缴纳费用的，以银行实际汇出日为缴费日。 多缴、重缴、错缴专利费用的，当事人可以自缴费日起3年内，向国务院专利行政部门提出退款请求，国务院专利行政部门应当予以退还。	Article 94 The fees provided for in the Patent Law and in these Implementing Regulations may be paid directly to the patent administration department under the State Council or paid by way of bank or postal remittance, or by way of any other means as prescribed by the patent administration department under the State Council. Where any fee is paid by way of bank or postal remittance, the applicant or the patentee shall indicate on the money order at least the correct filing number or the patent number and the name of the fee paid. If the requirements as prescribed in this paragraph are not complied with, the payment of the fee shall be deemed not to have been made. Where any fee is paid directly to the patent administration department under the State Council, the date on which the fee is paid shall be the date of payment; where any fee is paid by way of postal remittance, the date of remittance indicated by the postmark shall be the date of payment; where any fee is paid by way of bank transfer, the date on which the transfer of the fee is done shall be the date of payment. Where any patent fee is paid in excess of the amount as prescribed, paid repeatedly or wrongly, the party making the payment may, within three years from the date of payment, request a refund from the patent administration department under the State Council, and the patent administration department under the State Council shall return it.

Implementing Regulations (Chinese)	Implementing Regulations (English translation)
第九十五条 申请人应当自申请日起2个月内或者在收到受理通知书之日起15日内缴纳申请费、公布印刷费和必要的申请附加费；期满未缴纳或者未缴足的，其申请视为撤回。	Article 95 The applicant shall pay the filing fee, the printing fee for the publication of the application and the necessary additional fee for filing an application within two months from the filing date or fifteen days from the date of receipt of the notification of acceptance of the application from the patent administration department under the State Council. If the fees are not paid or not paid in full within the time limit, the application shall be deemed to be withdrawn.
申请人要求优先权的，应当在缴纳申请费的同时缴纳优先权要求费；期满未缴纳或者未缴足的，视为未要求优先权。	Where the applicant claims priority, he or it shall pay the fee for claiming priority at the same time with the payment of the filing fee. If the fee is not paid or not paid in full within the time limit, the claim for priority shall be deemed not to have been made.
第九十六条 当事人请求实质审查或者复审的，应当在专利法及本细则规定的相关期限内缴纳费用；期满未缴纳或者未缴足的，视为未提出请求。	Article 96 Where the party concerned makes a request for an examination *as* to substance or a reexamination, the relevant fee shall be paid within the lime limit as prescribed respectively for such requests by the Patent Law and these Implementing Regulations. If the fee is not paid or not paid in full within the time limit, the request is deemed not to have been made.
第九十七条 申请人办理登记手续时，应当缴纳专利登记费、公告印刷费和授予专利权当年的年费；期满未缴纳或者未缴足的，视为未办理登记手续。	Article 97 When the applicant goes through the formalities of registration of the grant of patent right, it or he shall pay a registration fee for the grant of patent right, printing fee for the announcement of grant of patent right and the annual fee of the year in which the patent right is granted. If such fees are not paid or not paid in full within the lime limit, the registration of the grant of patent right shall be deemed not to have been made.
第九十八条 授予专利权当年以后的年费应当在上一年度期满前缴纳。专利权人未缴纳或者未缴足的，国务院专利行政部门应当通知专利权人自应当缴纳年费期满之日起6个月内补缴，同时缴纳滞纳金；滞纳金的金额按照每超过规定的缴费时间1个月，加收当年全额年费的5%计算；期满未缴纳的，专利权自应当缴纳年费期满之日起终止。	Article 98 The annual fee of the patent right after the year in which the patent is granted shall be paid before the expiration of the preceding year. If the patentee fails to pay or pay in full the fee, the patent administration department under the State Council shall notify the patentee to pay the fee or to make up the insufficiency within six months from the expiration of the time limit within which the annual fee is due to be paid, and at the same time pay a surcharge. The amount of the surcharge shall be, for each month of late payment, 5% of the whole amount of the annual

Implementing Regulations (Chinese)	Implementing Regulations (English translation)
	fee of the year within which the annual fee is due to be paid. Where the fee and the surcharge are not paid within the time limit, the patent right shall lapse from the expiration of the time limit within which the annual fee should be paid.
第九十九条 恢复权利请求费应当在本细则规定的相关期限内缴纳；期满未缴纳或者未缴足的，视为未提出请求。	Article 99 The fee for requesting restoration of right shall be paid within the relevant time limit prescribed in these Implementing Regulations. If the fee is not paid or not paid in full within the time limit, the request shall be deemed not to have been made.
延长期限请求费应当在相应期限届满之日前缴纳；期满未缴纳或者未缴足的，视为未提出请求。	The fee for request of extension of a time limit shall be paid before the expiration of the relevant time limit. If the fee is not paid or not paid in full within the time limit, the request shall be deemed not to have been made.
著录事项变更费、专利权评价报告请求费、无效宣告请求费应当自提出请求之日起1个月内缴纳；期满未缴纳或者未缴足的，视为未提出请求。	The fee for a change in the bibliographic data, fee for requesting for evaluation report of patent and fee for request of invalidation of patent right shall be paid within one month from the date on which such request is filed. If the fee is not paid or not paid in full within the time limit, the request shall be deemed not to have been made.
第一百条　申请人或者专利权人缴纳本细则规定的各种费用有困难的，可以按照规定向国务院专利行政部门提出减缴或者缓缴的请求。减缴或者缓缴的办法由国务院财政部门会同国务院价格管理部门、国务院专利行政部门规定。	Article 100 Where any applicant or patentee has difficulties in paying the various fees prescribed in these Implementing Regulations, it or he may, in accordance with the prescriptions, submit a request to the patent administration department under the State Council for a reduction or postponement of the payment. Measures for the reduction and postponement of the payment shall be prescribed by the finance administration department under the State Council in conjunction with the price administration department under the State Council and the patent administration department under the State Council.
第十章　关于国际申请的特别规定	**Chapter 10 Special Provisions Concerning International Applications**
第一百零一条 国务院专利行政部门根据专利法第二十条规定，受理按照专利合作条约提出的专利国际申请。	Article 101 The patent administration department under the State Council receives international patent applications filed under the Patent Cooperation Treaty in accordance with the provisions of Article 20 of the Patent Law.

Implementing Regulations (Chinese)	Implementing Regulations (English translation)
按照专利合作条约提出并指定中国的专利国际申请（以下简称国际申请）进入国务院专利行政部门处理阶段（以下称进入中国国家阶段）的条件和程序适用本章的规定；本章没有规定的，适用专利法及本细则其他各章的有关规定。	For any international application filed under the Patent Cooperation Treaty designating China (hereinafter referred to as the international application), the requirements and procedures for entering the phase of process conducted by the patent administration department under the State Council (hereinafter referred to as entering the Chinese national phase), the provisions prescribed in this chapter shall apply. Where no provisions are made in this chapter, the relevant provisions in the Patent Law and in any other chapters of these Implementing Regulations shall apply.
第一百零二条 按照专利合作条约已确定国际申请日并指定中国的国际申请，视为向国务院专利行政部门提出的专利申请，该国际申请日视为专利法第二十八条所称的申请日。	Article 102 Any international application which has been accorded an international filling date in accordance with the Patent Cooperation Treaty and which has designated China shall be deemed as an application for patent filed with the patent administration department under the State Council, and the said international filing date shall be deemed as the filing date referred to in Article 28 of the Patent Law.
第一百零三条 国际申请的申请人应当在专利合作条约第二条所称的优先权日（本章简称优先权日）起30个月内，向国务院专利行政部门办理进入中国国家阶段的手续；申请人未在该期限内办理该手续的，在缴纳宽限费后，可以在自优先权日起32个月内办理进入中国国家阶段的手续。	Article 103 Any applicant for an international application entering the Chinese national phase shall, within 30 months from the priority date as referred to in Article 2 of the Patent Cooperation Treaty (referred to as "the priority date" in this chapter), go through the formalities for entering the Chinese national phase before the patent administration department under the State Council. If the applicant fails to go through the said formalities within the prescribed time limit, he or it may, after paying a surcharge for the late entry, go through the formalities for entering the Chinese national phase within the 32 months from the priority date.
第一百零四条 申请人依照本细则第一百零三条的规定办理进入中国国家阶段的手续的，应当符合下列要求： （一）以中文提交进入中国国家阶段的书面声明，写明国际申请号和要求获得的专利权类型；	Article 104 When the applicant goes through the formalities for entering the Chinese national phase in accordance with the provisions of Article 103 of these Implementing Regulations, it or he shall fulfill the following requirements: (1) submitting in Chinese a written statement for entering the Chinese national phase, indicating the international application number and the type of patent right sought;

Implementing Regulations (Chinese)	Implementing Regulations (English translation)
（二）缴纳本细则第九十三条第一款规定的申请费、公布印刷费，必要时缴纳本细则第一百零三条规定的宽限费； （三）国际申请以外文提出的，提交原始国际申请的说明书和权利要求书的中文译文； （四）在进入中国国家阶段的书面声明中写明发明创造的名称，申请人姓名或者名称、地址和发明人的姓名，上述内容应当与世界知识产权组织国际局（以下简称国际局）的记录一致；国际申请中未写明发明人的，在上述声明中写明发明人的姓名； （五）国际申请以外文提出的，提交摘要的中文译文，有附图和摘要附图的，提交附图副本和摘要附图副本，附图中有文字的，将其替换为对应的中文文字；国际申请以中文提出的，提交国际公布文件中的摘要和摘要附图副本； （六）在国际阶段向国际局已办理申请人变更手续的，提供变更后的申请人享有申请权的证明材料； （七）必要时缴纳本细则第九十三条第一款规定的申请附加费。 符合本条第一款第（一）项至第（三）项要求的，国务院专利行政部门应当给予申请号，明确国际申请进入中国国家阶段的日期（以下简称进入日），并通知申请人其国际申请已进入中国国家阶段。	(2) paying the filing fee and the printing fee for the publication of the application as provided in Article 93, paragraph one of these Implementing Regulations, and where necessary, the surcharge for the late entry as provided in Article 103 of these Implementing Regulation; (3) submitting the Chinese translation of the description and the claims of the initial international application where an international application is filed in a foreign language; (4) indicating in the written statement for entering the Chinese national phase the title of the invention-creation, the name or title of the applicant, the address of the applicant and the name of the inventor, all of which should be in conformity with those recorded with the International Bureau under the World Intellectual Property Organization (hereafter referred to as the International Bureau). Where the inventor is not indicated in the international application, the name of the inventor shall be indicated in the said statement; (5) where the international application is filed in a foreign language, submitting the Chinese translation of the abstract; submitting a copy of the drawings and a copy of the drawing of the abstract where there are drawings and the drawing of the abstract; the text matter in the drawings, if any, shall be replaced by the corresponding text matter in Chinese; where the international application is filed in Chinese, submitting a copy of the abstract and the drawing of the abstract as appeared in the documents of international publication; (6) where the applicant has gone through the formalities of changing the applicant before the International Bureau in the international phase, certifying documents shall be furnished to prove the right of the applicant after the change to the international application; (7) payment of the additional fee for application when necessary, as provided in Article 93, subparagraph (1) of these Implementing regulations. Where the requirements set forth in subparagraphs (1) to (3), paragraph one of this Article are met, the patent administration department under the State Council shall issue the filing number, indicate clearly the date of entry of the international application into the Chinese national phase (hereafter referred to as the date of entry), and notify the applicant that its or his international application has entered into the Chinese national phase.

Implementing Regulations (Chinese)	Implementing Regulations (English translation)
国际申请已进入中国国家阶段，但不符合本条第一款第（四）项至第（七）项要求的，国务院专利行政部门应当通知申请人在指定期限内补正；期满未补正的，其申请视为撤回。	Where, after entering the Chinese national phase, it is found that an international application does not meet the requirements as set forth in subparagraphs (4) to (7), paragraph one of this Article, the patent administration department under the State Council shall notify the applicant to make rectification within the specified time limit. If the applicant fails to do so, the application shall be deemed to have been withdrawn.
第一百零五条 国际申请有下列情形之一的，其在中国的效力终止： （一）在国际阶段，国际申请被撤回或者被视为撤回，或者国际申请对中国的指定被撤回的； （二）申请人未在优先权日起32个月内按照本细则第一百零三条规定办理进入中国国家阶段手续的； （三）申请人办理进入中国国家阶段的手续，但自优先权日起32个月期限届满仍不符合本细则第一百零四条第（一）项至第（三）项要求的。 依照前款第（一）项的规定，国际申请在中国的效力终止的，不适用本细则第六条的规定；依照前款第（二）项、第（三）项的规定，国际申请在中国的效力终止的，不适用本细则第六条第二款的规定。	Article 105 Where an international application has any of the following circumstances, the effect of the application in China shall cease: (1) where in the international phase, the international application has been withdrawn or was deemed to have been withdrawn, or the designation of China of the international application has been withdrawn; (2) where the applicant fails to go through the formalities for entry into the Chinese national phase within 32 months from the priority date in accordance with the provision of Article 103 of these Implementing Regulations; (3) while going through the formalities for entry into the Chinese national phase, the applicant fails to fulfil the requirements of Article 104, subparagraphs (1) to (3) of these Implementing Regulations at the expiration of the time limit of 32 months from the date of priority. Where the effect of an international application cease in China in accordance with the provision of the preceding paragraph, subparagraph (1), the provisions of Article 6 of these Implementing Regulations shall not apply. Where the effect of an international application cease in China in accordance with the provision of the preceding paragraph, subparagraph (2) or (3), the provisions of Article 6, paragraph two of these Implementing Regulations shall not apply.
第一百零六条 国际申请在国际阶段作过修改，申请人要求以经修改的申请文件为基础进行审查的，应当自进入日起2个月内提交修改部分的中文译文。在该期间内未提交中文译文的，对申请人在国际阶段提出的修改，国务院专利行政部门不予考虑。	Article 106 Where an international application was amended in the international phase and the applicant requests that the examination be based on the amended application, the Chinese translation of the amendments shall be furnished within two months from the date of entry. Where the Chinese translation is not furnished within the said time limit,

Implementing Regulations (Chinese)	Implementing Regulations (English translation)
	the amendments made in the international phase shall not be taken into consideration by the patent administration department under the State Council.
第一百零七条 国际申请涉及的发明创造有专利法第二十四条第（一）项或者第（二）项所列情形之一，在提出国际申请时作过声明的，申请人应当在进入中国国家阶段的书面声明中予以说明，并自进入日起2个月内提交本细则第三十条第三款规定的有关证明文件；未予说明或者期满未提交证明文件的，其申请不适用专利法第二十四条的规定。	Article 107 Where any invention-creation to which the international application relates has one of the events referred to in Article 24, subparagraph (1) or (2) of the Patent Law and where statements have been made in this respect when the international application was filed, the applicant shall indicate it in the written statement concerning entry into the Chinese national phase, and furnish the relevant certifying documents prescribed in Article 30, paragraph three of these Implementing Regulations within two months from the date of entry. If the applicant fails to indicate it or furnish the relevant certifying documents within the time limit, the provisions of Article 24 of the Patent Law shall not apply to its or his application.
第一百零八条 申请人按照专利合作条约的规定，对生物材料样品的保藏已作出说明的，视为已经满足了本细则第二十四条第（三）项的要求。申请人应当在进入中国国家阶段声明中指明记载生物材料样品保藏事项的文件以及在该文件中的具体记载位置。	Article 108 Where the applicant has made indications concerning deposited biological materials in accordance with the provisions of the Patent Cooperation Treaty, the requirements provided for in Article 24, subparagraph (3) of these Implementing Regulations shall be deemed to have been fulfilled. In the statement concerning entry into the Chinese national phase, the applicant shall indicate the documents recording the particulars of the deposit of the biological materials, and the exact location of the record in the documents.
申请人在原始提交的国际申请的说明书中已记载生物材料样品保藏事项，但是没有在进入中国国家阶段声明中指明的，应当自进入日起4个月内补正。期满未补正的，该生物材料视为未提交保藏。	Where particulars concerning the deposit of the biological materials are contained in the description of the international application as initially filed, but there is no such indication in the statement concerning the entry into the Chinese national phase, the applicant shall make corrections within four months from the date of entry. If the correction is not made at the expiration of the time limit, the biological materials shall be deemed not to have been deposited.
申请人自进入日起4个月内向国务院专利行政部门提交生物材料样品保藏证明和存活证明的，视为在本细则第二十四条第（一）项规定的期限内提交。	Where, within four months from the date of entry, the applicant has submitted the certificates of the deposit and the viability of the biological materials to the patent administration department under the

Implementing Regulations (Chinese)	Implementing Regulations (English translation)
	State Council, the deposit of biological materials shall be deemed to have been furnished within the time limit as provided for in Article 24, subparagraph (1) of these Implementing Regulations.
第一百零九条 国际申请涉及的发明创造依赖遗传资源完成的，申请人应当在国际申请进入中国国家阶段的书面声明中予以说明，并填写国务院专利行政部门制定的表格。	**Article 109** Where an invention-creation has been developed relying on the use of genetic resources for which the international application is filed, the applicant shall indicate the fact in the written statement for entering the Chinese national phase, and fill in the forms provided by the patent administration department under the State Council.
第一百一十条 申请人在国际阶段已要求一项或者多项优先权，在进入中国国家阶段时该优先权要求继续有效的，视为已经依照专利法第三十条的规定提出了书面声明。 申请人应当自进入日起2个月内缴纳优先权要求费；期满未缴纳或者未缴足的，视为未要求该优先权。 申请人在国际阶段已依照专利合作条约的规定，提交过在先申请文件副本的，办理进入中国国家阶段手续时不需要向国务院专利行政部门提交在先申请文件副本。申请人在国际阶段未提交在先申请文件副本的，国务院专利行政部门认为必要时，可以通知申请人在指定期限内补交；申请人期满未补交的，其优先权要求视为未提出。	**Article 110** Where the applicant claims one or multiple priorities in the international phase and such claims remain valid at the time when the application enters the Chinese national phase, the applicant shall be deemed to have submitted the written declaration in accordance with the provisions of Article 30 of the Patent Law. The applicant shall pay a fee for the claim of priority within two months from the date of entry. If the fee is not paid or not paid in full within the time limit, the priority shall be deemed not to have been claimed. Where the applicant has submitted a copy of the earlier application in the international phase in accordance with the provisions of the Patent Cooperation Treaty, he or it shall be exempted from submitting a copy of the earlier application to the patent administration department under the State Council at the time of going through the formalities for entering the Chinese national phase. Where the applicant has not submitted a copy of the earlier application in the international phase, and if the patent administration department under the State Council deems necessary, it may notify the applicant to submit a copy of the earlier application within the specified time limit. If no copy is submitted at the expiration of the time limit, his or its claim for priority shall be deemed not to have been made.
第一百一十一条 在优先权日起30个月期满前要求国务院专利行政部门提前处理和审查国际申请的，申请人除应当办理进入中国国家阶段手续外，还应当依照专利合作条约第二十三条第二款规定提出请求。国际局尚未向国务	**Article 111** Where, before the expiration of 30 months from the priority date, the applicant files a request with the patent administration department under the State Council for early processing and examination of his or its international application, he or it shall, in

Implementing Regulations (Chinese)	Implementing Regulations (English translation)
院专利行政部门传送国际申请的，申请人应当提交经确认的国际申请副本。	addition to going through the formalities for entering the Chinese national phase, submit a request in accordance with the provisions in Article 23, paragraph two of the Patent Cooperation Treaty. Where the international application has not been transmitted by the International Bureau to the patent administration department under the State Council, the applicant shall submit a certified copy of the international application.
第一百一十二条 要求获得实用新型专利权的国际申请，申请人可以自进入日起2个月内对专利申请文件主动提出修改。 要求获得发明专利权的国际申请，适用本细则第五十一条第一款的规定。	Article 112 With regard to an international application for a patent for utility model, the applicant may amend the patent application documents on its or his own initiative within two months from the date of entry. With regard to an international application for a patent for invention, the provisions of Article 51, paragraph one of these Implementing Regulations shall apply.
第一百一十三条 申请人发现提交的说明书、权利要求书或者附图中的文字的中文译文存在错误的，可以在下列规定期限内依照原始国际申请文本提出改正： （一）在国务院专利行政部门作好公布发明专利申请或者公告实用新型专利权的准备工作之前； （二）在收到国务院专利行政部门发出的发明专利申请进入实质审查阶段通知书之日起3个月内。 申请人改正译文错误的，应当提出书面请求并缴纳规定的译文改正费。 申请人按照国务院专利行政部门的通知书的要求改正译文的，应当在指定期限内办理本条第二款规定的手续；期满未办规定手续的，该申请视为撤回。	Article 113 Where the applicant finds that there are mistakes in the Chinese translation of the description, the claims or the text matter in the drawings as filed, he or it may correct the translation in accordance with the international application as filed within the following time limits: (1) before the completion of technical preparations for publication of an application for a patent for invention or announcement of patent right for utility model by the patent administration department under the State Council; (2) within three months from the date of receipt of the notification sent by the patent administration department under the State Council, stating that the application for a patent for invention has entered into the substantive examination phase. Where the applicant intends to correct the mistakes in the translation, he or it shall file a written request and pay the prescribed fee for the correction of the translation. Where the applicant makes correction of the translation in accordance with the notification of the patent administration department under the State Council, he or it shall, within the specified time limit, go through the formalities prescribed in paragraph two of this Article. If the prescribed formalities are not gone through at the expiration of the time limit, the international application shall be deemed to be withdrawn.

Implementing Regulations (Chinese)	Implementing Regulations (English translation)
第一百一十四条 对要求获得发明专利权的国际申请，国务院专利行政部门经初步审查认为符合专利法和本细则有关规定的，应当在专利公报上予以公布；国际申请以中文以外的文字提出的，应当公布申请文件的中文译文。	Article 114 With regard to any international application for a patent for invention, if the patent administration department under the State Council, after preliminary examination, considers it in compliance with relevant provisions of the Patent Law and these Implementing Regulations, it shall publish it in the Patent Gazette; where the international application is filed in a language other than Chinese, the Chinese translation of the international application shall be published.
要求获得发明专利权的国际申请，由国际局以中文进行国际公布的，自国际公布日起适用专利法第十三条的规定；由国际局以中文以外的文字进行国际公布的，自国务院专利行政部门公布之日起适用专利法第十三条的规定。	Where the international publication of an international application for a patent for invention by the International Bureau is in Chinese, the provisions of Article 13 of the Patent Law shall apply from the date of the international publication. If the international publication by the International Bureau is in a language other than Chinese, the provisions of Article 13 of the Patent Law shall apply from the date of the publication of the Chinese translation by the patent administration department under the State Council.
对国际申请，专利法第二十一条和第二十二条中所称的公布是指本条第一款所规定的公布。	With regard to an international application, the publication referred to in Articles 21 and 22 of the Patent Law means the publication referred to in paragraph one of this Article.
第一百一十五条 国际申请包含两项以上发明或者实用新型的，申请人可以自进入日起，依照本细则第四十二条第一款的规定提出分案申请。	Article 115 Where two or more inventions or utility models are contained in an international application, the applicant may, from the date of entry, submit a divisional application in accordance with the provisions in Article 42, paragraph one of these Implementing Regulations.
在国际阶段，国际检索单位或者国际初步审查单位认为国际申请不符合专利合作条约规定的单一性要求时，申请人未按照规定缴纳附加费，导致国际申请某些部分未经国际检索或者未经国际初步审查，在进入中国国家阶段时，申请人要求将所述部分作为审查基础，国务院专利行政部门认为国际检索单位或者国际初步审查单位对发明单一性的判断正确的，应当通知申请人在指定期限内缴纳单一性恢复费。期满未缴纳或者未足额缴纳的，国际申请中未经检索或者未经国际初步审查的部分视为撤回。	Where, in the international phase, some parts of the international application have not been the subject of international search or international preliminary examination because the International Searching Authority or the International Preliminary Examination Authority considers that the international application does not comply with the requirement of unity of invention prescribed in the Patent Cooperation Treaty, and the applicant fails to pay the additional fee, whereas at the time of going through the formalities for entering the Chinese national phase, the applicant requests that the said parts be the basis of examination, the patent

Implementing Regulations (Chinese)	Implementing Regulations (English translation)
	administration department under the State Council, finding that the decision concerning unity of invention made by the International Searching Authority or the International Preliminary Examination Authority is justified, shall notify the applicant to pay the restoration fee for unity of invention within the specified time limit. Where the fee is not paid or not paid in full at the expiration of the prescribed time limit, those parts of the international application which have not been searched or have not been the subject of international preliminary examination shall be deemed to be withdrawn.
第一百一十六条 国际申请在国际阶段被有关国际单位拒绝给予国际申请日或者宣布视为撤回的，申请人在收到通知之日起2个月内，可以请求国际局将国际申请档案中任何文件的副本转交国务院专利行政部门，并在该期限内向国务院专利行政部门办理本细则第一百零三条规定的手续，国务院专利行政部门应当在接到国际局传送的文件后，对国际单位作出的决定是否正确进行复查。	Article 116 Where an international application in the international phase has been refused to be accorded an international filling date or has been declared to be deemed withdrawn by an international authority concerned, the applicant may, within two months from the date on which he or it receives the notification, request the International Bureau to send the copy of any document in the file of the international application to the patent administration department under the State Council, and shall go through the formalities prescribed in Article 103 of these Implementing Regulations within the said time limit before the patent administration department under the State Council. After receiving the documents sent by the International Bureau, the patent administration department under the State Council shall review the decision made by the international authority concerned to find whether it is correct.
第一百一十七条 基于国际申请授予的专利权，由于译文错误，致使依照专利法第五十九条规定确定的保护范围超出国际申请的原文所表达的范围的，以依据原文限制后的保护范围为准；致使保护范围小于国际申请的原文所表达的范围的，以授权时的保护范围为准。	Article 117 With regard to a patent right granted on the basis of an international application, if the extent of protection determined in accordance with the provisions of Article 59 of the Patent Law exceeds the scope of the international application in its original language because of incorrect translation, the extent of protection granted on the international application shall be determined according to what is limited in the original language of the application; if the extent of protection granted on the international application is narrower than the scope of the application in its original language, the extent of protection shall be determined according to the patent when it is granted.

Implementing Regulations (Chinese)	Implementing Regulations (English translation)

第十一章　附则

Chapter 11　Supplementary Provisions

第一百一十八条
经国务院专利行政部门同意，任何人均可以查阅或者复制已经公布或者公告的专利申请的案卷和专利登记簿，并可以请求国务院专利行政部门出具专利登记簿副本。

已视为撤回、驳回和主动撤回的专利申请的案卷，自该专利申请失效之日起满2年后不予保存。

已放弃、宣告全部无效和终止的专利权的案卷，自该专利权失效之日起满3年后不予保存。

Article 118

Any person may, after approval by the patent administration department under the State Council, consult or copy the files of the published or announced patent applications and the Patent Register. Any person may request the patent administration department under the State Council to issue a copy of extracts from the Patent Register.

The files of the patent applications which have been withdrawn or deemed to be withdrawn or which have been rejected, shall not be preserved after expiration of two years from the date on which the applications cease to be valid.

Where the patent right has been abandoned, wholly invalidated or ceased, the files shall not be preserved after expiration of three years from the date on which the patent right ceases to be valid.

第一百一十九条
向国务院专利行政部门提交申请文件或者办理各种手续，应当由申请人、专利权人、其他利害关系人或者其代表人签字或者盖章；委托专利代理机构的，由专利代理机构盖章。

请求变更发明人姓名、专利申请人和专利权人的姓名或者名称、国籍和地址、专利代理机构的名称、地址和代理人姓名的，应当向国务院专利行政部门办理著录事项变更手续，并附具变更理由的证明材料。

Article 119

Any patent application which is filed with, or any formality which is gone through before, the patent administration department under the State Council shall be signed or sealed by the applicant, the patentee, any other interested person or his or its representative. Where any patent agency is appointed, it shall be sealed by such agency.

Where a change in the name of the inventor, or in the title or name, nationality and address of the applicant or the patentee, or in the title and address of the patent agency and the name of patent agent is requested, a request for a change in the bibliographic data shall be made to the patent administration department under the State Council, together with the relevant certifying documents.

第一百二十条
向国务院专利行政部门邮寄有关申请或者专利权的文件，应当使用挂号信函，不得使用包裹。
除首次提交专利申请文件外，向国务院专利行政部门提交各种文件、办理各种手续的，应当标明申请号或者专利号、发明创造名称和申请人或者专利权人姓名或者名称。

Article 120

The document relating to a patent application or patent right which is mailed to the patent administration department under the State Council shall be mailed by registered letter, not by parcel.

Except for any patent application filed for the first time, any document which is submitted to and any formality which is gone through before the patent administration department under the State Council, the filing number or the patent number, the title of the invention-creation and the title or name of the applicant or the patentee shall be indicated.

Implementing Regulations (Chinese)	Implementing Regulations (English translation)
一件信函中应当只包含同一申请的文件。	Only documents relating to the same application shall be included in one letter.
第一百二十一条 各类申请文件应当打字或者印刷，字迹呈黑色，整齐清晰，并不得涂改。附图应当用制图工具和黑色墨水绘制，线条应当均匀清晰，并不得涂改。	Article 121 Various kinds of application documents shall be typed or punted. All the characters shall be in black ink, neat and clear. They shall be free from any alterations. The drawings shall be made in black ink with the aid of drafting instruments. The lines shall be uniformly thick and well defined, and free from alterations.
请求书、说明书、权利要求书、附图和摘要应当分别用阿拉伯数字顺序编号。	The request, description, claims, drawings and abstract shall be numbered separately in Arabic numerals and arranged in numerical order.
申请文件的文字部分应当横向书写。纸张限于单面使用。	The written language of the application shall run from left to right. Only one side of each sheet shall be used.
第一百二十二条 国务院专利行政部门根据专利法和本细则制定专利审查指南。	Article 122 The patent administration department under the State Council shall formulate Guidelines for Examination in accordance with the Patent Law and these Implementing Regulations.
第一百二十三条 本细则自2001年7月1日起施行。1992年12月12日国务院批准修订、1992年12月21日中国专利局发布的《中华人民共和国专利法实施细则》同时废止。	Article 123 These Implementing Regulations shall enter into force on July 1, 2001. The Implementing Regulations of the Patent Law of the People's Republic of China approved by the State Council on December 12, 1992 and promulgated by the Patent Office of the People's Republic of China on December 21, 1992 shall be repealed at the same time.

APPENDIX 3

Interpretation by the Supreme People's Court on Several Issues Regarding Legal Application in the Adjudication of Patent Infringement Cases

最高人民法院关于审理侵犯专利权纠纷案件应用法律若干问题

Effective January 1, 2010

为正确审理侵犯专利权纠纷案件，根据《中华人民共和国专利法》、《中华人民共和国民事诉讼法》等有关法律规定，结合审判实际，制定本解释。	To facilitate proper adjudication of patent infringement disputes, in accordance with the relevant provisions of the Patent Law of the People's Republic of China, the Civil Procedure Law of the People's Republic of China and other laws, and combining the actual practice of trials, this interpretation is promulgated.
第一条　人民法院应当根据权利人主张的权利要求，依据专利法第五十九条第一款的规定确定专利权的保护范围。权利人在一审法庭辩论终结前变更其主张的权利要求的，人民法院应当准许。	1. The people's court shall based on the claims asserted by the right holder in accordance with Article 59(1) of the Patent Law, determine the scope of protection of the patent rights. If the right holder changes the claim which he asserts before the end of the submissions of the first instance trial, the People's Court shall permit this.
权利人主张以从属权利要求确定专利权保护范围的，人民法院应当以该从属权利要求记载的附加技术特征及其引用的权利要求记载的技术特征，确定专利权的保护范围。	If the right holder requests a determination of the scope of protection of the patent rights based on a dependent claim, the People's Court shall determine the scope of protection of the patent rights based upon the additional technical limitations recited in the dependent claim as well as the technical limitations of the claim it relies upon.

第二条　人民法院应当根据权利要求的记载，结合本领域普通技术人员阅读说明书及附图后对权利要求的理解，确定专利法第五十九条第一款规定的权利要求的内容。	2. The people's court shall based on what is recited in the claims combined with the understanding of a person of ordinary skill in the art who reads the specification and figures confirm, based on the provisions of Article 59(1) of the Patent Law, the contents of the claim.
第三条　人民法院对于权利要求，可以运用说明书及附图、权利要求书中的相关权利要求、专利审查档案进行解释。说明书对权利要求用语有特别界定的，从其特别界定。	3. The people's court may use the specification, figures, relevant claims of the patent, and the patent examination file to interpret a claim. If the specification contains a special definition regarding terminology in the claim, it shall be specially defined as such.
以上述方法仍不能明确权利要求含义的，可以结合工具书、教科书等公知文献以及本领域普通技术人员的通常理解进行解释。	If using the above methods it is still not possible to clearly determine the meaning of the claim, interpretation can conducted using a combination of literature available to the public such as reference books and textbooks, as well as the ordinary meaning understood by an ordinary skilled man.
第四条　对于权利要求中以功能或者效果表述的技术特征，人民法院应当结合说明书和附图描述的该功能或者效果的具体实施方式及其等同的实施方式，确定该技术特征的内容。	4. Where the claim describes a technical limitation though functions or effects, the people's court shall determine the contents of the technical limitation according to the specific embodiments and the equivalent embodiments of the functions or effects described by the specification and figures.
第五条　对于仅在说明书或者附图中描述而在权利要求中未记载的技术方案，权利人在侵犯专利权纠纷案件中将其纳入专利权保护范围的，人民法院不予支持。	5. Regarding a technical scheme which has only been described in the specification or figures and has not been recited in the claims, and the right holder in a patent infringement suit seeks to include it in the scope of protection of patent rights, the people's court will not support it.
第六条　专利申请人、专利权人在专利授权或者无效宣告程序中，通过对权利要求、说明书的修改或者意见陈述而放弃的技术方案，权利人在侵犯专利权纠纷案件中又将其纳入专利权保护范围的，人民法院不予支持。	6. If a patent applicant or a patent right holder in the course of grant or invalidation, abandoned a technical scheme through amendments to the claims or specifications or in a statement of opinion, and the right holder in a patent infringement suit seeks to include it in the scope of protection of patent rights, the people's court will not support it.
第七条　人民法院判定被诉侵权技术方案是否落入专利权的保护范围，应当审查权利人主张的权利要求所记载的全部技术特征。	7. When a people's court adjudicates whether an alleged infringing technical scheme falls into the scope of protection of patent rights, it shall examine all the technical limitations recited in the claims asserted by the right-holder.
被诉侵权技术方案包含与权利要求记载的全部技术特征相同或者等同的技术特征的，人民法院应当认定其落入专利权的保护范围；被诉侵权技术方案的技术特征与权利要求记载的全部技术特征相比，缺少权利要求记载的一个以上的技术特	If the alleged infringing technical scheme includes all the technical limitations or equivalent technical limitations recited in a claim, the people's court shall determine that the accused infringing technical scheme falls into the scope of protection of the patent rights. When comparing the technical

征，或者有一个以上技术特征不相同也不等同的，人民法院应当认定其没有落入专利权的保护范围。	limitations of an alleged infringing technical scheme and all the technical limitations recited in the claim, if one or more of the technical limitations recited in the claim are missing, or if one or more of the technical limitation are not identical or equivalent, the people's court shall determine that the accused infringing technical scheme does not fall into the scope of protection of the patent rights.
第八条 在与外观设计专利产品相同或者相近种类产品上，采用与授权外观设计相同或者近似的外观设计的，人民法院应当认定被诉侵权设计落入专利法第五十九条第二款规定的外观设计专利权的保护范围。	8. Where a product of the same or similar type to the product of the design patent uses a design which is identical or similar to the granted design patent, the people's court shall determine the alleged infringing design patent falls into the scope of protection of design patents of Article 59(2), of the Patent Law
第九条 人民法院应当根据外观设计产品的用途，认定产品种类是否相同或者相近。确定产品的用途，可以参考外观设计的简要说明、国际外观设计分类表、产品的功能以及产品销售、实际使用的情况等因素。	9. The people's court shall based on the purpose of the product of the design patent, determine whether the type of product is identical or similar. To determine the purpose of the product, the People's Court may refer to the brief description of the design, the International Classification for Industrial Designs, the function of the product as well as factors such as the circumstances of sale and actual use of the products.
第十条 人民法院应当以外观设计专利产品的一般消费者的知识水平和认知能力，判断外观设计是否相同或者近似。	10. The people's court shall, deciding whether the design is identical or similar, using the intellectual level and cognitive ability of ordinary consumers of the product the subject of the design patent.
第十一条 人民法院认定外观设计是否相同或者近似时，应当根据授权外观设计、被诉侵权设计的设计特征，以外观设计的整体视觉效果进行综合判断；对于主要由技术功能决定的设计特征以及对整体视觉效果不产生影响的产品的材料、内部结构等特征，应当不予考虑。	11. The people's court in determining whether a design is identical or similar, shall according to the design features of the granted design and the accused infringing design patent, conduct a comprehensive determination based on the total visual effect of the design; however, design features that are determined mainly by technical functions as well as features that which do not affect the total visual effect such as materials and internal construction shall not be considered.
下列情形，通常对外观设计的整体视觉效果更具有影响： （一）产品正常使用时容易被直接观察到的部位相对于其他部位； （二）授权外观设计区别于现有设计的设计特征相对于授权外观设计的其他设计特征。 被诉侵权设计与授权外观设计在整体视觉效果上无差异的，人民法院应当认定两者相同；在整体视觉效果上无实质性差异的，应当认定两者近似。	The following conditions usually have more influence on the total visual effect of a design: (a) Parts of the product that in normal use are easily observed directly relative other parts; (b) Design features of the granted design that differ from existing designs relative to other design features of the granted design. If the alleged infringing design does not differ from the granted design in terms of total visual effect, the People's Court shall determine the two to be the same; if no substantial difference in total visual effect exists, the two shall be determined to be similar.

第十二条　将侵犯发明或者实用新型专利权的产品作为零部件，制造另一产品的，人民法院应当认定属于专利法第十一条规定的使用行为；销售该另一产品的，人民法院应当认定属于专利法第十一条规定的销售行为。	12. If a product which infringes invention or utility model patent rights has been used as a component to manufacture another product, the people's court shall determine that it constitutes an act of use under Article 11 of the Patent Law. If such other product is sold, the people's court shall determine that it constitutes and act of selling under Article 11 of the Patent Law.
将侵犯外观设计专利权的产品作为零部件，制造另一产品并销售的，人民法院应当认定属于专利法第十一条规定的销售行为，但侵犯外观设计专利权的产品在该另一产品中仅具有技术功能的除外。	If a product which infringes a design patent right has been used as a component to manufacture and sell anther product, the people's court shall determine that it constitutes an act of selling under Article 11 of the Patent Law, subject to the exception however where the infringing design patent product only has technical functions in said other product.
对于前两款规定的情形，被诉侵权人之间存在分工合作的，人民法院应当认定为共同侵权。	Regarding the situations provided in the two preceding paragraphs, if there exists division of labour and cooperation between alleged infringers, the people's court shall determine this to be joint infringement.
第十三条　对于使用专利方法获得的原始产品，人民法院应当认定为专利法第十一条规定的依照专利方法直接获得的产品。	13. With regard to an original product obtained through the use of a patented process, the people's court shall determine this to constitute a product directly obtained through the patented process under Article 11 of the Patent Law.
对于将上述原始产品进一步加工、处理而获得后续产品的行为，人民法院应当认定属于专利法第十一条规定的使用依照该专利方法直接获得的产品。	With regard to the acts of further processing or treating the above original product to obtain a further product, the people's court shall determine this to constitute use under Article 11 of the Patent Law by which a product is directly obtained by the patented process.
第十四条　被诉落入专利权保护范围的全部技术特征，与一项现有技术方案中的相应技术特征相同或者无实质性差异的，人民法院应当认定被诉侵权人实施的技术属于专利法第六十二条规定的现有技术。	14. If all the technical characteristics alleged to fall within the scope of protection of a patent right are identical or without substantial differences to corresponding technical characteristics of a prior art technical scheme, the people's court shall determine that the technology implemented by the alleged infringer constitutes prior art under Article 62 of the Patent Law.
被诉侵权设计与一个现有设计相同或者无实质性差异的，人民法院应当认定被诉侵权人实施的设计属于专利法第六十二条规定的现有设计。	If an alleged infringing design is identical to or without substantial differences to a prior design, the People's Court shall determine the design implemented by the alleged infringer constitutes a prior design under Article 62 of the Patent Law.
第十五条　被诉侵权人以非法获得的技术或者设计主张先用权抗辩的，人民法院不予支持。	15. If an alleged infringer asserts a prior art defence based on a technology or design which has been illegally obtained, the People's Court shall not support it.

有下列情形之一的，人民法院应当认定属于专利法第六十九条第（二）项规定的已经作好制造、使用的必要准备：

（一）已经完成实施发明创造所必需的主要技术图纸或者工艺文件；
（二）已经制造或者购买实施发明创造所必需的主要设备或者原材料。

专利法第六十九条第（二）项规定的原有范围，包括专利申请日前已有的生产规模以及利用已有的生产设备或者根据已有的生产准备可以达到的生产规模。

先用权人在专利申请日后将其已经实施或作好实施必要准备的技术或设计转让或者许可他人实施，被诉侵权人主张该实施行为属于在原有范围内继续实施的，人民法院不予支持，但该技术或设计与原有企业一并转让或者承继的除外。

第十六条 人民法院依据专利法第六十五条第一款的规定确定侵权人因侵权所获得的利益，应当限于侵权人因侵犯专利权行为所获得的利益；因其他权利所产生的利益，应当合理扣除。

侵犯发明、实用新型专利权的产品系另一产品的零部件的，人民法院应当根据该零部件本身的价值及其在实现成品利润中的作用等因素合理确定赔偿数额。

侵犯外观设计专利权的产品为包装物的，人民法院应当按照包装物本身的价值及其在实现被包装产品利润中的作用等因素合理确定赔偿数额。

In any of the following situations, the people's court shall determine that it constitutes "already made the necessary preparations for manufacturing or using" under Article 69(2) of the Patent Law.

(1) The main technical drawings or technical documents needed for implementing the invention-creation have already been completed.
(2) The main equipment or raw materials required for implementing the invention-creation have been manufactured or purchased.

The original scope under Article 69(2) of the Patent Law includes the existing manufacturing scale as well as the manufacturing scale which can be reached using the existing manufacturing equipment or based on the existing preparations for manufacturing before the date of application for the patent.

If the prior use rights holder after the patent application date, transfers or licenses the technology or design for existing implementation or for the preparation for implementation to a third party to be implemented, and if the alleged infringer asserts such act of implementation constitutes continued implementation within the original scope, the people's court shall not support it, except, however, where the technology or design and the original company have been simultaneously transferred or succeeded to.

16. When the people's court determines the profit obtained due to the infringement by the infringer under Article 65(1) of the Patent Law, it shall be limited to the profit obtained due to the acts of infringement by the infringer; all other profits produced by other rights shall be reasonably deducted.

Where the product which infringes invention or utility model patent rights is the component of another product, the people's court shall in accordance with factors such as the value of such part itself as well as its role in producing the profit of the final product reasonably determine the amount of damages.

Where the product infringing a design patent is a packaging, the people's court shall in accordance with factors such as the value of packaging itself as well as its role in producing the profit of the packaged product reasonably determine the amount of damages

第十七条 产品或者制造产品的技术方案在专利申请日以前为国内外公众所知的，人民法院应当认定该产品不属于专利法第六十一条第一款规定的新产品。	17. If a product or the technical scheme of a product is known to the domestic or overseas public before the application date of a patent, the People's Court shall deem that the product does not fall within the "new product" under Article 61(1) of the Patent Law.
第十八条 权利人向他人发出侵犯专利权的警告，被警告人或者利害关系人经书面催告权利人行使诉权，自权利人收到该书面催告之日起一个月内或者自书面催告发出之日起二个月内，权利人不撤回警告也不提起诉讼，被警告人或者利害关系人向人民法院提起请求确认其行为不侵犯专利权的诉讼的，人民法院应当受理。	18. Where a right holder issues to a third party a patent infringement warning, if the party which has been warned or an related injured party has in writing demanded the right holder to exercise its right to sue, and if within one month from the right holder receiving said written demand notice or within two months from the sending of said demand notice, the right holder does not withdraw the warning and does not file a suit, if the party which has been warned or the related injured party files a suit to the people's court to request a determination that its acts do not infringe patent rights, the People's Court shall accept the case.
第十九条 被诉侵犯专利权行为发生在2009年10月1日以前的，人民法院适用修改前的专利法；发生在2009年10月1日以后的，人民法院适用修改后的专利法。 被诉侵犯专利权行为发生在2009年10月1日以前且持续到2009年10月1日以后，依据修改前和修改后的专利法的规定侵权人均应承担赔偿责任的，人民法院适用修改后的专利法确定赔偿数额。	19. If an alleged act of patent infringement took place before 1 October 2009, the people's court shall apply the Patent Law before the amendment; if it takes place after 1 October 2009, the people's court shall apply the amended Patent Law. Where the alleged acts of patent infringement occurred prior to 1 October 2009 and continue after 1 October 2009, and the infringer shall be liable to pay compensation in accordance with the provisions of the Patent Law pre-amendment and post-amendment, the People's Court shall apply the post-amendment Patent Law to determine the amount of compensation.
第二十条 本院以前发布的有关司法解释与本解释不一致的，以本解释为准。	20. In case of any inconsistencies with relevant judicial interpretations previously issued by this court, this Interpretation shall control.

APPENDIX 4

Several Provisions of the Supreme People's Court on Issues Relating to Application of Law to Adjudication of Cases of Patent Disputes

最高人民法院关于审理专利纠纷案件 适用法律问题的若干规定

（2001年6月19日最高人民法院审判委员会第1180 次会议通过）

(Adopted on 19 June 2001 at the 1180th Meeting of the Adjudication Committee of the Supreme People's Court)

为了正确审理专利纠纷案件，根据《中华人民共和国民法通则》（以下简称民法通则）、《中华人民共和国专利法》（以下简称专利法）、《中华人民共和国民事诉讼法》和《中华人民共和国行政诉讼法》等法律的规定，作如下规定：

With a view to correctly adjudicating patent dispute cases, in accordance with the legal provisions of the General Principles of the Civil Law of the People's Republic of China (hereinafter General Principles of the Civil Law), the Patent Law of the People's Republic of China, (hereinafter Patent Law), the Civil Procedure Law of the People's Republic of China and the Administrative Procedure Law of the People's Republic of China and other laws, the following regulations are made:

第一条
人民法院受理下列专利纠纷案件：
1. 专利申请权纠纷案件；
2. 专利权权属纠纷案件；
3. 专利权、专利申请权转让合同纠纷案件；
4. 侵犯专利权纠纷案件；
5. 假冒他人专利纠纷案件；
6. 发明专利申请公布后、专利权授予前使用费纠纷案件；

Article 1
The people's courts accept following cases of patent disputes:
1. Patent entitlement cases;
2. Patent ownership cases;
3. Patent and patent application assignment dispute cases;
4. Patent infringement cases;
5. Patent counterfeiting cases;
6. Disputes over the fee use of a patent after publication of the application for a patent for invention and before the patent grant;

7. 职务发明创造发明人、设计人奖励、报酬纠纷案件；
8. 诉前申请停止侵权、财产保全案件；
9. 发明人、设计人资格纠纷案件；
10. 不服专利复审委员会维持驳回申请复审决定案件；
11. 不服专利复审委员会专利权无效宣告请求决定案件；
12. 不服国务院专利行政部门实施强制许可决定案件；
13. 不服国务院专利行政部门实施强制许可使用费裁决案件；
14. 不服国务院专利行政部门行政复议决定案件；
15. 不服管理专利工作的部门行政决定案件；
16. 其他专利纠纷案件。

7. Disputes over the reward and remuneration for the inventor-creators of service inventions or designers;
8. Pre-action applications for ceasing infringement or for property preservation;
9. Disputes over the qualifications of inventors or designers;
10. Cases of dissatisfaction with the re-examination decisions of the Patent Re-examination Board to uphold rejection of applications;
11. Cases of dissatisfaction with the re-examination decisions by the Patent Re-examination Board on requests for invalidation of the patent right;
12. Cases of dissatisfaction with decisions by the Patent Administrative Organ under the State Council on execution of compulsory licenses;
13. Cases of dissatisfaction with the adjudication by the Patent Administrative Organ under the State Council on the use fees for execution of compulsory licenses;
14. Cases of dissatisfaction with the administrative re-examination decisions by the Patent Administrative Organ under the State Council;
15. Cases of dissatisfaction with the administrative decisions by the administrative authorities for patent affairs; and
16. Any other patent dispute cases.

第二条
专利纠纷第一审案件，由各省、自治区、直辖市人民政府所在地的中级人民法院和最高人民法院指定的中级人民法院管辖。

Article 2
Patent dispute cases of first instance shall be under the jurisdiction of the intermediate people's courts of the seats of the People's Government of the Provinces, Autonomous Regions and Municipalities directly under the Central Government and intermediate people' courts designated by the Supreme People's Court.

第三条
当事人对专利复审委员会于2001年7月1日以后作出的关于实用新型、外观设计专利权撤销请求复审决定不服向人民法院起诉的，人民法院不予受理。

Article 3
Where any party dissatisfied with a re-examination decision made by the Patent Re-examination Board after 1 July 2001 on the requests for revocation of a patent for utility model or design, institutes a lawsuit in the people's court, the people's court will not accept it.

第四条
当事人对专利复审委员会于2001年7月1日以后作出的关于维持驳回实用新型、外观设计专利申请的复审决定，或者关于实用新型、外观设计专利权无效宣告请求的决定不服向人民法院起诉的，人民法院应当受理。

Article 4
Where any party dissatisfied with a re-examination decision made by the Patent Re-examination Board after 1 July 2001 to uphold the rejection of the application for patent for utility model or design or with the decision on the request for invalidation of the patent right for utility model or design, institutes a lawsuit in the people's court, the people's court shall accept the lawsuit.

第五条

因侵犯专利权行为提起的诉讼，由侵权行为地或者被告住所地人民法院管辖。侵权行为地包括：被控侵犯发明、实用新型专利权的产品的制造、使用、许诺销售、销售、进口等行为的实施地；专利方法使用行为的实施地，依照该专利方法直接获得的产品的使用、许诺销售、销售、进口等行为的实施地；外观设计专利产品的制造、销售、进口等行为的实施地；假冒他人专利的行为实施地。上述侵权行为的侵权结果发生地。

Article 5

Lawsuits instituted against acts of patent infringement shall be under the jurisdiction of the people's court of the place where the defendant has its domicile or the place of infringement. Places of infringement include: places where acts take place of manufacturing, using, offering for sale, selling or importing products accused of infringing a patent for invention or utility model; places where the acts of using a patented process takes place and where acts take place of using, offering for sale, selling or importing products acquired directly according to the patented process; places where acts of manufacturing, selling or importing products of patented designs; places where acts of counterfeiting patents of other persons take place. Places where consequences of the preceding infringing acts arise.

第六条

原告仅对侵权产品制造者提起诉讼，未起诉销售者，侵权产品制造地与销售地不一致的，制造地人民法院有管辖权；以制造者与销售者为共同被告起诉的，销售地人民法院有管辖权。

销售者是制造者分支机构，原告在销售地起诉侵权产品制造者制造、销售行为的，销售地人民法院有管辖权。

Article 6

Where a plaintiff takes action against the manufacturer of an infringing product, but not against the seller and the places where the infringing products are manufactured and sold are not the same place, the people's court of the place of the manufacture has jurisdiction; where the action is taken with both the manufacturer and seller as the co-defendants, the people's court of the place of sale has jurisdiction.

Where the seller is a subordinate organisation of the manufacturer and the plaintiff takes action against the acts of the manufacturer of the infringing products to manufacture and selling the product, the people's court of the place of sale has jurisdiction.

第七条

原告根据1993年1月1日以前提出的专利申请和根据该申请授予的方法发明专利权提起的侵权诉讼，参照本规定第五条、第六条的规定确定管辖。

人民法院在上述案件实体审理中依法适用方法发明专利权不延及产品的规定。

Article 7

Where a plaintiff institutes an infringement lawsuit in relation to a of process invention patent granted for a patent application filed before 1 January 1993, jurisdiction is determined by reference to the provisions of Articles 5 and 6 of these Provisions.

The people's court, in substantive hearing of the preceding cases, shall apply the rule that a process invention patent does not extend to the product.

第八条

提起侵权实用新型专利权诉讼的原告，应当在起诉时出具由国务院专利行政部门作出的检索报告。

Article 8

Any plaintiff who takes action for infringement of a utility model patent shall when filing the suit produce the search report made by the Patent Administrative Organ under the State Council.

侵犯实用新型、外观设计专利权纠纷案件的被告请求中止诉讼的，应当在答辩期内对原告的专利权提出宣告无效的请求。	Any defendant to a case of infringement of a utility model patent or external design who requests a stay of the action shall within the time limited for filing a defence, file a request for invalidation of the plaintiff's patent right.
第九条 人民法院受理的侵犯实用新型、外观设计专利权纠纷案件，被告在答辩期间内请求宣告该项专利权无效的，人民法院应当中止诉讼，但具备下列情形之一的，可以不中止诉讼：	Article 9 In a case accepted by the people's court for infringement of a utility model patent or external design, where the defendant files a request for invalidation of the patent right within the time limited for filing a defence, the people's court shall stay the proceedings. However, under any one of the following circumstances, the legal proceedings may decline to stay the proceedings:
（一）原告出具的检索报告未发现导致实用新型专利丧失新颖性、创造性的技术文献的； （二）被告提供的证据足以证明其使用的技术已经公知的； （三）被告请求宣告该项专利权无效所提供的证据或者依据的理由明显不充分的； （四）人民法院认为不应当中止诉讼的其他情形。	(1) where in the search report produced by the plaintiff that there is not discovered any technical documentation to lead to the loss of novelty or inventiveness of the patent or utility model; (2) where the evidence submitted by the defendant is sufficient to prove that the technology it uses was already common knowledge; (3) where the evidence or grounds the defendant has submitted for requesting the invalidation of the patent right in question is obviously insufficient; or (4) any other circumstances where the people's court considers that the proceedings should not be stayed.
第十条 人民法院受理的侵犯实用新型、外观设计专利权纠纷案件，被告在答辩期间届满后请求宣告该项专利权无效的，人民法院不应当中止诉讼，但经审查认为有必要中止诉讼的除外。	Article 10 In a case accepted by a people's court for infringement of a utility model or external design, where the defendant files a request for invalidation of the patent right in question after the expiration of the time for making defence, the people's court shall not stay the proceedings, except where after examination it considers it is necessary to stay the proceedings.
第十一条 人民法院受理的侵犯发明专利权纠纷案件或者经专利复审委员会审查维持专利权的侵犯实用新型、外观设计专利权纠纷案件，被告在答辩期间内请求宣告该项专利权无效的，人民法院可以不中止诉讼。	Article 11 Where in a case accepted by a people's court for infringement of an invention patent or for a case of infringement of a utility model patent or external design where the Patent Re-examination Board has upheld the patent right, the defendant has within the period for filing a defence files an application to invalidate the patent, the people's court may decline stay the proceedings.

第十二条

人民法院决定中止诉讼，专利权人或者利害关系人请求责令被告停止有关行为或者采取其他制止侵权损害继续扩大的措施，并提供了担保，人民法院经审查符合有关法律规定的，可以在裁定中止诉讼的同时一并作出有关裁定。

Article 12.

Where the people's court decides to stay the proceedings, the patentee or the related injured party requests for an order that the defendant cease the relevant act or for taking other measures to stop the spread of damage caused by the infringement and provides security, the people's court, upon consideration, finds it in compliance with the provisions of the relevant laws, the people's court may at the same time as deciding to stay the proceedings make a related ruling.

第十三条

人民法院对专利权进行财产保全，应当向国务院专利行政部门发出协助执行通知书，载明要求协助执行的事项，以及对专利权保全的期限，并附人民法院作出的裁定书。

对专利权保全的期限一次不得超过六个月，自国务院专利行政部门收到协助执行通知书之日起计算如果仍然需要对该专利权继续采取保全措施的，人民法院应当在保全期限届满前向国务院专利行政部门另行送达继续保全的协助执行通知书。保全期限届满前未送达的，视为自动解除对该专利权的财产保全。

人民法院对出质的专利权可以采取财产保全措施，质权人的优先受偿权不受保全措施的影响；专利权人与被许可人已经签订的独占实施许可合同，不影响人民法院对该专利权进行财产保全。

人民法院对已经进行保全的专利权，不得重复进行保全。

Article 13

Where the people's court conducts property preservation in relation to a patent right, it shall send the Patent Administrative Organ under the State Council a notification for assistance in execution of the property preservation, indicating the matters for which assistance is sought and the duration of the patent right preservation, with the people's court written decision attached.

The period for patent right preservation that shall not last more than six months for each occasion, the term is counted from the date the Patent Administrative Organ under the State Council receives the notification of assistance for execution. If it is still necessary to continue to take measures for patent right preservation, the people's court shall serve the Patent Administrative Organ under the State Council with the notification of assistance for executing the continued preservation before the expiration of the time limit fixed for the preservation. Where such notification is not served before the expiration of the time limit fixed for the preservation, the property preservation of the patent right will be deemed to have been automatically cancelled.

The people's court may take the property preservation measures for pledged patent rights, the pledgee's priority of compensation is not affected by the preservation measure; the exclusive licensing contract concluded between the patentee and the licensee does not affect the people's court's conduct property preservation of a patent right.

The people's court shall not preserve a second time a patent right that has already been preserved.

第十四条

2001年7月1日以前利用本单位的物质技术条件所完成的发明创造，单位与发明人或者设计人订有合同，对申请专利的权利和专利权的归属作出约定的，从其约定。

Article 14

Where in respect of any invention-creation completed before 1 July 2001 by making use of the material and/or technical conditions of the entity to which the inventor or creator belongs, and the

	entity and the inventor or creator has concluded a contract, making provision for the ownership of the right to apply for patent and of the patent right, the provisions shall be observed.
第十五条 人民法院受理的侵犯专利权纠纷案件，涉及权利冲突的，应当保护在先依法享有权利的当事人的合法权益。	Article 15 The people's court in any case accepted for patent infringement where there is a conflict of rights, should protect the legitimate rights and interests of the party that enjoys the prior right according to law.
第十六条 专利法第二十三条所称的在先取得的合法权利包括：商标权、著作权、企业名称权、肖像权、知名商品特有包装或者装潢使用权等。	Article 16 The prior legitimate rights referred to in Article 23 of the Patent Law include: trademark rights, copyright, enterprise name rights, portrait rights and the right to use the well known packaging or decorations of goods, etc.
第十七条 专利法第五十六条第一款所称的"发明或者实用新型专利权的保护范围以其权利要求的内容为准，说明书及附图可以用于解释权利要求"，是指专利权的保护范围应当以权利要求书中明确记载的必要技术特征所确定的范围为准，也包括与该必要技术特征相等同的特征所确定的范围。 等同特征是指与所记载的技术特征以基本相同的手段，实现基本相同的功能，达到基本相同的效果，并且本领域的普通技术人员无需经过创造性劳动就能够联想到的特征。	Article 17 "The extent of protection of the right for invention or utility model shall be determined by the terms of the claims. The description and the appended drawings may be used to interpret the claims" mentioned in Article 56(1) of the Patent Law means that the scope of protection of patent right should be determined based on the necessary technical features expressly stated in the claims, and also includes the scope as determined by the features equivalent to the necessary technical features. The equivalent features refer to the features which uses substantially the same means, perform substantially the same function and produce substantially the same results and which can be contemplated by an ordinarily skilled person in the art without inventive labour.
第十八条 侵犯专利权行为发生在2001年7月1日以前的，适用修改前专利法的规定追究民事责任；发生在2001年7月1日以后的，适用修改后专利法的规定追究民事责任。	Article 18 Where any act of patent infringement takes place before 1 July 2001, the provisions Patent Law before amendment shall apply when seeking civil liability; where such act takes place after 1 July 2001, the provisions of the amended Patent Law shall apply to seek civil liability.
第十九条 假冒他人专利的，人民法院可以依照专利法第五十八条的规定追究其民事责任。管理专利工作的部门未给予行政处罚的，人民法院可以依照民法通则第一百三十四条第三款的规定给予民事制裁，适用民事罚款数额可以参照专利法第五十八条的规定确定。	Article 19 Where there is counterfeiting of another person's patent, the people's court may impose civil liability in accordance with the provisions of Article 58 of the Patent Law. Where the administrative authority for patent work does not impose any administrative penalty, the people's court may impose civil penalty

pursuant to the provision of Article 134(3) of the General Principles of the Civil Law, and the amount of the applicable civil fine may be determined by reference to the provisions of Article 58 of the Patent Law.

第二十条

人民法院依照专利法第五十七条第一款的规定追究侵权人的赔偿责任时，可以根据权利人的请求，按照权利人因被侵权所受到的损失或者侵权人因侵权所获得的利益确定赔偿数额。

权利人因被侵权所受到的损失可以根据专利权人的专利产品因侵权所造成销售量减少的总数乘以每件专利产品的合理利润所得之积计算。权利人销售量减少的总数难以确定的，侵权产品在市场上销售的总数乘以每件专利产品的合理利润所得之积可以视为权利人因被侵权所受到的损失。

侵权人因侵权所获得的利益可以根据该侵权产品在市场上销售的总数乘以每件侵权产品的合理利润所得之积计算。侵权人因侵权所获得的利益一般按照侵权人的营业利润计算，对于完全以侵权为业的侵权人，可以按照销售利润计算。

第二十一条

被侵权人的损失或者侵权人获得的利益难以确定，有专利许可使用费可以参照的，人民法院可以根据专利权的类别、侵权人侵权的性质和情节、专利许可使用费的数额、该专利许可的性质、范围、时间等因素，参照该专利许可使用费的1至3倍合理确定赔偿数额；没有专利许可使用费可以参照或者专利许可使用费明显不合理的，人民法院可以根据专利权的类别、侵权人侵权的性质和情节等因素，一般在人民币5000元以上30万元以下确定赔偿数额，最多不得超过人民币50万元。

Article 20

When the people's court imposes liability for compensation on the infringer according to the provision of Article 57(1) of the Patent Law, it may, in accordance with the request of the right holder, determine the amount of compensation according to the losses suffered by the right holder due to the infringement or the profit made by the infringer from the infringement.

The losses suffered by the right holder due to the infringement may be computed by the total of the infringing products sold in the market times the reasonable profit of each infringing product. Where it is difficult to determine the total reduction in the volume of sale by the right holder, the total of the infringing products sold in the market times the reasonable profit of each infringing product may be deemed to the losses suffered by the right holder due to the infringement.

The profit of the infringer from the infringement may be computed according to the total of infringing products sold in the market times the reasonable profit of each infringing product. The profit of the infringer from the infringement is generally calculated according to the business profit of the infringer. As for the infringer who solely engages in infringement as its entire business, the profit may be computed according to its sales profit.

Article 21

Where the losses of the infringee or the income of the infringer is difficult to determine, the people's court may, where there is a patent royalty that may be referred to, determine the reasonable amount of compensation according to the kind of patent right involved, the nature and facts of the infringement by the infringer, the amount of the patent royalty, the nature, extent and time of the patent license with reference to one to three times the patent licensing fee; where there is no patent licensing fee to be referred to or the license fee is obviously unreasonable, the people's court may, according to the factors, such as the kind of the patent right, the nature and facts of the infringement, determine the amount of compensation of more than RMB 5,000 yuan and less than RMB 300,000 yuan, but not exceeding RMB 500,000 yuan at most.

第二十二条 人民法院根据权利人的请求以及具体案情，可以将权利人因调查、制止侵权所支付的合理费用计算在赔偿数额范围之内。	Article 22 The people's court may, on the request of the right holder or according to the specific situation of a case, include the reasonable expenses paid for investigation or for stopping the infringement in the amount of compensation.
第二十三条 侵犯专利权的诉讼时效为二年，自专利权人或者利害关系人知道或者应当知道侵权行为之日起计算。权利人超过二年起诉的，如果侵权行为在起诉时仍在继续，在该项专利权有效期内，人民法院应当判决被告停止侵权行为，侵权损害赔偿数额应当自权利人向人民法院起诉之日起向前推算二年计算。	Article 23 The limitation for action against patent right infringement is two years, computed from the date when the patentee or the related injured party knew about or had reasonable grounds to know about the infringing act. Where the right holder does not take action after two years and the infringing act is continuing when action is taken, the people's court shall, within the term of validity of the patent right in question, rule that the defendant desist from infringing acts, and the amount of compensation for the infringement shall be computed from two years before the date when the right holder instituted legal proceedings in the people's court.
第二十四条 专利法第十一条、第六十三条所称的许诺销售，是指以做广告、在商店橱窗中陈列或者在展销会上展出等方式作出销售商品的意思表示。	Article 24 The offering for sale referred to in Articles 11 and 63 of the Patent Law means the expression of willingness to sell by way of advertisement, shop window display or exhibition.
第二十五条 人民法院受理的侵犯专利权纠纷案件，已经过管理专利工作的部门作出侵权或者不侵权认定的，人民法院仍应当就当事人的诉讼请求进行全面审查。	Article 25 Where the people's court accepts a case of dispute arising from patent infringement in which the administrative authority for patent affairs has made a determination of infringement or non-infringement, the people's court should still carry out comprehensive examination in accordance with the litigation requests of the parties.
第二十六条 以前的有关司法解释与本规定不一致的，以本规定为准。	Article 26 Where there is any discrepancy between the former relevant judicial interpretations and these Provisions, these Provisions shall prevail.

APPENDIX 5

Several Provisions of the Supreme People's Court for the Application of Law to Pre-trial Cessation of Infringement of Patent Right

最高人民法院关于对诉前停止侵犯专利权行为适用法律问题的若干规定

(2001年6月5日最高人民法院审判委员会第1179次会议通过)

(Adopted at the 1179th Meeting of the Adjudication Committee of the Supreme People's Court on 5 June 2001)

为切实保护专利权人和其他利害关系人的合法权益，根据《中华人民共和国民法通则》、《中华人民共和国专利法》（以下简称专利法)、《中华人民共和国民事诉讼法》（以下简称民事诉讼法）的有关规定，现就有关诉前停止侵犯专利权行为适用法律若干问题规定如下：

With a view to protecting the legitimate rights and interests of patentees and other related injured parties, in accordance with the relevant provisions of the General Principles of the Civil Law of the People's Republic of China, the Patent Law of the People's Republic of China (hereafter referred to as the Patent Law), the Civil Procedure Law of the People's Republic of China (hereafter referred to as the Civil Procedure Law) these Several Provisions for the Application of Law to Pre-action Cessation of Infringement of Patent Right are hereby made as follows:

第一条
根据专利法第六十一条的规定，专利权人或者利害关系人可以向人民法院提出诉前责令被申请人停止侵犯专利权行为的申请。

Article 1
In accordance with the provisions of Article 61 of the Patent Law, a patentee or related injured party may file an application with the people's court for ordering pre-action the respondent to cease acts infringing the patent right.

提出申请的利害关系人，包括专利实施许可合同的被许可人、专利财产权利的合法继承人等。专利实施许可合同被许可人中，独占实施许可合同的被许可人可以单独向人民法院提出申请；排他实施许可合同的被许可人在专利权人不申请的情况下，可以提出申请。	The related injured party that files an application includes, the licensee of a licensing contract for exploitation of the patent, and the legal successor to the property right of the patent, etc. Among the licensees of the licensing contract for exploitation of the patent, the licensee of an exclusive patent licensing contract may file an application with the people's court; the licensee of a sole licensing contract in the circumstances where the patentee does not apply, may file an application.
第二条 诉前责令停止侵犯专利权行为的申请，应当向有专利侵权案件管辖权的人民法院提出。	**Article 2** An application for pre-action cessation of infringement of the patent right shall be filed with a people's court that has the jurisdiction over patent infringement cases.
第三条 专利权人或者利害关系人向人民法院提出申请，应当递交书面申请状； 申请状应当载明当事人及其基本情况、申请的具体内容、范围和理由等事项。 申请的理由包括有关行为如不及时制止会使申请人合法权益受到难以弥补的损害的具体说明。	**Article 3** Any patentee or related injured party who files an application with the people's court shall submit the application in writing, the application shall clearly indicate the parties as well as their basic information, the specific contents, scope and reasons for the application. The reasons for the application include a specific explanation of why irreparable harm will be caused to the applicant's legitimate rights and interests if the relevant acts are not stopped.
第四条 申请人提出申请时，应当提交下列证据： (一) 专利权人应当提交证明其专利权真实有效的文件，包括专利证书、权利要求书、说明书、专利年费交纳凭证。提出的申请涉及实用新型专利的，申请人应当提交国务院专利行政部门出具的检索报告。 (二) 利害关系人应当提供有关专利实施许可合同及其在国务院专利行政部门备案的证明材料，未经备案的应当提交专利权人的证明，或者证明其享有权利的其他证据。排他实施许可合同的被许可人单独提出申请的，应当提交专利权人放弃申请的证明材料。专利财产权利的继承人应当提交已经继承或者正在继承的证据材料。	**Article 4** The applicant when filing the application, shall submit the following evidence: (1) The patentee shall submit documents proving the authenticity and validity of its patent right, including the patent certificate, claims, description and receipt of payment of the patent annuity. Where the application filed by the applicant relates to a patent for utility model, the applicant shall submit a search report made by the Patent Administrative Department under the State Council. (2) The related injured party shall submit the related patent licensing contract and proof that it has been recorded with the Patent Administrative Department under the State Council, where it has not been recorded a certificate from the patentee or other evidence proving that it enjoys the rights shall be filed. Where the licensee of an exclusive licensing contract files an application on its own, it shall submit evidence of the patentee abandoning making an application. The legal successor to property rights in the patent shall submit evidence that has already succeeded to or is in the process of succession.

（三）提交证明被申请人正在实施或者即将实施侵犯其专利权的行为的证据，包括被控侵权产品以及专利技术与被控侵权产品技术特征对比材料等。	(3) Evidence to prove that the respondent is committing or will commit an act infringing its patent right, including materials such as the alleged infringing product and comparisons of the technical features of the patented technology and the alleged infringing product.
第五条 人民法院作出诉前停止侵犯专利权行为的裁定事项，应当限于专利权人或者利害关系人申请的范围。	Article 5 The ruling made by the people's court to cease an act of patent infringement pre-action shall be confined to the scope of the application filed by the patentee or related injured party.
第六条 申请人提出申请时应当提供担保，申请人不提供担保的，驳回申请。 当事人提供保证、抵押等形式的担保合理、有效的，人民法院应当准予。 人民法院确定担保范围时，应当考虑责令停止有关行为所涉及产品的销售收入，以及合理的仓储、保管等费用；被申请人停止有关行为可能造成的损失，以及人员工资等合理费用支出；其他因。	Article 6 The applicant when making an application shall provide security; where the applicant does not provide security, the application shall be rejected. Where the security provided by a party is in the form of a mortgage etc and is reasonable and valid, the people's court shall approve. When the people's court determines the scope of the security, it shall consider the sales turnover of the product the relevant acts related to which are to be injuncted as well as reasonable costs of storage and safekeeping; the losses that may be caused by the respondent ceasing the relevant act as well as other reasonable costs, such as the wages or salaries; and other factors.
第七条 在执行停止有关行为裁定过程中，被申请人可能因采取该项措施造成更大损失的，人民法院可以责令申请人追加相应的担保。申请人不追加担保的，解除有关停止措施。	Article 7 Where in the process of enforcing the ruling to cease the relevant act, the respondent may be caused greater losses due to the adoption of the measures, the people's court may order the applicant to provide an appropriate supplementary security. Where the applicant does not supplement the security, the measure to cease the relevant act shall be cancelled.
第八条 停止侵犯专利权行为裁定所采取的措施，不因被申请人提出反担保而解除。	Article 8 Any measures taken to execute the ruling to cease the act of patent infringement will not be removed because the respondent provides counter security.
第九条 人民法院接受专利权人或者利害关系人提出责令停止侵犯专利权行为的申请后，经审查符合本规定第四条的，应当在四十八小时内作出书面裁定；裁定责令被申请人停止侵犯专利权行为的，应当立即开始执行。	Article 9 The people's court after receiving an application filed by a patentee or related injured party to order to cease the act of patent infringement, after examination for conformity with Article 4 of these provisions, shall within 48 hours issue a ruling in writing; where a ruling is made to order the respondent to stop its act of patent infringement, enforcement shall be commenced without delay.

人民法院在前述期限内，需要对有关事实进行核对的，可以传唤单方或双方当事人进行询问，然后再及时作出裁定。	Where the people's court within the aforementioned time limit, needs to verify relevant facts, it may summon and make inquiries of one or both parties, and then promptly make a ruling.
人民法院作出诉前责令被申请人停止有关行为的裁定，应当及时通知被申请人，至迟不得超过五日。	The people's court making a ruling pre-action to order respondent to cease the relevant act, shall promptly notify the respondent, at the latest it should not exceed 5 days.
第十条 当事人对裁定不服的，可以在收到裁定之日起十日内申请复议一次。复议期间不停止裁定的执行。	Article 10 Where a party is not satisfied with the ruling, it may apply once for review within 10 days from the date of the receipt of the ruling. The review period shall not suspend the execution of the ruling.
第十一条 人民法院对当事人提出的复议申请应当从以下方面进行审查： （一）被申请人正在实施或即将实施的行为是否构成侵犯专利权； （二）不采取有关措施，是否会给申请人合法权益造成难以弥补的损害； （三）申请人提供担保的情况； （四）责令被申请人停止有关行为是否损害社会公共利益	Article 11 The people's court shall examine the application for reconsideration filed by a party as to the following aspects: (1) Whether or not the act of the respondent that is being committed or will be committed constitutes infringement of patent right; (2) Whether or not not taking the relevant measure will cause irreparable harm to the legitimate rights and interests of the applicant; (3) The conditions of the security provided by the applicant; and (4) Whether or not ordering the respondent to cease the relevant act would harm the public interest.
第十二条 专利权人或者利害关系人在人民法院采取停止有关行为的措施后十五日内不起诉的，人民法院解除裁定采取的措施。	Article 12 Where the patentee or related injured party does not institute legal proceedings within 15 days after the people's court takes measures to cease the relevant act, the people's court shall cancel enforcement of the measures of the ruling.
第十三条 申请人不起诉或者申请错误造成被申请人损失的，被申请人可以向有管辖权的人民法院起诉请求申请人赔偿，也可以在专利权人或者利害关系人提起的专利权侵权诉讼中提出损害赔偿的请求，人民法院可以一并处理。	Article 13 Where an applicant does not institute legal proceedings or the application is in error causing losses to the respondent, the respondent may institute legal proceedings in a people's court having the jurisdiction requesting the applicant to pay compensation; or may also file a request for damages during the patent infringement litigation instituted by the patentee or related injured party, the people's court may simultaneously handle the request.

| 第十四条 停止侵犯专利权行为裁定的效力，一般应维持到终审法律文书生效时止。人民法院也可以根据案情，确定具体期限；期限届满时，根据当事人的请求仍可作出继续停止有关行为的裁定。 | Article 14
The validity of the ruling ordering to cease the infringement of patent right, generally shall continue until and cease after the final legal instrument comes into effect. The people's court may also according to the facts of the case confirm a specific time limit; at the expiration of the time limit, in accordance with the request of a party the people's court may make a ruling for continued cessation of the relevant act. |
|---|---|
| 第十五条 被申请人违反人民法院责令停止有关行为裁定的，依照民事诉讼法第一百零二条规定处理。 | Article 15
Where the respondent breaches the ruling made by the people's court to order the cessation of the relevant act, the matter shall be handled according to the provisions of Article 102 of the Civil Procedure Law. |
| 第十六条 人民法院执行诉前停止侵犯专利权行为的措施时，可以根据当事人的申请，参照民事诉讼法第七十四条的规定，同时进行证据保全。

人民法院可以根据当事人的申请，依照民事诉讼法第九十二条、第九十三条的规定进行财产保全。 | Article 16
The people's court when executing pre-trial measures to cease the act of patent infringement, may in accordance with the application of a party, by reference to the provisions of Article 74 of the Civil Procedure Law simultaneously conduct evidence preservation.

The people's court may, in accordance with an application of a party, pursuant to Articles 92 and 93 of the Civil Procedure Law conduct property preservation. |
| 第十七条 专利权人或者利害关系人向人民法院提起专利侵权诉讼时，同时提出先行停止侵犯专利权行为请求的，人民法院可以先行作出裁定。 | Article 17
Where the patentee or the related injured party when filing patent infringement litigation simultaneously files a request for ceasing an act of patent infringement in advance, the people's court may first make a ruling. |
| 第十八条 诉前停止侵犯专利权行为的案件，申请人应当按照《人民法院诉讼收费办法》及其补充规定交纳费用。 | Article 18
For a case to stop infringement of a patent, the applicant shall in accordance with the People's Court Litigation Charges Measures and its supplementary provisions pay fees. |

APPENDIX 6

Supreme People's Court Opinion on Certain Issues with Respect to Intellectual Property Judicial Adjudication Under the Current Economic Situation

最高人民法院关于当前经济形势下知识产权审判服务大局若干问题的意见

(April 21, 2009)

各省、自治区、直辖市高级人民法院,解放军军事法院,新疆维吾尔自治区高级人民法院生产建设兵团分院:	The Higher People's Courts of all provinces, autonomous regions, directly controlled municipalities, PLA Military Courts, the Production and Construction Corps Branch of the Higher People's Court of Xinjiang Uygur Autonomous Region:
现将《最高人民法院关于当前经济形势下知识产权审判服务大局若干问题的意见》印发给你们,请结合审判工作实际,认真贯彻执行。	Now the "Supreme People's Court Opinion on Certain Issues with Respect to Intellectual Property Judicial Adjudication Under the Current Economic Situation" is issued to you, please actually and seriously implement it during trial work.
当前,我国国民经济继续保持平稳较快发展,改革开放深入推进,社会事业加快发展,人民生活进一步改善,但同时也面临着严重的困难和挑战。为深入贯彻全国"两会"精神,落实国家知识产权战略,使知识产权审判更好地服务于有效应	At present, our countries' national economy is maintaining steady and rapid development, reform and opening are being further promoted, social undertakings are developing fast and people's lives are further improving, but at the same time we also face serious difficulties and challenges. To better

对国际金融危机冲击，促进经济平稳较快发展的大局，为"保增长、保民生、保稳定"作出更加积极的贡献，现就当前经济形势下人民法院做好知识产权审判工作的若干问题，提出如下意见：	implement the "two sessions" spirit, the implementation of national intellectual property strategy, and to allow intellectual property trials during international financial crisis to better serve to respond effectively and to promote stable and rapid economic development of the overall situation, in order to make more positive contributions "to maintain economic growth and maintain the people's livelihood and maintaining stability" and under the current economic situation to handle better a number of issues in intellectual property trial work by the people's courts, we issue the following opinion:
一、立足实际，突出重点，努力增强知识产权审判服务大局的针对性和有效性	I. Based on actuality, with a prominent focus, strive hard to enhance the overall relevance and effectiveness of intellectual property adjudication
1、充分认识知识产权保护对于促进经济平稳较快发展的重要性，切实增强服务大局的使命感。知识产权是国家科技创新能力和水平的集中体现，是国家发展的战略性资源，是提高国际竞争力的核心要素。现代经济竞争归根结底也是知识产权的竞争。加强知识产权保护，提高知识产权的创造、运用和管理水平，对于加快经济结构调整、转变发展方式、推进自主创新、深化改革、提高对外开放水平，从而保持经济平稳较快发展，都具有重要意义。历史经验表明，经济危机常常伴随着科技革命，科技革命又成为推动新一轮经济增长和繁荣的重要引擎。在当前经济形势下加强知识产权保护，对于有效推动科技创新和科技革命，为催生新兴产业、创造新的市场需求、培育新的经济增长点和引领经济发展新方向，具有重大作用。	1. Fully understand the importance of intellectual property protection in promoting stable and rapid economic development and increase the sense of serving the overall situation. Intellectual property is a collective expression of the level of national scientific and technological innovation ability; is a strategic resource for national development; and, is a core element in improving international competitiveness. In the final analysis, modern economic competition is intellectual property competition. Strengthening intellectual property protection, improving intellectual property creation use and management levels are of great significance to speeding up economic restructuring and changing patterns of development, promoting independent innovation, deepening reform and improving the level of opening so as to maintain stable and rapid economic development. Historical experience shows that economic crises are often associated with scientific and technological revolutions; technological revolution has become an important engine for the new round of economic growth and prosperity. In the current economic situation, strengthening intellectual property protection has a significant role to promote effectively technological innovation and scientific and technological revolutions, the birth of new industries and create new market demands, cultivate new economic growth points and lead the new directions of economic development.
2、高度关注国际国内经济形势变化对于知识产权审判的新需求，切实增强服务大局的针对性、有效性和主动性。当前经济形势对于知识产权审判提出了更新更高的要求和期待。知识产权司法保护只能加强和	2. Pay high attention to the changes in international and domestic economic situation and new demands for intellectual property adjudication to effectively serve to enhance the overall situation with validity, efficiency and initiative. The current economic

提升，不能削弱和放松。各级法院务必要增强危机意识、忧患意识、宏观意识和大局意识，更加注重拓展创新空间，促进培育自主知识产权、自主品牌和新的经济增长点，增强企业的市场竞争力，提高国家的核心竞争力；更加注重营造开放自由的贸易和投资环境，规范市场秩序，维护公平竞争，完善社会主义市场经济体制，大力推动诚信社会的建设，在应对挑战、化危为机中充分发挥知识产权审判的独特职能作用。	situation has created newer and higher requirements and expectations for intellectual property adjudication. Courts at all levels must enhance the sense of crisis and sense of urgency, their overall macro-consciousness and awareness, make greater effort to expand room for innovation, promote nurturing intellectual property rights brands and new economic growth points, enhance market competitiveness of enterprises and enhance the country's core competitiveness; focus more attention to create an open and liberal trade and investment environment, standardize market order, safeguard fair competition, improve the socialist market economic system, vigorously promote the building of a society with integrity and in addressing the challenges, turn crisis into an opportunity to fully enhance the unique function of intellectual property adjudication.
二、加大专利权保护力度，着力培育科技创新能力和拓展创新空间，积极推进自主创新	II. Increase the strength of patent protection, efforts to cultivate and expand space for innovative scientific and technological innovation and actively promote independent innovation
3、以贯彻新修订的专利法为契机，高度重视专利审判工作，全面提高专利审判水平。以专利为核心的科技创新成果构成了企业和国家的核心竞争力，加强专利权保护对于科技进步和自主创新具有最直接、最重要的促进作用。各有关法院要以提高创新能力和建设创新型国家的责任感和使命感，高度重视专利案件的审理，把提高专利审判水平作为一项重点工作。要深刻领会和正确把握专利法立法宗旨和精神，加强调查研究，及时发现新情况，解决新问题，确保修订后的专利法的正确贯彻实施。	3. Use the implementation of the newly revised patent law as an opportunity to place great importance on patent trials, and comprehensively improve the level of patent adjudication. Patents as the core scientific and technological innovations form the core of enterprises' and national competitiveness and play the most direct and important role in strengthening patent protection for scientific and technological progress and independent innovation. Every relevant court, based on a sense of responsibility and mission to improve innovation capability and build an innovative country, needs to attach great importance to the trial of patent cases and to raise the level of patent adjudication as a priority. It is necessary to deeply understand and correctly grasp the legislative purpose and spirit of the patent law, strengthen research and ensure correct implementation of the revised patent law when new situations are discovered and resolve new problems.
4、准确把握专利司法政策，切实加强专利权保护。要从我国国情出发，根据我国科技发展阶段和产业知识产权政策，依法确定合理的专利司法保护范围和强度，既要使企业具有投资创新的动力，使个人具有创造热情，使社会富有创造活力，又不能使专利权成为阻碍技术进步、不正当打击竞争对手的工具；既能够充分调动、配置	4. Accurately grasp patent justice policies and strengthen protection of patent rights. It is necessary from China's national conditions, in accordance with the stage of development of China's industrial technology and industrial intellectual property policies, in accordance with law to confirm a reasonable scope for strengthening the judicial protection of patents, so as to enable enterprises to

全社会的资本和技术资源，又能够加速技术信息的传播和利用。要正确适用专利侵权判定原则和方法，进一步总结审判经验，完善权利要求解释规则和侵权对比判定标准。正确解释发明和实用新型专利的权利要求，准确界定专利权保护范围，既不能简单地将专利权保护范围限于权利要求严格的字面含义，也不能将权利要求作为一种可以随意发挥的技术指导，应当从上述两种极端解释的中间立场出发，使权利要求的解释既能够为专利权人提供公平的保护，又能确保给予公众以合理的法律稳定性。凡写入独立权利要求的技术特征，均应纳入技术特征对比之列。对于权利人在专利授权确权程序中所做的实质性的放弃或者限制，在侵权诉讼中应当禁止反悔，不能将有关技术内容再纳入保护范围。严格等同侵权的适用条件，探索完善等同侵权的适用规则，防止不适当地扩张保护范围。依法认真审查各种不侵权抗辩事由和侵权责任抗辩事由，合理认定先用权，依法支持现有技术抗辩。	invest in innovation, to enable individuals to have creative enthusiasm, to enable full creative vitality of the community, but also not to enable patents to become an obstacle to technological progress, and a tool for unfair competition against competitors; to mobilise and configure fully the capital and technology resources of the whole of society, and to accelerate the dissemination and use of technical information. It is necessary to correctly apply the principles and methods of deciding patent infringement and further coordinate adjudication and improve the standards of patent claim interpretation and infringement comparison. To correctly interpret the claims of invention patents and utility models and properly delineate the scope of patent protection, one cannot simply limit the scope of patent protection to the strict literal meaning of the claims, nor can one use claims freely as technical guidance, instead one must set out from the middle of these two extreme positions, so that the interpretation of the claims can provide fair protection of patent holders, but also to ensure that the law gives the public reasonable stability. Whatever technical features are in the independent claim should be included among the technical features compared. If a patentee has specifically excluded features from the scope of the patent during the prosecution or validity proceedings, they shall be estopped in infringement proceedings and cannot include these features within the scope of protection. Strictly apply the provisions of the doctrine of equivalents, explore and improve the application of equivalent infringement rules to prevent inappropriate expansion of the scope of protection. According to law, seriously review the various non-infringement defences and infringement defences, reasonably identify first use rights and according to law support the prior art defence.
三、加强商业标识保护，积极推动品牌经济发展，规范市场秩序和维护公平竞争	III. Strengthen the protection of commercial indicators, actively promote the economic development of brands and standardize the market order and defend fair competition
5、充分尊重知名品牌的市场价值，依法加强知名品牌保护。知名品牌凝聚了企业的竞争优势，是企业参与国内国际市场竞争的利器，代表着核心的经济竞争力，是企业和国家的战略性资产，也是引领市场消费方向的主要因素。人民法院要通过依法加强商标权保护和制止不正当竞争，为知名品牌的创立和发展提供和谐宽松的法律环境，促进品牌经济发展，刺激和创造消费需求，拉动经济增长，增强我国企业的国内和国际竞争力。	5. Fully respect the market value of well-known brands and in accordance with the law strengthen the protection of well known brands. Well-known brands embody competitive advantage for enterprises, are an advantageous tool for enterprises to participate in domestic and international market competition, represent the core of the economic competitiveness, are enterprises' and the nation's strategic assets and also are one of the key elements to drive market consumption. People's courts need, through strengthening trademark protection and

preventing unfair competition, in order to provide a harmonious and relaxed legal environment to promote the creation of famous brands and the economic development of brands, to stimulate and create consumer demand, stimulate economic growth and increase our nation's enterprises domestic and international competitiveness.

6、完善商标司法政策，加强商标权保护，促进自主品牌的培育。正确把握商标权的专用权属性，合理界定权利范围，既确保合理利用商标资源，又维护公平竞争；既以核定使用的商品和核准使用的商标为基础，加强商标专用权核心领域的保护，又以市场混淆为指针，合理划定商标权的排斥范围，确保经营者之间在商标的使用上保持清晰的边界，使自主品牌的创立和发展具有足够的法律空间。未经商标注册人许可，在同一种商品上使用与其注册商标相同的商标的，除构成正当合理使用的情形外，认定侵权行为时不需要考虑混淆因素。认定商品类似和商标近似要考虑请求保护的注册商标的显著程度和市场知名度，对于显著性越强和市场知名度越高的注册商标，给予其范围越宽和强度越大的保护，以激励市场竞争的优胜者，净化市场环境，遏制不正当搭车、模仿行为。	6. Perfect trademark judicial policies, strengthen trademark right protection and enhance and promote the cultivation of own brands. Correctly grasp the exclusive nature of trademark rights, reasonably define the scope of rights, both to ensure the reasonable use of trademarks resources, and safeguard fair competition; based only on goods for which use is approved and trademarks for which use is approved, strengthen the core areas of trademark protection, but also using market confusion as a guide, reasonably delineate the exclusive scope of trademark rights, to ensure that that there are clear boundaries in the use of trademarks by business operators, so that the creation and development of own brands has sufficient legal space. Where without the permission of trademark registrant, a trademark is used on the same products for which the trademark is registered, except where this produces conditions of fair reasonable use, in confirming this is an infringing act it is not necessary to consider elements of confusion. When determining whether the trademarks are similar, or whether the products bearing the different trademarks are similar types of products, take into consideration the distinctiveness and public recognition of the registered trademark for which protection is sought and offer stronger and broader protection to trademarks that are more distinctive or better recognized in the market place, assist the leaders in market competition and clean the market environment and stop acts for unfair free-riding and copying.
7、妥善处理注册商标实际使用与民事责任承担的关系，使民事责任的承担有利于鼓励商标使用，激活商标资源，防止利用注册商标不正当地投机取巧。请求保护的注册商标未实际投入商业使用的，确定民事责任时可将责令停止侵权行为作为主要方式，在确定赔偿责任时可以酌情考虑未实际使用的事实，除为维权而支出的合理费用外，如果确无实际损失和其他损害，一般不根据被控侵权人的获利确定赔偿；注册人或者受让人并无实际使用意图，仅将注册商标作为索赔工具的，可以不予赔偿；注册商标已构成商标法规定的连续三年停止使用情形的，可以不支持其损害赔偿请求。	7. Properly handle relationship between actual use of a registered trademark and the bearing of civil liability, allow the bearing of civil liability to encourage the use of the trademarks and activate trademark resources and prevent the use of registered trademarks improperly and opportunistically. Where the trademark for which protection is requested has not entered actual commercial use, the main way of determining civil liability may be to order injunctions against infringement, in determining the liability for damages it is appropriate to consider the actual non-use of the trademark and, except for reasonable costs incurred to protect rights, if indeed there is no actual damages and other damage, generally do not

determine compensation based on the alleged infringer's profits; if the registrant or assignee has no real intention to use and the registered trademark is being used as a compensation tool, it is permissible not to order damages; where the registered trademark has reached three continuous years of non-use as provided by the Trademark Law it is permissible not to support a claim for compensation for damages.

8、加强驰名商标司法认定的审核监督，完善驰名商标司法保护制度，确保司法保护的权威性和公信力。严格把握驰名商标的认定范围和认定条件，严禁扩张认定范围和降低认定条件。凡商标是否驰名不是认定被诉侵权行为要件的情形，均不应认定商标是否驰名。凡能够在认定类似商品的范围内给予保护的注册商标，均无需认定驰名商标。对于确实符合法律要求的驰名商标，要加大保护力度，坚决制止贬损或者淡化驰名商标的侵权行为，依法维护驰名商标的品牌价值。认真贯彻《最高人民法院关于涉及驰名商标认定的民事纠纷案件管辖问题的通知》（法〔2009〕1号），凡通知下发以后不具有管辖权的法院受理的此类案件，均需移送有管辖权的法院审理；通知下发前受理、尚未审结的此类案件，要严格执行判前审核制度。各级法院均应加强已认定驰名商标的案件的评查和审判监督，对于伪造证据骗取驰名商标认定的案件，以及其他违法认定驰名商标的案件，均需通过审判监督程序予以纠正；当事人在涉及驰名商标认定的案件中有妨碍民事诉讼行为的，依法给予制裁。有管辖权的法院均应积极接受各有关方面对于驰名商标司法认定的监督，发现问题务必及时解决。有关驰名商标司法保护的司法解释颁布施行以后，各级法院要认真贯彻落实，使驰名商标司法保护更加规范化。

8. Strengthen the judicial determination and supervision of well-known trademarks and improve the system for protection of well-known trademark to ensure the authority and credibility of judicial protection. Strictly control the confirmation scope and confirmation conditions of well-known trademarks and strictly prohibit the expansion of the confirmation scope and reduction of confirmation conditions. Whenever it is possible to give protection to a registered trademark on the basis products are similar it is not necessary to determine whether a trademark well-known mark. Where a well-known trademark is confirmed to meet the legal requirements, the level of protection needs to be increased and resolutely put a stop to acts of infringement that are derogatory or dilute the well-known trademark and according to law safeguard the brand value of well-known trademarks. Conscientiously implement the "Supreme Court Notice Relating to jurisdiction in Civil Disputes Concerning Well Known Trademarks " (No. 1 of 2009). After the notice is issued cases accepted by a court without jurisdiction must be transferred to a court with jurisdiction to adjudicate. For cases accepted prior to issue of the notice, and where such cases have not yet concluded, the audit before decision system must be strictly implemented. Courts at all levels should strengthen the investigation and supervision of cases where well-known trademarks have already been confirmed, in relation to cases where well known trademarks have been confirmed based on fabrication of evidence or fraud, and other cases where well-known trademarks have been illegally confirmed, you should correct the cases through the procedure of trial supervision; parties involved in well-known trademark cases who perform acts which obstruct civil litigation, shall be subject to sanctions. Courts with jurisdiction should positively accept the various aspects of supervision in relation to judicial determination of well-known trademarks and problems that arise must be solved in a timely manner. After judicial interpretations for protection of well-known trademarks are promulgated, courts at all levels should conscientiously implement them so that the judicial protection of well-known trademarks is standardised.

9、加强商标授权确权案件的审判工作，正确处理保护商标权与维持市场秩序的关系。既要有效遏制不正当抢注他人在先商标行为，加强对于具有一定知名度的在先商标的保护，又要准确把握商标权的相对权属性，不能轻率地给予非驰名注册商标跨类保护。正确区分撤销注册商标的公权事由和私权事由，防止不适当地扩张撤销注册商标的范围，避免撤销注册商标的随意性。对于注册使用时间较长、已建立较高市场声誉和形成自身的相关公众群体的商标，不能轻率地予以撤销，在依法保护在先权利的同时，尊重相关公众已在客观上将相关商标区别开来的市场实际。要把握商标法有关保护在先权利与维护市场秩序相协调的立法精神，注重维护已经形成和稳定了的市场秩序，防止当事人假商标争议制度不正当地投机取巧和巧取豪夺，避免因轻率撤销已注册商标给企业正常经营造成重大困难。与他人著作权、企业名称权等在先财产权利相冲突的注册商标，因超过商标法规定的争议期限而不可撤销的，在先权利人仍可在诉讼时效期间内对其提起侵权的民事诉讼，但人民法院不再判决承担停止使用该注册商标的民事责任。

9. Strengthen trademark application review adjudication work, correctly handle the protection of trademark rights and their relationship to maintaining market order. It is necessary to effectively curb the improper acts of trade mark hijacking by others, strengthen the protection of prior trademarks with a certain amount of fame, and also accurately grasp the relative strengths of trademarks and not give cross category protection to non-well-known trademarks. Correctly distinguish between the right to cancel a registered trademark based on public and private rights, prevent the inappropriate expansion of the scope of a registered trademark and avoid the arbitrary revocation of registered trademarks. Trademarks which have been used for a relatively long time and have established a relatively high reputation in the market and created their own groups of related marks can not be lightly revoked, at the same time as protecting the earlier rights according to law, respect the market reality that the related public has already objectively formed a separation between the related marks. It is necessary to grasp the legislative spirit of the procedures of the Trademark Law relating to protection of prior rights and protecting the market order and focus on maintaining the procedures that have already established and stabilized the market order to prevent parties creating fake trademark disputes to opportunistically and predatorily take advantage and avoid hastily revoking a registered trademark causing great hardship to an enterprise's ordinary course of business. For trademarks which conflict with other's prior copyright, business names and other property rights, which have exceeded the period for dispute under the Trademark Law and cannot be cancelled, the prior right holder can still within the limitation period bring civil litigation, but the People's Court can no longer issue a decision of civil liability to stop use of the said registered trademark.

10、妥善处理注册商标、企业名称与在先权利的冲突，依法制止"傍名牌"等不正当竞争行为。除注册商标之间的权利冲突民事纠纷外，对于涉及注册商标、企业名称与在先权利冲突的民事纠纷，包括被告实际使用中改变了注册商标或者超出核定使用的商品范围使用注册商标的纠纷，只要属于民事权益争议并符合民事诉讼法规定的受理条件，人民法院应予受理。凡被诉侵权商标在人民法院受理案件时尚未获得注册的，均不妨碍人民法院依法受理和审理；被诉侵权商标虽为注册商标，但被诉侵权行为是复制、摹仿、翻译在先驰名商标的案件，人民法院应当依法受理。

10. Properly handle the conflict between registered trademarks, enterprise names and prior rights according to the law stop "near the famous" and other acts of unfair competition. In addition to civil disputes relating to conflicts between registered trademarks, in relation to civil disputes over conflicts between registered trademarks, enterprise names and prior rights, including disputes where the Defendant has in actual use changed the registered trademark or used the registered trademark exceeding the scope of the goods for which it is registered, as long as it is a dispute over civil rights and interests and also meets the requirements in civil procedure rules to be accepted, people's courts

should accept the case. Wherever the alleged infringing mark is not registered at the time of acceptance, the people's court should not be impeded from accepting and hearing the case. In cases where the alleged infringing mark has been registered but the alleged infringing act is copy, imitating or translating a prior well-known trademark, the people's court should accept the case.

按照诚实信用、维护公平竞争和保护在先权利等原则，依法审理该类权利冲突案件。有工商登记等的合法形式，但实体上构成商标侵权或者不正当竞争的，依法认定构成商标侵权或者不正当竞争，既不需要以行政处理为前置条件，也不应因行政处理而中止诉讼。在中国境外取得的企业名称等商业标识，即便其取得程序符合境外的法律规定，但在中国境内的使用行为违反我国法律和扰乱我国市场经济秩序的，按照知识产权的独立性和地域性原则，依照我国法律认定其使用行为构成商标侵权或者不正当竞争。企业名称因突出使用而侵犯在先注册商标专用权的，依法按照商标侵权行为处理；企业名称未突出使用但其使用足以产生市场混淆、违反公平竞争的，依法按照不正当竞争处理。对于因历史原因造成的注册商标与企业名称的权利冲突，当事人不具有恶意的，应当视案件具体情况，在考虑历史因素和使用现状的基础上，公平合理地解决冲突，不宜简单地认定构成商标侵权或者不正当竞争；对于权属已经清晰的老字号等商业标识纠纷，要尊重历史和维护已形成的法律秩序。对于具有一定市场知名度、为相关公众所熟知、已实际具有商号作用的企业名称中的字号、企业或者企业名称的简称，视为企业名称并给予制止不正当竞争的保护。因使用企业名称而构成侵犯商标权的，可以根据案件具体情况判令停止使用，或者对该企业名称的使用方式、使用范围作出限制。因企业名称不正当使用他人具有较高知名度的注册商标，不论是否突出使用均难以避免产生市场混淆的，应当根据当事人的请求判决停止使用或者变更该企业名称。判决停止使用而当事人拒不执行的，要加大强制执行和相应的损害赔偿救济力度。

In accordance with good faith, maintain fair competition and protection of the principle of prior rights, in accordance with the law try such cases of conflict of rights. Where there is a legal form of registration with the administration of industry and commerce etc, but in fact this constitutes trademark infringement or unfair competition, according to the law determine this constitutes trademark infringement or unfair competition, there is no need for administrative handling as a precondition, and there is no need to stay litigation because of administrative handling. For commercial indicators such as enterprise names that have been registered outside China, even if its procedures for acquisition complied with the overseas laws and regulations, but the use in China is a violation of our laws and disrupts of the market economic order, based on the principles of independence and territoriality of intellectual property, in accordance with our laws confirm the acts of use constitute trademark infringement or unfair competition. Where an enterprise name conflicts with and infringes the exclusive right of a prior registered trademark, in accordance with the law handle it as trademark infringement; where a company name does not conflict but its use is sufficient to produce market confusion, and is anti-competitive, in accordance with the law handle it as unfair competition. Where for historical reasons trademark registrations and business name rights conflict and the parties do not have bad faith, the specific circumstances of the case should be considered, based on considering the historical factors and current use, reach a fair settlement of the conflict, it should no simply be assumed to constitute trademark infringement or unfair competition; in relation to where an old indicator has a clear identity and other commercial indicator disputes, it is necessary to respect the history and the maintain the legal order already established. In relation to indicators that are part of an enterprise name and simplifications of enterprises names that have a certain market reputation, are well known to the relevant public and have an actual role as a trade description, they should be deemed to be enterprise names and given protection against unfair competition. Where use of an enterprise name has constituted trademark infringement, you may according to the specific circumstances of the case issue an order to stop using, or in relation to the method of use of such enterprise name impose restrictions on the scope of use. Where use of an enterprise name has unfairly used another person's relatively well known registered trademark, without considering whether it has produced conflict and difficult to avoid market confusion, you should in accordance with the claims of the party order the cessation of use of the name or that the enterprise name be changed. Where an order is made for cessation and the party refuses execution, increase compulsory enforcement and consequential compensation for damages.

11、加强不正当竞争和反垄断审判，统筹兼顾自由竞争与公平竞争的关系，积极促进市场结构完善和社会主义市场经济体制的健全。妥善处理专利、商标、著作权等知识产权专门法与反不正当竞争法的关系，反不正当竞争法补充性保护不能抵触专门法的立法政策，凡专门法已作穷尽规定的，原则上不再以反不正当竞争法作扩展保护。凡反不正当竞争法已在特别规定中作穷尽性保护的行为，一般不再按照原则规定扩展其保护范围；对于其未作特别规定的竞争行为，只有按照公认的商业标准和普遍认识能够认定违反原则规定时，才可以认定构成不正当竞争行为，防止因不适当地扩大不正当竞争范围而妨碍自由、公平竞争。妥善处理保护商业秘密与自由择业、涉密者竞业限制和人才合理流动的关系，维护劳动者正当就业、创业的合法权益。高度重视反垄断法的执行，依法审理好各类垄断纠纷案件，遏制垄断行为，维护公平竞争，为企业提供自由宽松的创业和发展环境。

11. Strengthen unfair competition and anti-monopoly trials, fully consider the relationship between free competition and fair competition, actively promote improvement in the market structure and development of the socialist market economic system. Properly deal with the relationship between patent, trademark, copyright and other intellectual property laws and the anti-unfair competition law; unfair competition law's supplementary protection nature cannot clash with the legislative policy of specialist laws, where the special provisions of law have been exhausted, in principle the Anti-Unfair Competition Law should not be used to extend protection. Where the Anti-Unfair Competition Law has special provisions which provide exhaustive protection for certain acts, generally the provisions setting out basic principles should not be used to expand its scope of protection; in relation to acts of competition where specific provision has not been made, only in accordance with generally accepted business standards and awareness is it possible to determine violation of provisions setting out general principles and determine they constitute acts of unfair competition; prevent unfair competition by improperly expanding the scope of unfair competition and thereby hinder free and fair competition. Properly address the protection of trade secrets and freedom of choice of occupation, restrictions on employment to protect confidentiality and reasonable circulation of talent, safeguard the legitimate right of employment of workers and the legitimate rights and interests of entrepeneurs. Attach great importance to the implementation of the Anti-Monopoly Law, according to the law handle well all kinds of monopoly dispute cases, curb monopolistic behavior, maintain fair competition and provide a free and relaxed environment entrepreneurship and development.

四、完善知识产权诉讼制度，着力改善贸易和投资环境，积极推动对外开放水平的提高	IV. Improve the intellectual property litigation system, make efforts to improve the trade and investment environment, and actively promote the improvement of the level of opening to the outside
12、加强诉权保护，畅通诉讼渠道。依法加强诉权保护，凡符合受理条件的起诉均应及时受理；凡经权利人明确授权代为提起诉讼的律师，均可以权利人的名义提起诉讼，并考虑境外当事人维权的实际，不苛求境外权利人在起诉书上签章。结合知识产权审判实际，完善各种诉讼制度，简化救济程序，积极施行各项便民利民措施，增强司法救济的有效性。	12. Strengthen the protection of the right to bring proceedings and make litigation channels smooth. According to law, protect the right to bring proceedings, all proceedings which meet the conditions to be accepted shall be promptly accepted; where a right holder has expressly authorized a lawyer to sue on their behalf, he can bring proceedings in the name of the right holder; also consider the actual circumstances of right holders outside china protecting their rights and not demand the right holders outside china sign and/or chop on the complaint. Bring together the actual practice of intellectual property trial practice, improve various litigation systems, and simplify processes for providing relief and implement measures for the convenience and benefit of the people so as to enhance the effectiveness of judicial relief.
13、完善确认不侵权诉讼制度，遏制知识产权滥用行为，为贸易和投资提供安全宽松的司法环境。继续探索和完善知识产权领域的确认不侵权诉讼制度，充分发挥其维护投资和经营活动安全的作用。除知识产权权利人针对特定主体发出侵权警告且未在合理期限内依法提起诉讼，被警告人可以提起确认不侵权诉讼以外，正在实施或者准备实施投资建厂等经营活动的当事人，受到知识产权权利人以其他方式实施的有关侵犯专利权等的警告或威胁，主动请求该权利人确认其行为不构成侵权，且以合理的方式提供了确认所需的资料和信息，该权利人在合理期限内未作答复或者拒绝确认的，也可以提起确认不侵权诉讼。探索确认不侵犯商业秘密诉讼的审理问题，既保护原告的合法权益和投资安全，又防止原告滥用诉权获取他人商业秘密。	13. Improve the confirmation of non-infringement lawsuit system to curb acts of abuse of intellectual property rights so as to provide a judicial environment for the security of trade and investment. Continue to explore and improve the confirmation of non-infringement litigation system in the field of intellectual property to give full play to secure its role to maintain investment and business activities. In addition to the situation where a right holder has issued a warning to a particular subject and has not within a reasonable time according to the law brought suit, so the warned party can bring an action to confirm the non-infringement, a party, who is implementing or preparing to implement investment and construct factories and other such business activities and receives from the intellectual property right holder in some other way a related patent infringement etc warning or threat, and takes the initiative to request the right holder confirm that its behavior does not constitute infringement, and provides in a reasonable manner the information required and materials to make such a confirmation and the right holder does not within a reasonable period reply or refuses to provide confirmation, a lawsuit for confirmation of non-infringement may also be brought. When investigating the trial of confirmation of non-infringement of trade secrets, both protect the plaintiff's legal rights and investment safety, but also prevent the abuse of the litigation by the plaintiff to obtain trade secrets of others.

14、严格把握法律条件,慎用诉前停止侵权措施。采取诉前停止侵权措施既要积极又要慎重,既要合理又要有效,要妥善处理有效制止侵权与维护企业正常经营的关系。诉前停止侵权主要适用于事实比较清楚、侵权易于判断的案件,适度从严掌握认定侵权可能性的标准,应当达到基本确信的程度。在认定是否会对申请人造成难以弥补的损害时,应当重点考虑有关损害是否可以通过金钱赔偿予以弥补以及是否有可执行的合理预期。担保金额的确定既要合理又要有效,主要考虑禁令实施后对被申请人可能造成的损失,也可以参考申请人的索赔数额。严格审查被申请人的社会公共利益抗辩,一般只有在涉及公众健康、环保以及其他重大社会利益的情况下才予考虑。诉前停止侵权涉及当事人的重大经济利益和市场前景,要注意防止和规制当事人滥用有关权利。应考虑被诉企业的生存状态,防止采取措施不当使被诉企业生产经营陷入困境。特别是在专利侵权案件中,如果被申请人的行为不构成字面侵权,其行为还需要经进一步审理进行比较复杂的技术对比才能作出判定时,不宜裁定责令诉前停止侵犯专利权;在被申请人依法已经另案提出确认不侵权诉讼或者已就涉案专利提出无效宣告请求的情况下,要对被申请人主张的事实和理由进行审查,慎重裁定采取有关措施。根据案件进展情况,注意依法适时解除诉前停止侵权裁定。加强在诉前停止侵权措施申请错误时对受害人的救济,申请人未在法定期限内起诉或者已经实际构成申请错误,受害人提起损害赔偿诉讼的,应给予受害人应有的充分赔偿。对于为阻碍他人新产品上市等重大经营活动而恶意申请诉前停止侵权措施,致使他人的市场利益受到严重损害的情形,要注意给予受害人充分保护。

14. Strictly grasp the provisions of law and cautiously use preliminary injunction measures. Adopting preliminary injunctions need to be done actively but also cautiously, and need to be not only reasonable but also effective, to properly handle and maintain effective suppression of infringement and protect the ordinary course of enterprises business relations. Preliminary injunctions are suitable mainly in cases where the facts are relatively clear and infringement easy to judge, and by strictly applying the criteria for infringement you should reach a level of basic confidence. In determining if the applicant would suffer irreparable harm, the key consideration should be whether the damage can be compensated by monetary damages and whether enforcement of a judgment can be reasonably expected. The determination of the amount of bond needs to be reasonable and needs to be effective, the main consideration is the loss the respondent may suffer after being injuncted, but reference can be made to the amount of the applicant's claim for compensation. Critically review a respondent's public interest defence, generally it should only be considered in relation to public health, environmental protection and other circumstances of major social interests. The existing conditions of defendant companies should be considered, so as to avoid taking measures that would unfairly cause trouble to the production and operations of the enterprise sued. Especially in patent infringement cases, if the alleged infringing activity does not constitute literal infringement and a relatively more complex comparison of technology is needed, preliminary injunctions should not be ordered. Where the respondent has requested a declaratory judgment of non-infringement, or has initiated invalidation proceedings, the court shall investigate these claims and cautiously decide to adopt relevant measures. In accordance with the way in which the case has progressed, pay attention to cancelling in accordance with the law preliminary injunction orders at an appropriate time. Strengthen measures to provide relief to those who suffer from wrongfully applied for preliminary injunction measures: where the applicant has not brought suit within the legally provided time period or has in fact has made a wrongful application, where the injured party brings a claim for compensation, the injured party should be given adequate compensation. Where in order to stop major business activities such as discouraging others from putting new products on the market a malicious application for preliminary injunctions is made, resulting in the serious damage to the market interests others, it is necessary to pay attention to giving full protection of the injured party.

15、充分发挥停止侵害的救济作用，妥善适用停止侵害责任，有效遏制侵权行为。根据当事人的诉讼请求、案件的具体情况和停止侵害的实际需要，可以明确责令当事人销毁制造侵权产品的专用材料、工具等，但采取销毁措施应以确有必要为前提，与侵权行为的严重程度相当，且不能造成不必要的损失。如果停止有关行为会造成当事人之间的重大利益失衡，或者有悖社会公共利益，或者实际上无法执行，可以根据案件具体情况进行利益衡量，不判决停止行为，而采取更充分的赔偿或者经济补偿等替代性措施了断纠纷。权利人长期放任侵权、怠于维权，在其请求停止侵害时，倘若责令停止有关行为会在当事人之间造成较大的利益不平衡，可以审慎地考虑不再责令停止行为，但不影响依法给予合理的赔偿。

15. Give full play to the role of injunctive relief, the responsibility to properly apply for injunctions, and effectively curb infringing acts. In accordance with the litigation claims of the parties, the concrete circumstances of the case and the actual need to stop infringement, parties can be clearly ordered to destroy materials and molds etc specifically used to manufacture infringing products. However, before adopting destruction measures, the precondition of necessity must apply, there should be comparable gravity to the infringing acts and not cause unnecessary losses. If stopping the relevant conduct will cause a significant imbalance of interests between the parties, or is contrary to public interest, or in fact can not be performed, you may in accordance with the specific situation of the case proceed to balance the interests and decide not to stop the infringing acts and adopt more substantial compensation or alternative measures such as economic compensation. Where the right holder has for a long period of time acquiesced in infringement and not enforced its rights, at the time it makes a claim for cessation of damage, if ordering cessation of the act would result in a relatively large imbalance between the interests of the parties, you may consider carefully not to order cessation of infringing acts but without affecting giving reasonable compensation in accordance with law.

16、增强损害赔偿的补偿、惩罚和威慑效果，降低维权成本，提高侵权代价。在确定损害赔偿时要善用证据规则，全面、客观地审核计算赔偿数额的证据，充分运用逻辑推理和日常生活经验，对有关证据的真实性、合法性和证明力进行综合审查判断，采取优势证据标准认定损害赔偿事实。积极引导当事人选用侵权受损或者侵权获利方法计算赔偿，尽可能避免简单适用法定赔偿方法。对于难以证明侵权受损或侵权获利的具体数额，但有证据证明前述数额明显超过法定赔偿最高限额的，应当综合全案的证据情况，在法定最高限额以上合理确定赔偿额。除法律另有规定外，在适用法定赔偿时，合理的维权成本应另行计赔。适用法定赔偿时要尽可能细化和具体说明各种实际考虑的酌定因素，使最终得出的赔偿结果合理可信。根据权利人的主张和被告无正当理由拒不提供所持证据的行为推定侵权获利的数额，要有合理的根据或者理由，所确定的数额要合情合理，具有充分的说服力。注意参照许可费计算赔偿时的可比性，充分考虑正常许可与侵权实施在实施方式、时间和规模等方面的区别，并体现侵权赔偿金适当高

16. Enhance the compensatory, punitive and deterrent effect of damages, reduce the cost of defending rights and increase the price to be paid for infringing. In determining damages make good use of the rules of evidence, comprehensively and objectively examine the evidence to calculate the amount of compensation, fully use logical reasoning and everyday life experience, conduct a full review and examination of the authenticity, legitimacy and probative value of the evidence and adopt advantageous standards of evidence to determine the facts of damages. Actively guide parties to choose damages calculations based on loss caused or profits made, as far as possible avoid simply using the statutory damages method. Where it is difficult to prove the loss caused or profits made but there is evidence it is significantly more than the statutory maximum amount of compensation, this should be combined with the actual case situation, and reasonable compensation greater than the statutory maximum determined. Unless otherwise provided in laws, in applying statutory compensation, the reasonable costs of protecting rights should be calculated separately. When applying statutory compensation as far as possible give a detailed and

于正常许可费的精神。注意发挥审计、会计等专业人员辅助确定损害赔偿的作用，引导当事人借助专业人员帮助计算、说明和质证。积极探索知识产权损害赔偿专业评估问题，在条件成熟时适当引入由专业机构进行专门评估的损害赔偿认定机制。	specific explanation of the discretionary elements of each practical matter considered, so that the final amount of compensation resulting is reasonable and credible. When, in accordance with the request of the right holder, you are calculating profit made from the infringement and the defendant without good reason refuses to provide evidence of its acts, there must be reasonable grounds or reasons for the amount determined and it needs to be convincing and reasonable. Pay attention to comparability when referring to licensing fees when calculating compensation, fully consider normal licensing and the way in which infringement actually occurred, and differences between the timing and scale etc, and reflect the spirit that infringement damages should be appropriately higher than normal licensing fees. Pay attention to the role played by auditing, accounting and other professionals in determining damages, guide parties to seek the help of professionals to help the calculation, description, and cross-examination. Actively explore the issue of professional assessment of intellectual property damages, when conditions are appropriate introduction of a system of expert assessment of damages by a professional organization.
17、注意研究经济领域的知识产权新问题，积极促进科技兴贸基地和服务外包基地建设。	17. Pay attention and research new issues in economic field of intellectual property rights and actively promote the development of the science and technology trade base and service outsourcing base.
加强科技兴贸基地和服务外包基地建设所涉及的知识产权保护问题的调查研究，有针对性地加强相关知识产权的司法保护，为促进科技兴贸基地和服务外包基地建设提供优良的司法环境。加大对信息、软件、医药、新材料、航空航天、精细化工等高新技术领域的知识产权保护力度，积极促进科技兴贸基地建设。引导高技术企业进一步增强自主创新能力，拥有自主知识产权，大力支持具有自主品牌和自主知识产权的高新技术产品出口，进一步提高出口产品国际市场竞争力。深入研究服务外包中的知识产权法律问题，促进服务外包基地建设。通过司法裁判引导服务外包企业树立知识产权保护意识，建立健全企业知识产权保护制度，提高外包服务的竞争力。	Strengthen investigation and research of science of intellectual property protection issues related to the technology trade base and development of service outsourcing, in a targeted manner strengthen judicial protection of related intellectual property rights, in order to provide a good judicial environment for promoting the trade and science and technology base and serve the outsourcing base. Increase the strength of intellectual property protection in the areas of information, software, pharmaceuticals, new materials, aerospace, fine chemicals and other high-tech fields of, and actively promote the development of the science and technology trade base. Guide high-tech enterprises to further enhance independent innovation capability, possess independent intellectual property rights, strongly support the export of high tech exports with independent brands and independent intellectual property rights to further enhance the international competitiveness of export products. Deeply research legal issues in service outsourcing, further the construction of the service outsourcing base. Through judicial decisions guide service

	outsourcing enterprises to establish intellectual property protection awareness, establish a sound corporate intellectual property protection system, and improve the competitiveness of outsourcing services.
18、完善有关加工贸易的司法政策，促进加工贸易健康发展。认真研究加工贸易中的知识产权保护问题，抓紧总结涉及加工贸易的知识产权案件的审判经验，解决其中存在的突出问题，完善司法保护政策，促进加工贸易的转型升级。妥善处理当前外贸"贴牌加工"中多发的商标侵权纠纷，对于构成商标侵权的情形，应当结合加工方是否尽到必要的审查注意义务，合理确定侵权责任的承担。	18. Improve relevant judicial policies on processing trade, and promote the healthy development of processing trade. Seriously study intellectual property protection issues in the processing trade, pay close attention to pull together experience of adjudicating intellectual property cases in the processing trade and resolve prominent problems that exist, improve the judicial protection policies, promote transformation and upgrading of processing trade. Properly handle the current multiple trademark infringement disputes in "OEM" foreign trade, in relation to the situations where there is trademark infringement, you should strike a balance as to whether the processor had an obligation that required it to investigate and reasonably impose infringement liability.
19、坚持平等保护原则，坚决反对任何形式的保护主义。严格依法办案，平等保护本地与外地、本国与外国当事人的合法权益，坚决遏制地方保护和部门保护，促进国内市场的统一开放，完善投资环境和增强投资信心，提高国际声誉和树立良好形象，提高对外开放水平。统筹好国内国际两个大局，妥善处理与贸易有关的重大知识产权纠纷，积极服务于国内国际两个市场、两种资源的统筹利用，既确保遵循相关国际公约和国际惯例，促进国际经贸合作，又始终注意维护国家利益和经济安全，激励和促进自主创新，提升我国的知识产权综合能力和国际竞争力。正确处理对外关系与具体案件审理的关系，无论普通涉外案件还是引起国际关注的敏感性案件，都要严格依法办案，不能为盲目迎合片面的外部舆论而牺牲公正司法。	19. Adhere to the equal protection principle and resolutely oppose any form of protectionism. Handle cases in strict accordance with the law, equal protection of the local and non-local, national and foreign parties' legitimate rights and interests, resolutely curb local protectionism and departmental protectionism, promote unified opening of the domestic market, improve the investment environment and enhance investor confidence, improve the international reputation and establish a good image and improve the level of opening to the outside. Co-ordinate domestic and international situations, appropriately handle major trade-related intellectual property disputes, actively serve both domestic and international markets and make overall use of both resources, both to ensure compliance with relevant international conventions and international practices, to promote international trade and economic cooperation, at the same time always paying attention to safeguard national interests and economic security, encourage and promote independent innovation, enhance the total capability of China's intellectual property and international competitiveness. Correctly handle the relationship between the hearing of specific cases and international relationships, no matter whether it is an ordinary foreign-related case or a sensitive case that has drawn international attention, they should all be handled strictly according to law, you can not be blind-sided by outside opinion to sacrifice the fair administration of justice.

20、加强同类案件和关联案件的协调指导，规范司法行为，维护法治统一。加强同类案件的调查研究和业务指导，加大司法解释力度，完善司法政策，积极推行典型案例指导制度，不断明确和完善法律适用标准。强化对法官行使自由裁量权的约束和规范机制，细化正当行使自由裁量权的标准。对于法律问题相同、裁判定性不一的案件，强化审级监督，充分发挥二审和再审的纠错功能。加强关联案件的协调指导力度，完善协调处理机制。对于涉及同一法律事实或者同一法律关系的关联案件，需要移送的，应当依照法律规定移送管辖和合并审理。健全关联案件审理法院之间的相互沟通制度和报请共同上级法院协调指导制度。在后受理的法院，应积极主动加强沟通并及时报请上级法院进行协调，避免作出相互矛盾的判决。

20. Strengthen the coordinated guidance for cases of a similar type and related cases, standardize judicial practices and defend a unified rule of law. Strengthen investigation and research and operational guidance for cases of a similar type, increase the strength of judicial interpretations, perfect judicial policy, and actively implement the guidance system of typical cases, continue to clarify and improve laws and applicable standards. Strengthen the binding and standardised system for the exercise of discretionary power by judges and refine proper standards for the exercise of discretion. For cases where the legal issues are the same but judgments are not the same, strengthen trial level supervision, give full play to function of error correction of second instance trials and retrials. Strengthen the strength of the coordination and guidance of related cases, and improve coordination mechanisms. Cases involving the same legal facts or cases associated with the same legal relationship, which need to be transferred to another court, shall be transferred to another court in accordance with the provisions governing jurisdiction and joinder. For related cases develop the communication between the trial courts handling related cases and a coordination and guidance system for reporting jointly to higher courts. A court that has accepted a case after another, should be proactive in strengthening communication and timely report to the higher court to coordinate and avoid conflicting contradictory rulings.

APPENDIX 7
List of Courts with Jurisdiction to Handle Patent Cases

At the end of 2010, there were 76 courts designated by the Supreme People's Court with jurisdiction to handle patent cases, including 75 intermediate people's courts and one primary people's court. All Higher People's Courts have jurisdiction to handle patent cases. The Intermediate Courts and the Primary Court were:

Beijing (2): No 1 and No 2 Intermediate People's Courts
Shanghai (2): No 1 and No 2 Intermediate People's Courts
Tianjin (2): No 1 and No 2 Intermediate People's Courts
Chongqing (2) No 1 and No 5 Intermediate People's Courts
Zhejiang (9): Hangzhou, Wenzhou, Jinhua, Ningbo, Taizhou, Jiaxing, Huzhou, Shaoxing Intermediate People's Courts and Yiwu Primary People's Court
(Note: Yiwu court is a pilot program where a Primary People's Court can handle patent cases involving utility model and design patents)
Guangdong (8): Guangzhou, Shenzhen, Zhuhai, Shantou, Foshan, Dongguan Jiangmen, Zhongshan Intermediate People's Courts
Jiangsu (7): Nanjing, Suzhou, Nantong, Zhenjiang, Yancheng, Wuxi, Changzhou Intermediate People's Courts
Shandong (6): Jinan, Qingdao, Yantai, Weifang, Zibo, Dongying Intermediate People's Courts
Fujian (3): Fuzhou, Xiamen, Quanzhou Intermediate People's Courts
Jiangxi (3): Nanchang, Jingdezhen, Yichun Intermediate People's Courts
Liaoning (3): Shenyang, Dalian, Huludao Intermediate People's Courts
Xinjiang (1): Urumqi Intermediate People's Court

Xinjiang Production and Construction Corps (2): Agricultural 8th and 12th Divisions Intermediate People's Courts
Hubei (3): Wuhan, Yichang, Xiangfan Intermediate People's Court
Hunan (2): Changsha, Zhuzhou Intermediate People's Court
Inner Mongolia (2): Hohhot, Baotou Intermediate People's Courts
Sichuan (2): Chengdu, Mianyang Intermediate People's Court
Heilongjiang (2): Harbin, Qiqihar Intermediate People's Court
Guangxi (2): Nanning, Liuzhou Intermediate People's Courts
Hebei (1): Shijiazhuang Intermediate People's Court
Shanxi (1): Taiyuan Intermediate People's Court
Shaanxi (1): Xi'an Intermediate People's Court
Henan (1): Zhengzhou Intermediate People's Court
Anhui (1): Hefei Intermediate People's Court
Jilin (1): Changchun Intermediate People's Court
Hainan (1): Haikou Intermediate People's Court
Guizhou (1): Guiyang Intermediate People's Court
Yunnan (1): Kunming Intermediate People's Court
Tibet (1): Lhasa Intermediate Court
Gansu (1): Lanzhou Intermediate People's Court
Qinghai (1): Xining Intermediate People's Court
Ningxia (1): Yinchuan Intermediate People's Court

TABLE OF CASES

Beijing University Founder (Group) Co. v. Beijing Gaoshu Technology Co., ... 114–115
Changzhou Huasheng v. Eli Lilly. 101
China Environmental Project Tech Inc. v. Fujikasui Engineering Co.,
    Huayang Electric Power Co., ... 153–154
CHINT v. Schneider Electronics Co., ... 156n15, 157
Dalian Xinyi Jiancai Co. v. Dalian Renda Xinxing Qiangti Building
    Material Factory 126–128
Fugui v. Zhang Wenlin, Cao Yanpeng (Fugui). 138
Guo Jinlian v. Li Xincai. 112n26
Honda v. Shijiazhuang Shuanhuan 101
Hu Yunping v. Chongqing Sanlida Electronics Co., ... 129
Jialun Industry (Shenzhen) Co. v. Roman Tam. 114n31
Nantong Jiangong Group Co. Hainan Subsidiary v. He Xiaoming. 114n31
Sankyo v. Wansheng 137
Shanghai Meijia Industrial Co. v. Shanghai Zhongling Daily Use Articles Co., ... 135
Shanghai Zhongti Real-Estate Co. v. Shanghai Guangchuan Construction Design
    Consulting Co., ... 113n30
Suzhou Longbao v. Suzhou Langli 101
Zhejiang Holley Telecommunication Group Co. v. Shenzhen Samsung
    Kejian Mobile Technology Co., ... 157

TABLE OF LEGISLATION

LEGISLATION

Administrative Litigation Law (10/1/90) 8, 25, 76
Civil Procedure Law (4/1/08) 3, 8, 70, 82, 84–88, 93, 101, 105–106,
108–111, 151, 160
General Principles of Civil Law (1/1/87) 3, 8, 91, 121, 151, 152
Patent Law (1986)..................... 3, 7–12, 23, 31–39, 42, 45n7, 142. *See also specific provisions in General Index*

REGULATIONS

Implementing Regulations of the Patent Law, effective February 1, 2010...... 7, 36, 41–44,
57–59, 64–65, 67, 120, 141–142

JUDICIAL INTERPRETATIONS AND OPINIONS

Guidelines on the Application of the Law Regarding Trials of Patent Infringement Cases,
  issued by the Supreme People's Court on June 19, 2001........7, 94, 102, 120, 121–123,
154–155
Provisions of the Supreme People's Court on Certain Issues Concerning the
  Application of the Statute of Limitations to Civil Case Trials, effective on
  September 1, 2008... 8, 91, 93
Several Provisions of the Supreme People's Court for the Application of Law
  to Pretrial Cessation of Infringement of Patent Right, effective
  July 1, 2001.. 7–8, 97–100, 109n19
Several Provisions of the Supreme People's Court on Evidence in Civil Proceedings,
  effective April 1, 2002... 9, 83, 106–111, 113n30
Supreme Court Interpretation on Several Issues regarding Legal Application in the
  Adjudication of Patent Infringement Cases, effective January 1, 2010 .... 7, 100–101,
119–125, 128–129, 133–134, 139–140,
148–150, 152–153, 156–158
Supreme Court Opinion on Handling of Certain Issues in Intellectual Property Cases
  During the Current Economic Situation, effective April 21, 2009.............8, 8n2, 11,
98–99, 101, 125, 159, 162

ADMINISTRATIVE REGULATIONS

Guidelines for Patent Examination, effective February 1, 2010 ..... 8, 34–38, 41–62, 63–78
Measures for Administrative Enforcement of Patents, effective
    February 1, 2011 .... 8, 22–25
Regulations for Intellectual Property Customs Protection,
    effective April 1, 2010 .... 9, 27–29, 119

INDEX

Absence of party, 82
Absolute novelty, 10
Acts of infringement
    design patents, 147–149
    patents and utility models, 119–120
Adjudication Committee, 19–20, 85
Administration of Industry and Commerce (SAIC), 106
Administrative enforcement, 21–29
    overview, 13, 21
    GAC role in, 13, 21, 27–29
    mediation by SIPO, 15, 22, 25–27
    SIPO administrative actions, 13, 21, 22–25
Administrative system, 13. *See also* State Intellectual Property Office (SIPO)
Amendments to patent applications, 56–58, 146
Amendments to patent, 66
Amendments to Patent Law. *See also* Table of Legislation
    2009 provisions, 9–10, 137, 146, 147, 152–153
    Transitional Rules, 9–10
Anti-Monopoly Law, as defense, 138–139
Apology, 159
Appeals, in civil litigation
    appellate court decisions, 86
    deadlines, 85
    effect of, 87
    new evidence, 87
    notice of appeal, 86
    procedures, 86
    review of decisions, 87–88
Appeals, of PRAB decisions
    within judicial system, 14, 18, 25, 75–77

    re-examination decisions, 38–39
    timelines, 25
Asset-freezing orders, 100

Basic Standards of Judges Professional Ethics, 19
Best evidence rule, 107
Bonds, 28–29, 98–100
Burden of proof
    evidence and, 69, 111
    plaintiff and, 82
    reverse burden of proof, 122

Case law, relevance of, 10–11
Chaoyang Xingnuo Company, 139
China Environmental Project Tech Inc., 153–154
Civil liability. *See* Remedies
Civil litigation (China), 79–88
    absence of party, 82
    appeals of decisions, 85–88
    civil proceedings, 79–80
    complaint procedures, 80–81
    evidence, 83–84
    filing fees, 79–80, table 3
    filing of defense, 82, 82n11
    judging panels, 79
    judgments, 85
    Supreme Court review, 87–88
    trials, 84–85
Civil proceedings,
    summary, 79–80
Claim interpretation, 122–125, 129
Claims
    rectification of claims, 129
    supported by descriptions, 54–56
    technical features in, 58–59

Clinical trials, 136–137
Communist Party, 19–20
Complaints
    acceptance of, 81
    filing procedures, 80–81
    limitation periods and, 92
    service of, 81, 103
Confidentiality examinations, 43–44
Constitution (China), 5, 18
Corruption, 4, 5, 19
Counterbonds, 29
Counterfeiting, 15, 60
Customs, 13, 21, 27–29

Dalian Renda Xinxing Qiangti Building Material Factory, 126–128
Dalian Xinyi Jiancai Co., 126–128
Damages. *See also* Remedies
    administrative enforcement, 25
    apportionment of, 156–157
    design patents and, 150
    judicial enforcement, 159
    mediation by SIPO and, 25
    post-grant infringement and, 154–158
    preliminary injunctions wrongly granted, 99
    statutory damages, 10, 156
Declaration of non-infringement, 100–101
Defence, filing of, 80, 82, 93, 141
Defenses, 131–140
    breach of Anti-Monopoly Law, 138–139
    clinical trials, 136–137
    exhaustion of rights, 134
    innocence, 131, 137–138
    invalidity, 132
    limitation defense, 92–93, 138
    non-infringement, 132–133
    patent incorporated into standards, 139–140
    prior art defense, 64, 133–136, 150
    scientific research and experimentation, 136
    statutory defenses, 131–132
    temporary entry into China, 136
    types of, 131–132
Democratic Centralism, 20
Design, definition of, 32
Design patents, 141–150. *See also* Defenses; Patents
    acts of infringement, 147–149
    amendments and, 57, 146
    conflict with prior legal rights, 145
    customs seizures and, 27
    definition of, 32, 142
    designs incorporated into other products, 149
    drawings/photographs, 146
    filing requirements, 33
    grounds for invalidation, 141–143
    identical invention-creation, 147
    identical/not substantially different designs, 143–145
    infringement damages, 150
    law/morality/public interest and, 146–147
    search reports, 96–97
    statutory damages and, 10
    stay of infringement proceedings, 102–103, 141
    two-dimensional designs as indicators, 145–146
Divisional applications, 59
Doctrine of equivalents, 126–128, 132–133
Doctrine of precedent (lack of), 10, 11

Economic growth, 1–2
Elimination of ill effects, 159
Embassies/consulates (Chinese)
    notarization/legalization of foreign evidence, 108
    powers of attorney, 90
Enablement, 53–54
Enforcement. *See also* Administrative enforcement; State Intellectual Property Office (SIPO)
    of damage awards, 159
    of injunctions, 159–160
European patents, 72
Evidence, 105–115
    admissibility of pretext/trap purchases, 114–115
    best evidence rule, 107
    burden of proof, 111
    court collection of, 111
    evidence exchange, 83–84
    expert evidence, 74, 108–109
    foreign evidence, 71–72, 108
    foreign language evidence, 72, 108
    importance of, 105–106
    inadmissibility of illegally obtained evidence, 113–114

insufficient evidence as non-infringement defense, 132
investigations by parties, 112–113
notarization of, 23, 71–72, 107–108
orders for party to produce, 111
from outside mainland China, 71–72, 108
in patent invalidation, 69–74
penalties for destruction of, 111–112
permitted evidence, 106–107
preservation orders, 109–110
in SIPO proceedings, 23
Evidence Preservation Orders, 109–110
Exhaustion of rights, 134
Existing technology, definition of, 45, 45n7
Expert evidence, 74, 108–109
External design patents. *See* Design patents

File wrapper estoppel, 128–129, 132
Filing fees, 79–80, table 3
Foreign evidence, 71–72, 108
Foreign language evidence, 72, 108
Foreign-related patent issues, 14, 108
Forum shopping, 94–95

General Administration of Customs (GAC), 13, 21, 27–29
Genetic resources, 61
Grace periods, 34

Higher People's Court, 11, 16–18, 94
Higher People's Court (Beijing)
 citation of, 10–11
 Patent Opinion (2001), 12, 120
 PRAB appeals to, 14, 18, 77
Higher People's Court (Jilin)
 on limitation defense, 138
Higher People's Court (Liaoning)
 on doctrine of equivalents, 126–127
 on patent incorporation into standards, 139
Higher People's Court (Shanghai)
 citation of, 10
 on damages and preliminary injunctions, 99
Hong Kong, patents in, 14–15, 71–72
Huayang Electric Power Co., 153–154

Indirect infringement, 120–121
Infringement. *See also* Non-infringement; Patent infringement litigation

damages for post-grant infringement, 154–158
design patents, 147–149, 150
utility models, 119–120
Injunctions
 court grants of, 97–100, 152–154
 damages for wrongful grant, 99
 deadlines for filing suits, 99–100
 enforcement of, 159–160
 pretrial/interim, 97–100
 security requirement, 98–99
 SIPO, 152
Innocence defense, 131, 137–138
Intellectual property chambers, 17
Intermediate People's Court, 16–18, 27–28, 94, 96
Intermediate People's Court (Beijing No. 1)
 on clinical trials, 137
 PRAB appeals to, 11, 14, 18, 76, 157
Intermediate People's Court (Changchun)
 on limitation defense, 138
Intermediate People's Court (Chongqing No. 1)
 on claim of rectification, 129
Intermediate People's Court (Dalian)
 on doctrine of equivalents, 126–127
Intermediate People's Court (Hangzhou)
 on damage awards, 157
Intermediate People's Court (Shanghai No. 2)
 on trade fair sales jurisdiction, 96
Intermediate People's Court (Wenzhou)
 on damage awards, 157
Internet
 acts of infringement and, 147
 novelty disclosure on, 46
 publication dates on, 73
Invalidity, 132. *See also* Patent invalidation
Invention, definition of, 31
Invention patents. *See also* Patent infringement litigation; Patents
 definition of, 31
 filing requirements, 32–33
 grounds for invalidation, 69
 stay of infringement proceedings, 102
Invention-creations. *See* Patents
Inventiveness
 definition of, 48
 patent invalidation and, 48–51, 69
Investigations by parties, 112–113

Joint infringement, 121
Judges
    regulation of, 18–19
    as specialists in IP law, 5, 17
Judging panels, 79
Judgments, in civil litigation, 85
Judicial Appraisal, 84, 108–109
Judicial interpretations and opinions. *See* Table of Cases; Table of Legislation; *specific courts*
Judicial system. *See also* Civil litigation (China); *specific courts and actions*
    collection of evidence, 111
    infringement cases, 13, 17–18
    injunctions, 97–100, 152–154
    mediation, 82
    neutrality in, 4–5
    patent cases, 17–18
    PRAB appeals within, 14, 18, 25, 75–77
    structure of, 16–17
Jurisdiction
    first instance patent disputes, 94, 94*n*24
    generally, 93
    objection to, 94–96
    patent cases, 94

Legislation. *See* Table of Legislation
Limitation defense, 92–93, 138
Limitation periods
    agreements to waive, 93
    assertion of defense, 92–93
    continuous infringement and, 91
    making claims to courts, 92
    stopping of, 91–92
Local protectionism
    inconsistent decisions due to, 11
    national interest and, 162
    SIPO jurisdiction and, 23–24
    state-owned enterprises and, 5
Lower courts, 12. *See also specific courts*

Macau, patents in, 14, 15, 71–72
Media
    announcement publications in, 91, 91*n*12
    disclosure by publication, 46
    local protectionism campaigns in, 5
Mediation
    by judicial system, 82
    by SIPO, 15, 22, 25–27
Ministry of Public Security (MPS). *See* Public Security Bureau

Morality
    design patents and, 146–147
    patent invalidation and, 42, 60
    prohibited inventions and, 42

National Copyright Administration (NCA), 106
National Intellectual Property Rights Strategy (2008), 4
National People's Congress. *See also* Table of Legislation
    authorization of judicial interpretations, 11–12
    laws on prohibited inventions, 60
    passage of patent laws, 3, 7, 8
New product, definition of, 122
Non-infringement, 100–101, 132–133. *See also* Infringement
Nonpatentable subject matter, 32, 42, 59–61
Notable progress, 50
Notarization
    of evidence, 23, 71–72, 107–108
    of foreign evidence, 108
    powers of attorney and, 90
    of purchases of alleged infringing products, 113
Novelty
    absolute, 10
    date of issue/publication, 46
    definition of, 45, 45*n*7
    disclosure by publication, 46
    disclosure by use, 46
    earlier patent applications, 62
    examination criteria, 45, 47–48
    oral disclosure, 46
    patent invalidation and, 44–48
    prior art references, 47
    prior use outside China and, 10, 45

Objection to jurisdiction, 94–96
Official documents as evidence, 106
Oral hearings
    evidence submission prior to, 70–71
    PRAB and invalidation requests, 67–68, 74–75
    SIPO process for, 22, 24–25
    stages of, 74–75
    Supreme Court review, 18
Oral testimony, 73–74
Ordinary consumer test designs, 148

Patent Cooperation Treaty, 4
Patent Examination Guidelines, 8, 34–35, 38, 42–43, 45, 48–49
Patent infringement litigation, 117–130
  acts of infringement, 119–120
  claim interpretation, 122–125, 129
  doctrine of equivalents, 126–128, 132–133
  file wrapper estoppel, 128–129, 132
  indirect infringement, 120–121
  joint infringement, 121
  proving infringement, 129–130
  rectification of claims, 129
  reverse burden of proof, 122
  rights to bring action, 118
Patent invalidation, 41–62. *See also* Design patents; Patent Review and Adjudication Board (PRAB)
  amendments and, 56–58, 66
  application for revocation, 63–64
  claims supported by descriptions, 54–56
  confidentiality examinations, 43–44
  disclosure of prior art, 45
  divisional applications, 59
  effect of final decisions, 77–78
  essential technical features, 58–59
  evidence, 69–74
  Examination Guidelines on, 42–43
  examination principles, 45, 49
  genetic resources, 61
  grounds for, 68–69
  inventiveness, 48–51, 69
  law/morality/public interest, 42, 59–61
  novelty, 44–48, 62
  oral hearings, 67–68, 74–75
  patent revocation proceedings, 63–78
  practical applicability, 51–52
  procedures, 64–68
  prohibited inventions, 59–61
  statutory grounds, 41–42
  sufficiency of disclosure, 52–54
  utility models, 47–48
Patent law
  history of, 1–3
  politics and, 4–5, 11
  sources of, 7–12
Patent Review and Adjudication Board (PRAB). *See also* Patent invalidation; State Intellectual Property Office (SIPO)
  overview, 13, 15–16

appeals of decisions, 14, 18, 38–39, 75–77
applications for stay, 101–102
Examination Guidelines, 8, 34–35, 38, 42–43, 45, 48–49
re-examinations, 16, 34, 36, 38–39
SIPO establishment of, 16
validity, 64
Patents, 31–39
  amendments to, 56–58
  filing requirements, 32–33
  grace periods, 34
  nonpatentable subject matter, 32, 42, 59–61
  preliminary examination, 35–36
  re-examinations by PRAB, 16, 34, 36, 38–39
  substantive examination, 36–37
  term of protection, 33–34
  types of, 31–32
Plaintiff, and burden of proof, 82
Politics, influence on legal system, 4–5, 11
Powers of attorney, 89–90
Practical applicability, 51–52
Pre-grant third-party submissions, 64
Preliminary and interlocutory issues, 89–103
  asset-freezing orders, 100
  declaration of non-infringement, 100–101
  injunctions, 97–100
  jurisdiction, 93–96
  limitation periods, 90–93
  powers of attorney, 89–90
  search reports, 96–97
  stay of infringement proceedings, 101–103
Preliminary examination, 35–36
Primary People's Courts, 16–17, 18
Prior art and patent invalidation, 45, 47, 49–50
Prior art defense, 64, 133–136, 150
Prior use defense, 134–136
Priority claims, 33–34
Private investigators, 112–113
Prohibited inventions, 42, 59–61
Public interest
  design patents and, 146–147
  patent invalidation and, 60–61
  prohibited inventions and, 42
Public Security Bureau, 92, 112, 160

INDEX [291]

Redundant designation doctrine abolition of, 124–125
Re-examination by PRAB, 16, 34, 36, 38–39
Related injured parties, 23, 98, 118
Remedies, 151–160. *See also* Damages
   apology, 159
   damages for post-grant infringement, 154–158
   elimination of ill effects, 159
   enforcement of damage awards, 159
   enforcement of injunctions, 159–160
   injunctions, 152–154
   reasonable expenses, 157
   reasonable fee for pre-grant use, 154
   reasonable royalty and, 155
Renumbering of amended legislation, 9
Revocation. *See* Patent invalidation

Scientific research and experimentation, 136
Search reports, 96–97
Service
   of complaints, 81, 103
   noncompliance with deadlines of, 79
Standards, as defense, 139–140
State Council, 4, 14
State Intellectual Property Office (SIPO). *See also* Patent Review and Adjudication Board (PRAB); Patents
   overview, 14–15
   administrative enforcement, 13, 21, 22–25
   appeals of decisions, 25
   Examination Guidelines, 8, 34–35, 38
   filing requirements, 32–33
   injunctions, 152
   local branches of, 13, 15
   mediation by, 15, 22, 25–27
   oral hearings, 22, 24–25
   patent statistics, 3
   rejection of patent applications, 37–38
   search reports, 96–97
State-owned enterprises, 5
Statutory damages, 10, 156
Statutory defenses, 131–132
Stay of infringement proceedings, 101–103, 141
Substantive examination, 36–37
Sufficiency of disclosure, 52–54

Supreme Court of People's Procuratorate
   overview, 16–17
   civil litigation appeal reviews, 87–88
   making claims to, 92
Supreme People's Court. *See also* Table of Cases; Table of Legislation
   overview, 16–17
   citation of, 10
   civil litigation appeal reviews, 87–88
   on declaratory judgment actions, 101
   on doctrine of equivalents, 126–128
   on foreign complaint signatures, 81
   on injunctions, 152–154
   intellectual property chambers, 17
   interpretations and opinions, 11–12, 114
   oral hearings, 18
   on patent incorporation into standards, 139–140
   PRAB appeals to, 18, 77

Taiwan, patents in, 14, 15, 71–72, 90, 108
Temporary entry into China, 136
Term of protection, 33–34
Trade fairs, 96
Trade secrets, 84
Trademarks
   customs seizures and, 27–29
   design patents and, 145–146
   documentary evidence, 106
Transitional Provisions—2010 Amendments, 9–10. *See also* Table of Legislation
Translation of documentary evidence, 72, 108
Treaties
   foreign evidence and, 108
   Patent Cooperation Treaty, 4
   priority claims and, 33–34
   temporary entry into China and, 136
Trial procedures, 84–85

United Kingdom patents, 72
Utility models. *See also* Patent infringement litigation; Patents
   acts of infringement, 119–120
   amendments to patents, 57
   definition of, 32
   filing requirements, 32–33
   grounds for invalidation, 69

invention, definition of, 42–43
patent invalidation and, 47–48
search reports, 96–97
stay of infringement proceedings, 102–103

Wang Shengjun, 19, 20
Witnesses, 73–74, 106–107
World Intellectual Property Organization (WIPO), 4